The Concept of
Ambiguity—
the Example of James

The Concept of
Ambiguity—
the Example of James

Shlomith Rimmon

The University of Chicago Press

Chicago and London

SHLOMITH RIMMON was born in
Israel and earned her B.A. and M.A. degrees
from the Hebrew University of Jerusalem. She
received her Ph.D. at University College,
London, and is now teaching in the English
Department at the Hebrew University of
Jerusalem.

The University of Chicago Press, Chicago 60637
The University of Chicago Press, Ltd., London

81 80 79 78 77 987654321

Library of Congress Cataloging in Publication Data

Rimmon, Shlomith.
    The concept of ambiguity—the example of James.

    Based on the author's thesis, University of London,
1974.
    Bibliography: p.
    Includes index.
    1. James, Henry, 1843–1916—Criticism and Interpre-
tation.   2. Ambiguity in literature.   I. Title.
PS2127.A4R5   813'.4   77–2171
ISBN 0–226–72010–1

To my mother
and to the memory of my father

Contents

Preface

There are visual tricks that constantly tease the eye and never let our interpretative faculty come to rest. A slight shift of perspective can turn a rabbit into a duck, an urn into two profiles, a group of white birds flying in one direction into a group of black birds flying in the other. How is an image capable of representing different objects at the same time, and what happens to our minds while watching it? Here is Gombrich's description of the rabbit-or-duck figure:

> Clearly we do not have the illusion that we are confronted with a 'real' duck or rabbit. The shape on the paper resembles neither animal very closely. And yet there is no doubt that the shape transforms itself in some subtle way when the duck's beak becomes the rabbit's ears and brings an otherwise neglected spot into prominence as the rabbit's mouth. I say 'neglected', but does it enter our experience at all when we switch back to reading 'duck'? To answer this question, we are compelled to look for what is 'really there', to see the shape apart from its interpretation, and this, we soon discover, is not really possible. True, we can switch from one reading to another with increasing rapidity; we will also 'remember' the rabbit while we see the duck, but the more closely we watch ourselves, the more certainly will we discover that we cannot experience alternative readings at the same time. [1968, pp. 4–5]

A somewhat different technique was used to create Escher's "Night and Day" in which

> The white birds flying across the dark towards the black river come from another side of the world where there is still daylight and where black birds go the other way. And as we search for the dividing line between the two halves, we notice that there is none. It is the interstices between the

white birds—the ground—that gradually assume the shape of the black birds, and these checkered patterns merge downward into the fields of the countryside. Easy as it is to discover this transformation, it is impossible to keep both readings stable in one's mind. The day reading drives out the night from the middle of the sheet, the night reading turns the black birds of the same area into neutral ground. [1963, p. 154]

Some of the implications of Gombrich's observations are particularly important for my purpose.

1. The two interpretations are mutually exclusive. We see either a duck or a rabbit, either an urn or two profiles, either white birds flying in one direction or black birds flying in the other. Such puzzle-pictures should be distinguished from drawings of compound objects, in which the two parts are combined without initially excluding each other. This is how the eagle and the lion add up to create the fabulous figure of the griffin. The griffin is a complex of two figures, while the "rabbit or duck" is a stalemate in which the two figures alternate incessantly.

2. A stalemate indeed it is, for the meeting of the two readings creates an "impossible" situation for us: We cannot hold them both, yet we realize that they fit the image equally well and that there are no clues for choosing one rather than the other. All we can do is oscillate between the two conflicting readings as long as we join in the game.

3. It will be wrong to think that in such visual deadlocks *every* element yields itself to a double interpretation. Some elements do, like the duck's beak which transforms itself into the rabbit's ears. Other elements serve only one reading and escape notice in the opposite interpretation. This is the case of the mouth-spot, prominent when we read rabbit, neglected when we focus on the duck. As long as the number of such "singly directed" points is equal for both interpretations, the two remain equally tenable.

4. Among the techniques used to create such intriguing images are the omission of unequivocal information, the supply of conflicting clues, and the playing against each other of figure and ground (Gombrich 1968, pp. 260, 222, 238–42).

5. "Rabbit or duck," "urn or two profiles," "white birds or black birds" are all impossible objects. Impossible, because they keep our "imitative faculty" constantly busy (Gombrich 1968, p. 240); impossible also (and this is the cause of the former difficulty) because they are outside the range of our experience (p. 200). In reality, rabbits do not look like ducks, not even with the subtlest shift of perspective. Nor do the spaces between white birds create the shape of black birds. It is all "an affair, this fine symmetry, of artificial proportion" (James, *The Sacred Fount* 1959, p. 130).

The object of this study is a parallel phenomenon in literature, a phenomenon that even without the quotation from Henry James would instantly be recognized as "ambiguity." But because "ambiguity" is used in a very broad sense in literary criticism, I have chosen the oblique approach to describe the kind of "impossible object" with which I am concerned.

My work falls into two parts: the first is a tentative theory of narrative and verbal ambiguity, the second is an analysis of several Jamesian "impossible objects"—two tales, "The Lesson of the Master" (1888) and "The Figure in the Carpet" (1896); one *nouvelle*, *The Turn of the Screw* (1898); and one novel, *The Sacred Fount* (1901). The theoretical part of the study has a double aim: (1) a delimitation of the term *ambiguity* to cover only the relation obtaining between mutual exclusives, a definition of the formative principle underlying this relation, and a distinction between ambiguity in this sense and cognate phenomena like "double and multiple meaning," "openness," "vagueness," "symbolism"; (2) a description of the ways in which ambiguity operates at the level of narrative structure as well as at that of verbal realization. I define the basic narrative and verbal units which form the ambiguity and trace the network of linkages among them. The second part of the study applies the descriptive tools evolved in the first part to an analysis of the ambiguity in four of James's works, and it too has a double aim: (1) a detailed demonstration of the irresolvability of the ambiguity of these works, in the hope that such a demonstration will stop the endless debates among critics, debates motivated by a compulsion to choose between mutually exclusive hypotheses, when the very phenomenon of ambiguity makes such choice impossible and undesirable; (2) a description of the ways in which this unresolved ambiguity is created in each work by a specific handling of narrative composition and verbal texture. The works chosen for analysis are ambiguous to the reader, not only to a character or narrator as, for example, "The Liar," and their ambiguity is total, not just a "pocket" within the narrative, as in "The Aspern Papers," "The Friends of the Friends," and *The Wings of the Dove*.

I have found two nonliterary disciplines and two schools of literary study most helpful in the attempt to define ambiguity and its operation in the literary text: logic, linguistics, Formalism, and Structuralism. I have borrowed from logic and linguistics whatever is useful to my study, being careful to note any deviations in the use of terms. The logical notion of "conjunction," for example, is used somewhat differently in my definition of "ambiguity," and it is precisely this deviation from the propositional operation that characterizes the phenomenon. As for the Formalist and Structuralist schools, it is mainly they who have been interested in issues such as the nature of narrative, the definition of narrative units, the operation of informational gaps, and the distribution of clues to fill them in, issues upon which my perception of ambiguity basically rests, although in a modified form, intended to remedy some of the shortcomings of their notions.

This book is based on a doctoral dissertation submitted to the University of London in the summer of 1974. In revising the thesis for publication, I have omitted long sections surveying the various Jamesian critics and arguing with them. These, I felt, would be tedious for readers primarily interested in the theory of ambiguity and probably well known to readers primarily interested in James. However, my debt to traditional James critics should be evident from the text as well as from the bibliography.

I wish to acknowledge very gratefully the encouragement and help I have received from my supervisor, Professor J. F. Kermode, University College London (now at Kings' College, Cambridge) at all the stages of my work on both thesis and book. Professor Kermode took a genuine interest in my work, sustained me through various periods of doubt and frustration, and made many useful and stimulating comments on matters of theory as well as on my analysis of specific texts. To my friend and teacher, Professor Dorothea Krook, the Hebrew University of Jerusalem (now at Tel-Aviv University), I am indebted for an initiation into the world of Henry James, for numerous fascinating discussions of various issues in his fiction and in the theory of literature in general, as well as for a scrupulous and highly illuminating reading of the manuscript. I should also like to thank the examiners of my Ph.D. thesis, Dr. Roger Gard, Queen Mary College, London, and Dr. John Goode, Reading University, for their pertinent criticisms and suggestions. Particularly helpful were Dr. Gard's comments on chapter 6, comments which saved me from some dangerous exaggerations. I am equally grateful to some of my colleagues in the English Department of the Hebrew University of Jerusalem who have made perceptive comments on the manuscript at different stages: Dr. M. Chayen, Professor H.M. Daleski, Dr. P. Gaba, Professor R. Nevo, Professor S. Sandbank, and Dr. O. Segal. Miss A. Füredy and Mrs. M. Saguy were very helpful with some technical aspects of the book.

I am much indebted to the British Council whose kindness in granting financial support enabled me to study in London for two years and use the invaluable resources of the British Museum Library. The Hebrew University of Jerusalem gave me a supplementary grant which enabled me to concentrate on my research for another year, free of teaching duties.

1 The Concept of Ambiguity

1   Ambiguity: The Formative Principle

THE BASIC FORMULA

It is possible to describe ambiguity with the help of a concise formula, but because this formula is based on accepted logical operations, it is necessary to begin with an explanation of these operations themselves.

Preliminary Remarks: Some Notions and Operations in Logic

An important aspect of every science is the definition of its basic units and of the operations it allows in order to construct larger units out of the smaller ones. Both the units and the operations may be validated either by a correspondence to a "world" outside the science itself (for example, classifications and family groups in biology) or by the inner consistency of the science (for example, mathematics, logic) or by both (for example, physics, linguistics, literary theory). The science of logic confines itself to sentences which are "internally" verifiable as either true or false, and which it calls *propositions*.

It is on the basis of the truth-value of the individual propositions that the various *propositional operations*, that is, the "operations used to construct molecular sentences out of atomic sentences" (Reichenbach 1951, p. 23), are established. There are five propositional operations, one monary and four binary. The monary operation is that of 'negation'; the binary ones are 'conjunction', 'disjunction', 'implication', and 'equivalence'. Let a and b signify individual propositions. The five propositional operations can then be formulated in the following way (I adopt Reichenbach's notation):

monary   1. negation: $\bar{a}$ (not a)
binary   2. conjunction, product: $a.b$ (a and b)

3. disjunction, sum: $a \lor b$ (a or b)
4. implication: $a \supset b$ (a implies b)
5. equivalence: $a \equiv b$ (a is equivalent to b)

Every disjunction is expressed by 'or', but not every 'or' expresses a disjunction. A statement like "All literary criticism is either interpretative or evaluative" is not a disjunction, despite the fact that it contains the connective 'or'. It certainly does not mean "Either all literary criticism is interpretative or all literary criticism is evaluative"; it simply means that some works of criticism are interpretative and others are evaluative.

When 'or' does express a disjunction, it can have two meanings, corresponding to two kinds of disjunction: 'weak' or 'inclusive' and 'strong' or 'exclusive'. An inclusive 'or' means that at least one of the two sentences is true, leaving it open whether both are true. An exclusive 'or', on the other hand, rules out the possibility that both sentences are true, limiting truth to one and only one of the propositions. Correspondingly, in an inclusive disjunction one or the other or both disjuncts are true, whereas in an exclusive disjunction either one or the other, but not both, disjuncts are true. The statement "Customers who are teachers or college students are entitled to a special reduction," which one might find in a store, is an inclusive disjunction, since "it is not intended to refuse the reduction to a teacher who is at the same time a college student." On the other hand, when a child wants to be taken on a hike in the morning and to the theater in the afternoon, and his parents answer, "No, we are going on a hike or we are going to the theater," they have in mind an exclusive disjunction, since they "intend to comply with only one of the two requests" (Tarski 1940, p. 21).[1] Whereas in English both disjunctions are expressed by the word 'or', Latin has two different words corresponding to the two kinds of disjunction. The word *vel* expresses inclusive disjunction, while the word *aut* denotes the exclusive type. In the symbolism of logic, inclusive disjunction is marked by '$\lor$' (deriving from the Latin *vel*) and exclusive disjunction '$\land$'.

Exclusive disjunction can be expressed with the help of the other relational formulas and consequently should not be considered a separate type of propositional operation:

$$a \wedge b \equiv (a \vee b) . \overline{a.b} \equiv (a \vee b) . (\overline{a} \vee \overline{b}) \text{ (Reichenbach 1951, p. 43).}[2]$$

These equivalences can indeed be seen as definitions of the exclusive disjunction, so that we can write

$$a \wedge b =_{\text{Df.}} (a \vee b) . \overline{a.b} \text{ (p. 43)}.$$

In plain English, this expression says that an exclusive disjunction of a and b means "a or b and not a and b." Despite the reducibility of $a \wedge b$ to $(a \vee b) . \overline{a.b}$, I shall retain the separate notation for exclusive disjunction because it will simplify and clarify my definition of 'ambiguity'.[3]

Similarly, because of considerations of relevance to the literary theory to be proposed, I shall not reproduce the truth-tables of all the propositional operations, but only those of conjunction and disjunction. Truth-tables are a device for showing the truth-value of a propositional operation in relation to the truth-value of the separate propositions which it relates. The letters 'T' and 'F' in the tables stand for 'True' and 'False' respectively. For example:

a	b	$a.b$
T	F	F

means that if proposition a is 'true' and proposition b is 'false', the conjunction of the two will result in a 'false' proposition.

Conjunction

a	b	$a.b$
T	T	T
T	F	F
F	T	F
F	F	F

Disjunction (inclusive)

a	b	$a \lor b$
T	T	T
T	F	T
F	T	T
F	F	F

Disjunction (exclusive)

a	b	$a \land b$
T	T	F
T	F	T
F	T	T
F	F	F

Unlike the above tables, which inform us about restrictions for the truth-value of the elementary propositions, formulas which have 'F' for all possible values of the elementary propositions are 'empty'.[4] Take, for example, the case when one proposition is the negation of the other. The dependence between these propositions is such that b becomes $\bar{a}$; and if a is true, $\bar{a}$ cannot be true, and vice versa. The first and last rows in the regular truth-table are here impossible because a and $\bar{a}$ cannot both be true, and they cannot both be false. The reduced table of the conjunction of these propositions is the following.

a	$\bar{a}$	$a . \bar{a}$
T	F	F
F	T	F

Proposition $\bar{a}$ is the negation or denial of proposition a, and their conjunction will have only false substitution instances. The basic form of *contradiction*, $a.\bar{a}$, is guarded against by *the statement (or principle) of contradiction*. The statement of contradiction has the form $\overline{a.\bar{a}}$, that is, not both a and *not a*

can be true, or, in other words, no statement can be both true
and false.

The principle of contradiction, a cornerstone in logic, has
been objected to by Hegelians, Marxists, Maoists, "general
semanticists," and structural semanticists on the grounds that
there *are* contradictions, or situations in which contradictory
forces are at work, and that these contradictions are not simply
exceptions to the rule, but the rule itself. These objections,
which will be relevant to the discussion of ambiguity in literature, are based on a misuse of the term 'contradiction'. In fact,
not every opposition is a contradiction. Social classes or nations
or mechanical forces can be described as conflicting with each
other or opposing each other, but they do not negate or deny
each other, they do not 'contradict' each other. If we use the
term 'contradiction' in its strict logical sense, namely, the conjunction of two propositions one of which is a negation or denial
of the other, there can be no objection to the principle which
guards against it (Copi 1961, p. 272).

When conjoined, *a* and *ā* constitute a contradiction. But this
is not the only case in which two propositions are mutually
exclusive and yield an 'empty' conjunction. Logicians distinguish between 'contradictories' and 'contraries', defining them
in the following way: (1) "Two propositions are *contradictories* if one is the denial of the other, that is, if they cannot
both be true *and* they cannot both be false." (2) "Two propositions are said to be *contraries* if they cannot both be true,
though they might both be false" (Copi 1961, pp. 142–43).[5]
The statements "All judges are lawyers" and "Some judges are
not lawyers" are contradictories because they cannot both be
true and they cannot both be false. On the other hand, the
statements "All poets are idlers" and "No poets are idlers" are
contraries because although they cannot both be true, they
can both be false. In the realm of concepts, we can illustrate
contradictories by such oppositions as 'white vs. nonwhite',
'possible vs. impossible', and contraries by antonymic pairs like
'white vs. black', 'sweet vs. bitter', 'strong vs. weak' (Blanché
1966, p. 14). We can now reformulate the difference between
the two terms: Contradictories are both mutually exclusive and
exhaustive, while contraries are mutually exclusive but not

exhaustive (pp. 44–45). 'White' and 'nonwhite' do not only exclude each other but also, taken together, cover the whole field. 'White' and 'black', on the other hand, do indeed exclude each other, but they do not cover the whole field. Unlike contradictories, contraries are not subjected to the principle of the excluded middle,[6] but both contradictories and contraries are subjected to the principle of contradiction and can only be disjoined (contraries—inclusively; contradictories—exclusively). A conjunction of such propositions is empty, its logical product being inevitably null (pp. 50–51).

A Definition of Ambiguity

Ambiguity, in the sense in which I propose to employ the term, can be defined with the help of the following ad hoc formula: $a \wedge b$. The symbol '$\wedge$' is not simply a logical connector, but a relational sign which combines an exclusive disjunction and a conjunction in the following way: The exclusive disjunction is taken in its strict logical sense, while the conjunction is given the sense of copresence in the literary text. The '$\wedge$' sign implies that if the disjunction is true, the relation between a and b is such that if a is true b must be false and vice versa. As the truth-tables on pp. 5–6 have shown, when the interdependence between a and b is such that if one is true the other must be false, the truth-value of $a.b$ is 'F', while that of $a \wedge b$ is 'T', taking one of the following forms:

a	b	$a \wedge b$
T	F	T
F	T	T

But as soon as we are confronted with a specific ambiguous text and we wish to decide which member of the disjunction is true and which is false, a serious problem arises. On the one hand, we know that in an analogous life-situation we would have to choose between the two alternatives, logic instructing us that only one member of an exclusive disjunction is true and the other is false. On the other hand, there is in the case of ambiguity equal evidence for the truth and falsity of both a and b. We cannot decide whether a or b is the true proposition and, consequently, which of the two is the false one. Both possibilities thus remain equitenable and copresent. Although a conjunction in the logical sense would yield 'F' as its truth-value, the narrative or verbal expressions as a whole are "true" and so are their constituent "propositions." Thus some kind of "conjunction" is established between the exclusive disjunctions, and the incongruent '∧' marks precisely the tension we feel between the impulse to choose and the arrest of that impulse by the realization of the equitenability of mutual exclusives.

We can now introduce a further distinction: a and b in the formula can be either contradictories or contraries. In other words, $a \wedge b$ can take the form of either "This is white and this is nonwhite" (where 'this' refers to the same object and 'white' is used in the same sense in both propositions) or "This is white and this is red," but 'this is red' actually implies that it is also 'nonwhite'. 'Nonwhite' can have different manifestations (red, blue, yellow, $b, c, d \ldots$), all of which are mutually exclusive but *not* exhaustive. 'White' and 'nonwhite', on the other hand, are both mutually exclusive and exhaustive. What this means is that ambiguity can be the coexistence of contraries (mutually exclusive but not exhaustive) or the coexistence of contradictories (mutually exclusive and exhaustive). Because contraries are not exhaustive, there can be more than two mutually exclusive possibilities, but they presuppose the binary classification into a and $\bar{a}$. We must now clarify what the a and b or a and $\bar{a}$ stand for in the discussion of narrative and verbal ambiguity.

APPLICATION 1: NARRATIVE AMBIGUITY AND COGNATE PHENOMENA

The process of reading is largely an attempt to integrate the various data, to establish maximum relevance between the diverse details, to form hypotheses as to what happened, what is happening, and what is going to happen in the narrative, as well as to explain the characters' motives and the significance of the represented world.[7] The reader does not wait until the end of the narrative, but starts forming connections and constructing hypotheses at an early stage. In the process of integrating more and more items of information, he often comes to

reject false hypotheses which had the appearance of plausibility, to modify incomplete hypotheses, and to choose definitively the best hypothesis, namely, the one which accounts for
the greatest number of data in the most coherent, consistent,
and "simple" way.[8] These "finalized" hypotheses can be
summed up in a sentence or in a cluster of interrelated sentences which resemble logical propositions in that they are
subjected to the test of truth (truth, in this case, being determined by textual evidence). One sentence in the cluster is
always the basic "proposition" (or the major statement) on
which the other statements in the hypothesis depend, and it is
this sentence that is rendered by an abstract symbol (a, b, and
so on) in my basic formulas.

The degree of "finalization" varies from story to story. In
detective stories the end discloses one and only one solution to
the problem which the story sets out to solve: x is the murderer; y is the thief; z's death was caused by fire. But sometimes we close the book with more than one "finalized"
possibility in mind. It is here that the "propositional operations"
are relevant to define the variety of possible relations between
hypothesis a and hypothesis b (or between a, b, c and d, if more
than two exist). When the two hypotheses are mutually exclusive, and yet each is equally coherent, equally consistent,
equally plenary and convincing, so that we cannot choose between them, we are confronted with narrative ambiguity.

Henry James's *The Turn of the Screw* yields two "finalized"
hypotheses: a, It is a story about evil children who secretly
communicate with the ghosts of two corrupt servants but whose
souls are saved by the courageous governess who fights the
ghosts off (major statement: "The children communicate with
ghosts" or "There are real ghosts at Bly"); b, It is a story
about a mad governess who has hallucinations and who destroys
the children by subjecting them to her hysterical vagaries about
ghosts which they have never seen (major statement: "The
children do not communicate with ghosts" or "There are no
real ghosts at Bly"). Proposition a, "There are real ghosts at
Bly," and proposition b, "There are no real ghosts at Bly," are
clearly mutually exclusive, and yet they can both be equally supported by evidence from the text. When related, they should

form an exclusive disjunction, and yet they are also "conjoined," with the result of $a \wedge b$ or 'narrative ambiguity'. In this example, proposition b ("There are no real ghosts at Bly") is in fact a negation of proposition a ("There are real ghosts at Bly"), so that the elements to be combined are not simply a and b but a and $\bar{a}$, and the formula is that of a contradiction $(a.\bar{a})$. Given these basic contradictories, we can then recognize various contraries, that is, variations on the "no-ghosts" hypothesis.

A clearer example of the operation of contraries can be found in "The Figure in the Carpet." The two contradictory hypotheses are a, "There is a figure in Vereker's carpet"; $\bar{a}$, "There is no figure in Vereker's carpet." These propositions can be "realized" in various ways, and a whole network of a's and b's (based, of course, on the initial a and $\bar{a}$) can be formed. Each of these contraries has been proposed by critics as the best interpretation of the story. On the a side there are the following possibilities: (1) Corvick discovers the secret to Vereker's satisfaction and transmits it to Gwendolen who, in turn, withholds it from her second husband; (2) the secret exists, but all the "Virgilian intelligences" in the story fail to unearth it for reasons that are either personal (incapacity to love) or professional (wrong way of dealing with literature) or both; (3) the characters do not discover the secret, but it is indirectly communicated to us through the texture of James's story. On the $\bar{a}$ side there is a similar divergence into contrary b's: (1) Vereker "invented" the idea of the figure in order to impress the young critic (that is, Vereker lies); (2) Vereker is deluded about his own work; he believes it to contain a central 'figure', while in fact it has none; (3) Vereker ironically propounds the notion of the secret as a joke directed against the ridiculous game of literary criticism; (4) Corvick, on his part, only pretends to have found the figure in order to force Gwendolen into marriage, and Gwendolen later cheats the narrator because she knows that in fact there is nothing to know.

The concept of "finalized" hypotheses as well as the definition of 'narrative ambiguity' will be refined in chapter two. For the time being it is enough to note that my view is narrower than the current definition of 'ambiguity' as "having more than one interpretation." It seems to me that "having more than one interpretation" may involve various mechanisms, various "propositional operations," which should be distinguished from each other. Moreover, since the results of these operations all have names of their own, it seems unwise to create indiscriminate overlapping by lumping them all together under the heading 'ambiguity'. The one "operation" which, to my knowledge, has not been granted a separate term is the "conjunction" of exclusive disjuncts with which we have been concerned. I therefore propose to limit the term 'narrative ambiguity' to this relation between hypotheses, and to define its *differentia specifica* vis à vis the other relations.

'Ambiguity' should first be distinguished from the multiplicity of subjective interpretations given to a work of fiction. Almost every notable work of art has been given an enormous number of individual interpretations—some compatible with each other, some opposed to each other. Theorists holding a relativistic view of criticism conclude from this state of affairs that no two people understand a work of art in the same way, that there is no such thing as the work of art as object, and that there are as many works as there are readers. This is often referred to as the ultimate subjectivity or the "unescapable ambiguity" of all art (Stanford 1939, p. 87). The essential difference between this phenomenon and ambiguity proper is that while the subjectivity of reading is conditioned mainly by the psyche of the reader, ambiguity is a fact in the text—a double system of mutually exclusive clues.

The contemporary tendency to conceive of works as a "field of possibilities" rather than as fully determined objects is another way of giving free play to subjectivity. However, this is not simply a subjectivity of interpretation, determined by what the reader brings into the work, but a subjectivity of creation, invited by the work itself. Burrough's *Naked Lunch* is a work of this kind, a work which, in Burrough's own words, gives the reader "almost the same freedom as the writer" (quoted in Dawson 1965, p. 293). The reader can change the order of the episodes, can cut into the book at any point he wishes, and compose a "new" book out of it. Musical pieces like Stockhausen's *Klavierstück XI*, Berio's *Sequenza per flauto solo,* and Pousseur's *Scambi,* and visual "exercises" like Calder's mobiles, Munari's "painting in movement," and Agam's "tableaux transformables" also call for free reconstitution on the part of the consumer-become-creator (see Eco 1960, pp. 117–24). Such open forms are often referred to as 'ambiguous'. "Infinite Types of Ambiguity" is the title of Dawson's article on the subject, and Umberto Eco uses the expression "inépuisablement ambiguë" in his article "The Open Work and the Poetics of Indetermination" to describe these modern experiments (p. 124). But Eco's description unwittingly implies the difference between an open work and a work which is ambiguous in the strict sense. "L'oeuvre est ici inépuisablement ambiguë, parce qu'à un monde ordonné selon des lois universellement reconnues, s'est substitué un monde fondé sur l'équivoque. Ambiguïté: ici défaut de centres d'orientation; ambiguïté: positive et constante réversibilité des valeurs et des certitudes" (p. 124).

While an 'open work' or, in Barthes's words, a work characterized by 'infinite plurality' (1970, pp. 11–12) lacks (or deliberately eschews) centers of orientation, an ambiguous work possesses marked centers which polarize the data and create mutually exclusive systems. An open work does not have a definitive form; it is, in fact, "une série de formes virtuelle" (Eco 1960, p. 119). An ambiguous work, on the other hand, is characterized by a highly determined form, limiting the text's plurality by its organization of the data into two opposed systems which leave little or no room for further "play." 'Ambiguity' is the "conjunction" of mutual exclusives; Barthes's 'plurality' and Eco's 'openness', as exemplified by *Finnegans Wake* (1968, p. 166), are an endless generation of hypotheses without any necessary relation, any necessary "propositional operation" to link them.[9]

But let us return to more traditional concepts and define the differences between ambiguity and other long-standing manifestations of the multiplicity of meaning. The most classical device for conveying two meanings at the same time is allegory. *The Song of Songs* is said to be both about the love between a man and a woman and about the love between God and the people of Israel. Spenser's *The Faerie Queene,* Bunyan's *The*

Pilgrim's Progress, and Tennyson's *Idylls of the King* can all be read both as literal narratives and as figurative embodiments of spiritual meanings. In allegory, the literal reflects the figurative because the relation established between them is one of equivalence. In ambiguity, on the other hand, both alternatives are at the level of narrative literality (although both can have nonliteral implications), and the relation between them is not one of equivalence but of incompatibility. Allegory, in fact, can destroy a potential ambiguity, as Henry James's "The Private Life" amply proves.[10] Although the happenings in this story—the physical disappearance of Clare Vawdry when in society and of Lord Mellifont when left to himself—are supernatural, no question arises as to their reality because we immediately translate them into the language of allegory, taking the story to be about the absence of real personality on the part of the man of society and the absence of a social façade on the part of the writer.

But equivalence is not the only relation that can obtain between various readings of a literary text. Sometimes the "finalized" hypotheses complement each other or are integrated in a larger unit of meaning. The "operation" in these cases is a conjunction, and the accepted term is 'double meaning' or 'multiple meaning' (depending on the number of interpretations concerned). Examples of 'multiple meaning' are Shakespeare's *Hamlet,* Kafka's *Metamorphosis,* and Ionesco's *Amédée or How to Get Rid of It.* Ambiguity differs from double or multiple meaning in that its component alternatives cannot both be true, nor can they be subsumed in a larger unit which they conjoin to create or in which they are reconciled and integrated. Therefore 'double meaning' or 'multiple meaning' do not call for choice, while 'ambiguity' simultaneously calls for choice and makes it impossible.

Seemingly similar to ambiguity is the mixture of opposed elements in a complex whole. All too often a narrative is labeled 'ambiguous' because its characters or its represented world are neither wholly good nor wholly bad but a mixture of both (for example, Samuels 1971). The difference between this phenomenon and ambiguity has been acutely formulated by Roger Gard apropos criticism of James's *The Golden Bowl.* "James is not saying something like "people are complex and difficult to judge—neither wholly good nor wholly bad, but varying as your angle of vision or amount of information varies"—that would not be ambiguous. He is presenting two separate and complete, strongly contrasted but equally credible "realities" simultaneously. The effect therefore is not of a warning not to see people in simple blacks and whites, but of being asked to believe that some people are dark grey and light grey all over" (1963, p. 109). In 'ambiguity' both disjuncts refer to the totality, whereas in 'mixture' each refers to a different part of the totality, and the implicit 'or' is therefore nondisjunctive (see p. 4).

Real disjunction occurs in the case of irony. Here there are two opposed narratives—the one explicitly told and the other surreptitiously implied. They cannot both be true, but the reader usually has no doubt as to which of them is. Narrative irony consists not only of two opposed narratives, but also of two addressees (sometimes copresent in the same person), and the disjunction is not between two equally valid narratives, as it is in ambiguity, but between the invalid story of the narrator or character and the valid version established "behind his back" by the "implied author" and the reader. Irony is incompatible with ambiguity because its drift is unequivocally implied by the discourse. The very fact that we can identify a narrative as ironic implies a foregone choice of the correct reading, in the light of which we subvert every detail of the "false" version. The moment we can assert that a narrator or a character in a given narrative is unreliable and that our reading should proceed in direct opposition to his account, we have abandoned the realm of 'ambiguity' for that of 'irony'. Ambiguity exists in the in-between land of hesitation—a land where we cannot know whether the narrator is reliable or not and whether the events he records are to be taken on trust or to be treated with ironic disbelief. James's "A Light Man," "The Liar," "The Marriages" are only a few examples of stories in which the narrator or center of consciousness is made the butt of our irony. But what about "The Figure in the Carpet," *The Turn of the Screw,* and *The Sacred Fount?* Both reliability and unreliability, both credence and irony are equally possible. These are ambiguous works, and as such they teach us the nearly impossible lesson of being capable of belief and doubt at the same time.

At first sight it may seem possible to establish a progressive scale of "propositional operations" which will reveal a relation of direct proportion between the number of interpretations and the "flexibility" or "openness" of the work. One end of the scale will be 'univocality' and the other 'infinite plurality'. In between will be 'allegory', 'double meaning', 'ambiguity', 'multiple meaning'. But, as we shall see later, there is no such direct proportion between the number of interpretations and the openness of the work—at least not where 'ambiguity' is concerned. Ambiguity actually subjects all (or almost all) the data to its mutually exclusive hypotheses, thus leaving nothing (or almost nothing) for free play. A univocal work, on the other hand, usually contains elements which are not totally relevant, and these may contribute toward a flexibility greater than that of an ambiguous work.

APPLICATION 2: VERBAL AMBIGUITY AND
COGNATE PHENOMENA

Just as narrative ambiguity is the coexistence of mutually exclusive versions of the same happenings, so verbal ambiguity is the coexistence of mutually exclusive meanings of the same linguistic expression. The same formula of $a \wedge b$ can apply to verbal as well as to narrative ambiguity, and the same approach through "propositional operations" can be used to distinguish between verbal ambiguity and cognate verbal phenomena. The cognate verbal phenomena, like the cognate narrative phenomena, have often been treated as interchangeable with ambiguity, ambiguity having been defined rather broadly as "having more than one meaning." This broad use of the term has become the staple practice in the Anglo-American New Criticism since William Empson's pioneer *Seven Types of Ambiguity*. In this seminal book Empson defines the term as "any verbal nuance, however slight, which gives room to alternative reactions to the same piece of language" (1961, p. 1),[11] and the studies carried out by him and his disciples have had the great advantage of drawing our attention to a host of related phenomena, characteristic of the language of poetry, to which former schools of criticism have not done full justice. And yet the use of 'ambiguity' as a blanket term for all kinds of secondary meanings has also had a somewhat detrimental effect from the point of view of the precision and workability of critical terminology. It is this effect that I would like to remedy by trying to distinguish between similars and to confine 'ambiguity' to one type of "having more than one meaning."[12]

Taking $a \wedge b$ as the basic formula of ambiguity, we can now proceed to expound its implications in the form of a list of defining properties. This list can also be used as a scale of progressive discriminations and qualifications against which cognate phenomena can be measured and distinguished from 'ambiguity' proper. (I borrow this technique, but not the substance of the "conditions," from Perry 1969, pp. 40–82). While 'ambiguity' fulfills all the "conditions" listed below, other related phenomena fulfill only some.

1. An ambiguous expression has two or more distinct meanings operating in the given context.

2. The meanings of an ambiguous expression are not reducible to each other or to some common denominator, nor are they identifiable with each other or subsumable in a larger unit of meaning which they conjoin to create or in which they are reconciled and integrated.

3. The meanings of an ambiguous expression are mutually exclusive in the context, in the sense that if one applies, the other cannot apply, and vice versa.

4. Hence, an ambiguous expression calls for choice between its alternative meanings, but at the same time provides no ground for making the choice. The mutually exclusive meanings therefore coexist in spite of the either/or conflict between them.

The first defining property can be useful to distinguish between ambiguity and three cognate or seemingly cognate phenomena: the subjectivity of reading, ambivalence, and vagueness.

The subjectivity of reading, misleadingly called by Stanford "unescapable ambiguity" (1939, p. 139),[13] is mainly a function of what the reader brings into the verbal structure, whereas ambiguity is located in the verbal structure itself. The distinction is neither clear-cut nor absolute, for in both cases there is an interaction between the reader and the text. The difference lies mainly in emphasis; in the case of 'ambiguity' the verbal structure conditions our reaction, while in the case of 'subjectivity' our personal make-up determines a great deal of what we see in the verbal structure. The test of 'objectivity' is the "realization" of all the data of the text, while 'subjectivity' will usually select according to the reader's psychic constitution— "as a man is, so he sees." The use of 'ambiguity' for 'subjectivity of interpretation' also runs the risk of making all poems or, for that matter, all verbal messages ambiguous, thus rendering the term so general that it becomes practically meaningless.

The distinction between 'ambiguity' and 'ambivalence' can also be focused on the verb 'to have' in the first defining property. While ambiguity is a result of a quality or qualities *in* the object and in its interrelations with the context, ambivalence is the coexistence of contrasting emotions or attitudes *toward* the object. A clear example of the confusion of the two terms is the article by the psychologist Else Frenkel Brunswik (1954, pp. 509–38). Setting out to examine correlations between rigidity/flexibility of attitudes, tolerance of perceptual ambiguity, and various background factors, she makes comments like the following: "The evidence from both direct and indirect material thus suggests that children who tend to make unambiguous statements, either of total acceptance or of total rejection, seem to be aware of only one of two aspects co-existing within their dynamic, attitudinal make-up" (p. 519). Now, rejection or acceptance are elements of a person's "attitudinal make-up," and although they may be partly caused by qualities in the person or object toward which they are directed, they are not always completely or even partly equivalent to these qualities. In poetry, too, ambiguity and ambivalence may be related, but they may also be independent of each other. To quote Winifred Nowottny, "Though the language of poetry is often used to express or come to terms with ambivalence, and though in articulating ambivalence it may exploit the potential ambiguity of the common tongue, it is also true that ambivalence can be articulated without any such exploitation" (1962, p. 157). An example given by Nowottny is Catullus's "Odi et amo," in which the ambivalence of feeling is expressed by the contrary assertions that he loves and he hates (p. 158). It is equally true that there are poems in which "linguistic ambiguity is used for purposes other than the expression of the ambivalence of feeling" (p. 158).

Another term which can be distinguished from 'ambiguity' with the help of the first defining property is 'vagueness' or 'indeterminacy'—a term which is used in two different though related senses. Aristotle considered 'ambiguity' as a species of the fallacy of unclearness, and so did most of the Roman thinkers. Stanford, who sums up their views, himself sometimes treats 'ambiguity' and 'vagueness' as interchangeable, although, unlike the classicists he quotes, he employs both terms in a descriptive, nonevaluative sense: "In several cases it will be observed that the term ambiguity has been stretched to its widest limits to include vagueness and suggestiveness where they have appreciable dramatic force" (1939, p. 139).

Stephen Ullmann actually means 'vagueness', 'indeterminacy', 'lack of common consensus' when he speaks of the 'ambiguity' of such terms as 'sememe', 'morpheme', 'word', or 'context' (1957, pp. 5, 44, 60, passim). While it is true that both 'vagueness' and 'ambiguity' lack the crystal-clear finality of univocality and are susceptible of double (or multiple) interpretations, the difference between the two hinges on the verb 'to have' in my first defining property. While an ambiguous expression has various meanings in itself, a vague or indeterminate expression does not enter into the full commitment of any determined meaning, thereby making possible the projection of several interpretations upon it. Being more predominantly the reader's projection, the various interpretations of a vague expression are all equally *un*provable. The mutually exclusive interpretations of an ambiguous expression, on the other hand, are equally provable because equally anchored in the text. In terms of drawing, while ambiguity is a rabbit-or-duck figure, indeterminacy approaches the status of an inkblot used for Rorschach tests; it resembles no figure very clearly and therefore makes various projections possible.

The second meaning of 'vague' is derived from logic. In

logic a 'vague term' is one "referring to a quality that things can have in various degrees . . . such terms are vague when there is no general *rule* in the language to tell us *how much* of the quality a thing must have in order for the term to be applied to it" (Beardsley 1954, p. 46; Beardsley's italics). Good, bad, beautiful, ugly, rich are 'vague' terms in this sense. Indeed most words are, as the logician Copi, who defines the term somewhat differently, aptly puts it:

> Although the same word can be *both* vague and ambiguous, vagueness and ambiguity are two quite different properties. A term is ambiguous in a given context when it has two distinct meanings and the context does not make clear which one is intended. On the other hand, a term is *vague* when there exist "borderline cases" such that it cannot be determined whether the term applies to them or not. Most words are vague in the sense indicated. Scientists have been unable to decide whether certain viruses are "living" or "non-living", not because they do not know whether or not the virus has the powers of locomotion, or reproduction, etc., but because the word "living" is so vague a term. Perhaps more familiar is the difficulty in deciding whether or not a certain country is a "democracy", or whether a given work of art is "obscene" or not [1961, pp. 92–93; Copi's italics][14]

It is not only the difference between 'projection' and 'possession', hinted at by the verb 'to have', that distinguishes 'vagueness' in this sense from 'ambiguity'. The criterion of distinctness also contributes to the differentiation; whereas ambiguity (or indeed any form of multiple meaning) has two or more distinct interpretations, vagueness is characterized by a nebula of undefined "hovering" possibilities, rather than any single distinct meaning.

'Subjectivity', 'ambivalence', and 'vagueness' do not fulfill even the first defining property of 'ambiguity': they do not *have* (that is, possess in themselves) two or more *distinct* meanings. We can now proceed to verbal expressions which do have two or more distinct meanings but can be distinguished from 'ambiguity' on the basis of the other defining properties.

The second defining property postulates that the meanings of an ambiguous expression are not reducible to each other or to some common denominator. Thus 'ambiguity' is distinguished from expressions like "to count one's beads" or "as hard as nails" in which the difference between the two senses, prayers or rosary beads, fingernails or metal spikes, does not affect the meaning of the utterance as a whole (Ullmann 1962, p. 195).

Another part of the second defining property says that the meanings of an ambiguous expression are not identifiable with each other. We can thus take a further step from instances where the difference between meanings does not matter to instances where the difference does matter, but an identification between the various meanings is effected on some level of the text. To illustrate I shall quote William Empson's comment on Marvell's "Annihilating all that's made/To a green thought in a green shade" ("The Garden"). "This combines the idea of the conscious mind, including everything because understanding it, and that of the unconscious animal nature including everything because in harmony with it. Evidently the object of such a fundamental contradiction . . . is to deny its reality; the point is not that these are essentially different but that they must cease to be different so far as either is to be known. So far as he has achieved his state of ecstasy he combines them" (1935, pp. 119–20). The point of the stanza, according to Empson, is to identify these two different, even opposed, meanings, but such an identification dissolves the potential ambiguity of the expression.

Fulfilling all the above "conditions" and yet differing from 'ambiguity' are 'double meaning', 'multiple meaning', 'plurisignation', and 'complexity'. These phenomena neither reduce their various meanings to a basic common denominator nor identify them with each other, but maintain the distinctness of the meanings and let them operate conjointly. The adverb 'conjointly' actually hints at the difference between these manifestations of plurivocality and ambiguity in its strict sense. 'Double meaning', 'multiple meaning', 'plurisignation', and 'complexity' are based on a conjunction of "conjoinable" meanings, their formula being $a.b$ (or $a.b.c.d. . . .$). Ambiguity, on the other hand, is a "conjunction" of exclusive disjuncts, its formula being $a \wedge b$. It is the third defining property and its corollary, property 4, that are at the root of the difference between the two operations. In $a.b$ (or $a.b.c....$) the meanings are compatible with each other at some level of meaning—not always the literal—and can therefore be conjoined without giving rise to the issue of choice. In $a\wedge b$, on the other hand, the meanings are mutually exclusive, thus calling for disjunction and choice, but because the context provides no decisive grounds on which to base our choice, the meanings remain "conjoined."

The title of Empson's pioneer book is thus misleading. While purporting to be about 'ambiguity', the work actually analyzes the conjunction or "synthesis" or "fusion" (in the best Eliot-Richards-Graves tradition) of double or multiple meaning (for a similar point see Jensen 1965, 7271A). In the introduction Empson recognizes the advantage of narrower definitions: "Of course, I do not deny that the term had better be used as clearly as possible, and that there is a use for a separate term 'double meaning', for example, when a pun is not felt to be ambiguous in effect" (1961, p. xi).

But in the book itself he extends the term so much that "the ambiguity of 'ambiguity' " (1961, pp. 5–6) threatens to become a stumbling block rather than a convenience.[15] Philip Wheelwright, who coined the term 'plurisignation', defines the difference between it and 'ambiguity' and criticizes Empson's treatment of the two notions as interchangeable:

> Mr. William Empson in *Seven Types of Ambiguity* has made a survey of prominent types of plurisignation; unfortunately he has confused the matter by his misconception of ambiguity, which differs from plurisignation as "either-or" differs from "both-and." [1967, p. 252]

What is true of 'plurisignation' is also true of 'double meaning', 'multiple meaning' and 'complexity'—these terms being interchangeable, except that 'multiple meaning' designates more than two (that is, 'double') meanings, and that 'complexity' is actually the same phenomenon considered from the point of view of the result, rather than of the process of signification. An example of complexity created by multiple meaning or plurisignation is the title of Gide's *La symphonie pastorale*. As

Stephen Ullmann points out, the adjective *pastorale* conjoins three different meanings. At the literal level it refers to Beethoven's Pastoral Symphony, which the parson and his blind protégée attend at Neuchâtel. At the level of literary associations it brings the atmosphere of the idyllic and the bucolic to bear upon the narrated events, the effect being an ironic reminder that the friendship between the parson and Gertrude is not as innocent as it appears to him. A further nuance is added by the fact that this 'pastoral symphony' is the story of a Protestant *pastor*, French *pasteur* (1962, pp. 188–89). These three meanings of *pastorale* do not call for choice: they operate together, modify and enrich each other in their *a.b.c.* relationship. The title of Gide's novel is not ambiguous because it "fails" the test of mutual exclusiveness; it does not possess properties 3 and 4 of the proposed defining list.

The third defining property can also be used to distinguish between 'ambiguity' and what Winifred Nowottny calls "the possibility of cueing the reader to take a word as a referent both for some quality of a physical phenomenon and for some mental attitude toward it" (1962, p. 161). The example she cites is the word *candid,* which, in an anonymous poem published in a university magazine, retains both its etymological significance as 'white' and its modern meaning, denoting the quality of moral openness and frankness (p. 163). This device is a species of the simultaneous activation of the literal and figurative meanings of words, which in turn is closely related to the phenomenon of symbolism. In fact, the double meaning of the word *candid* in the student's poem, as well as any coexistence of the literal and the figurative, and likewise the related phenomenon of symbolism can be distinguished from ambiguity by the criterion of mutual exclusiveness.[16] Candid-white and candid-frank are not mutually exclusive, nor are the literal and figurative meanings of most expressions. Had they been mutually exclusive, the literal would have been incapable of suggesting the figurative.[17] These are cases of the coexistence, and often even equivalence ($a \equiv b$) of compatible meanings, whereas 'ambiguity' is the coexistence of incompatibles. Nowottny's broadening of 'ambiguity' to include the literal-figurative equation as well as the phenomenon of symbolism actually defeats her initial restrictive intention and takes us back to Empson's use of the term "for all kinds of secondary word-and-sentence meaning" (1962, p. 146). 'Extralocution', the term which she suggests instead of 'ambiguity' is made to mean *"having extra meaning* or leaving extra meaning in" (p. 156. Nowottny's italics). But this new term is also dangerously capable of suggesting that an ambiguous expression has one basic meaning plus secondary meanings *"outside* or apart from" it (p. 156. Nowottny's italics), while in fact both (or all) meanings of an ambiguous expression are equally basic and none of them is "extra."

Unlike the literal-figurative equivalence, symbols may, and often do, embrace mutually exclusive meanings. It is this kind of symbol as well as paradoxes and oxymora that fulfill all but one of the defining properties of ambiguity. Like 'ambiguity' they have two or more distinct meanings operating in the context. Like 'ambiguity' they do not reduce the various meanings to each other or to a basic common denominator, nor do they identify the meanings with each other. Like 'ambiguity', again, they give rise to a clash of mutually exclusive meanings. And yet they differ from 'ambiguity' because of the "condition" contained in the last part of the second defining property, namely, that the meanings of an ambiguous expression are not subsumable in a larger unit of meaning which they conjoin to create or in which they are reconciled and integrated. It is precisely such a reconciliation and integration that characterizes symbols, paradoxes, and oxymora. Here is Cleanth Brooks on the paradoxical treatment of divine and profane love in Donne's "The Canonization": "One type of union becomes a metaphor for the other. It may not be too far-fetched to see both as instances of, and metaphors for, the union which the creative imagination itself effects" (1949, p. 17). Paradox, says Brooks, is "the assertion of the union of opposites" (p. 194), a union which "represents not a residue but an achieved harmony" (pp. 178–79).[18]

Like paradox, an oxymoron unifies its contrary components at a level other than the literal. "Their silence is eloquent" (Cicero), "All nature is but art, unknown to thee" (Pope), and "I must be cruel only to be kind" (*Hamlet*) (Shipley

1966, s.v. "oxymoron")—each contain elements which are mutually incompatible at the literal level (silence/eloquence, nature/art, cruel/kind). And yet the contradiction is dissolved at a higher level, and the expressions make univocal sense ("their silence is expressive"; "Nature is a God-made 'object' just as Art is man-made"; "I must be cruel in order to make you realize things which will finally do you good"). In 'ambiguity', on the other hand, there is no resolution, and the mutually exclusive meanings coexist at the level of literality.

Verbal irony (like narrative irony) also differs from ambiguity, in spite of the mutually exclusive nature of its meanings. The difference between the two can be formulated with the help of the fourth property, namely, the possibility of choice. Irony is a disjunction of mutual exclusives $(a \land b)$ between which the reader can choose the "true" meaning concealed behind the overt "false" one. It is on the possibility of choice that the effect of irony depends, while ambiguity renders choice impossible and maintains both disjuncts in the openness of equitenability $(a \land b)$.

If even after these distinctions the reader is hesitant to adopt a terminology which upsets common usage, he can follow Kaplan and Kris in speaking of *types* of ambiguity, rather than of various cognate phenomena only one of which is 'ambiguity' proper. Five types are discerned by Kaplan and Kris (1948) in the most systematic study of ambiguity I have read, and I shall quote their own definitions:

1. *Disjunctive ambiguity:* "We call an ambiguity disjunctive when the separate meanings function in the process of interpretation as alternatives, excluding and inhibiting each other", for example, "The Duke yet lives that Henry shall depose" (p. 417).

2. *Additive ambiguity:* "the separate meanings, though still alternative, are no longer fully exclusive but are to some extent included one in the other . . . Several meanings differing only in degree or specificity or in what they add to the common core meaning" (p. 418). A word like 'rich' is ambiguous in this sense: it has different nuance-meanings which are "not fully distinct and exclusive, but overlap and merge into one another" (p. 418).

3. *Conjunctive ambiguity:* "When the separate meanings are jointly effective in the interpretation" (p. 419).

4. *Integrative ambiguity:* "when its manifold meanings evoke and support one another" (p. 420). Whereas in the conjunctive type the different meanings are connected but remain distinct, in the integrative type they are "fully reconstituted—integrated, in short, into one complex meaning", as in "the *shrunken* seas" from T.S. Eliot's "Sweeney among the Nightingales" (p. 420).

5. *Projective ambiguity* (and the authors themselves are not sure that this can legitimately be called a type of ambiguity): "The term is in such cases said to be 'hopelessly' vague, the meanings found being in fact imposed—projected —by the interpreter" (p. 421).

The parallels between this classification and my own set of distinctions are easy to establish. Kaplan and Kris's 'projective ambiguity' corresponds to 'the subjectivity of reading' and to extreme instances of 'vagueness' in the logical sense of the word. 'Conjunctive ambiguity' corresponds to some types of 'double meaning', 'multiple meaning', 'plurisignation', and 'complexity', while 'integrative ambiguity' corresponds to other instances of the same phenomena (depending on whether the various meanings are simply conjoined or also integrated in a larger unit of meaning) as well as to some types of symbols, to paradoxes, and to oxymora.[19] 'Disjunctive ambiguity' is the one type which corresponds to my strict definition of 'ambiguity', and the reader who prefers the Kaplan-Kris classification can read 'disjunctive ambiguity' wherever I say 'ambiguity' *tout court,* provided that he bear in mind the "conjunction" of exclusive disjuncts in this type of ambiguity.[20]

2 Ambiguity: The Concrete Realization

NARRATIVE AMBIGUITY

In chapter one it has been stated that an important aspect of every science is the definition of its basic units and of the operations it employs in order to construct larger units out of the smaller ones. Proceeding on similar lines, I have attempted a definition of ambiguity by specifying its constituent units and the "propositional operation" which obtains between them. In narrative ambiguity, the constituent elements, the *a* and *b* of the formula, were said to be the mutually exclusive "finalized hypotheses," and the operation obtaining between them was defined as a "conjunction" of exclusive disjuncts. But the "finalized hypotheses" and their "conjunction" are abstractions which convey the basic formative principle of ambiguity but cannot (and were not intended to) do justice to all its components and to the intricate relations among them. The purpose of this chapter is to trace—still at a general-theoretical level— the bridge between the most abstract macrostructural level of "the basic formula" and the most concrete microstructural units which constitute the ambiguity. The finalized *a* and *b* are generalizations from hundreds of smaller units which are related to each other in various logical, chronological, and spatial ways. I propose now to define these basic constituent units and to outline the possible relations among them.

Since narrative ambiguity is an aspect of narrative, and since narrative is an aspect or subcategory of "literary text," it could be convenient to base a theory of narrative ambiguity on fully developed and universally accepted theories of the literary text, and in particular of literary narrative. Unfortunately, no such theories exist. Research into the nature of narrative or of the literary text in general is relatively young and has not yet reached conclusive results. There exists, therefore, no unified body of definitions and distinctions on which we can base a demarcation of the components of narrative ambiguity. But there are several studies which may help us realize the nature of the problem, even though I cannot wholeheartedly accept their solutions. The studies I am about to survey deal with narrative units and narrative combinations in general, and I intend to examine their relevance to the definition of the basic units and linkages of which narrative ambiguity is constructed.

As soon as one wishes to survey existing definitions of narrative units, one is struck by an embarrassing lack of uniformity regarding the object defined by the various researchers who are, in fact, interested in different aspects of the text. I know of no systematic presentation of the various aspects amenable to unit analysis, and individual studies often omit an explicit statement of the aspect which they intend to examine, so that what seems a disagreement may simply be a selection of a different object for analysis. Therefore, it is with the aspects which condition the demarcation of units that I propose to begin.

Aspects of Narrative

Four distinctions mark four points of divergence between researchers:

1. Actional structure vs. texture
2. "*Langue*" vs. "*parole*"
3. "Deep structures" vs. "surface structures"
4. Totality vs. basic *armature*

Faute de mieux, the above terms are a concoction of linguistics, Formalism, and Structuralism, and they clearly call for explication.

Actional structure vs. texture.   A distinction has been made between the sum total of actions in a literary text and the way in which these actions are artistically organized and integrated in the accomplished work. The sum total of actions are in a sense preliterary and can be translated into different media of communication (film, for example). The texture, on the other hand, is the particular way in which the actions are handled in the literary work. The texture includes elements like organization, point of view, choice of narrator, handling of time, analogies, while the actional structure itself is an abstraction of the actions and a "mapping" of their "preartistic" relations. The actional structure is sometimes called "narrative structure," but I shall not adopt this term because the word *narrative* in my own study is not always used in this restricted sense.

"Langue" vs. "parole."   This is an application to the study of fiction of the linguistic terms coined by Ferdinand de Saussure in his famous *Cours de linguistique générale.* According to Saussure, *langue* is the code or system of language which all users have in common, while *parole* is the individual execution, the individual speech act (1969, pp. 36–39). In the study of narrative, the term *langue* refers to the system underlying all narratives and governing the generation of narratives, while the term *parole* designates the realization of the system in the framework of the individual narrative. The same distinction can be rephrased in Chomskian terminology as narrative "competence" versus narrative "performance" (without going here into the whole question of whether there is such a thing as "narrative competence").

"Deep structures" vs. "surface structures."   The terms are borrowed from generative-transformational grammar, which undertakes to enumerate (characterize) the infinite set of sentences of a language by positing a finite number of deep-structure (phrase-structure) rules containing a recursive element as well as a set of transformational rules which convert deep-structure strings to surface structures. Applying these concepts to the nonlinguistic "syntax" of narrative, we can distinguish between the "abstract" underlying structure of the action (its "deep structure") and its concrete realization in the particular work (its "surface structure").

Totality vs. basic armature.   Some studies deal with all the units of the given work, while others select only those units which combine to form the basic skeleton of the work, its structural "armature" (Barthes's term, 1966, p. 12).

All the cross combinations among the research directions contained in the above points of divergence are feasible, although some of them may overlap in practice, and some may be more frequent than others.

The distinction between actional structure and texture overlaps other useful distinctions, notably the Formalists' *fabula* vs. *sjužet* and the Structuralists' *histoire* vs. *discours*.

Of the two Formalist terms, *fabula* is clearly defined, while *sjužet* is given different (though obviously related) meanings by the different members of the group. According to Tomashevsky, the *fabula* is the sum total of events in their chronological and logical order, while the *sjužet* is the sum total of the same events in the order in which they are represented in the work (Lemon and Reis 1965, p. 66).[1] The criterion for Tomashevsky's distinction is temporal arrangement: the *fabula* is composed of events arranged in the order of occurrence, while the *sjužet* may follow the same order, as it does in simple stories like "Little Red Ridinghood," but it may also decompose and "deform" it for artistic purposes. An illuminating illustration of temporal displacements is the composition of the detective story. Take, for example, Conan Doyle's "The Sign of the Four." Whereas the *fabula* starts with the adventures concerning the Agra treasure, the *sjužet* delays these episodes to the very end. It tells first things last and last things first, thus maintaining suspense. Reversing the order of the *fabula*, Doyle starts with "The Statement of the Case" by Miss Morstan, and only at the end does he let Jonathan Small recount the story of the Agra treasure.

From the point of view of artistic creation, the *fabula* precedes the *sjužet*, the *fabula* being the raw material which can be artistically molded into various *sjužets*.[2] From the point of view of synopsis, on the other hand, the *sjužet* is the most concrete level which we can retell by selecting the cardinal events and establishing the correct links between them. A telling of the *fabula*, on the other hand, requires an abstraction and a reconstruction of a sequence of events which differs from that represented in the text before us.

But temporal arrangement is not the only way of turning a series of events into an artistic composition, and some Formalist studies use the term *sjužet* in a broader sense which includes point of view, analogies, digressions. Thus, for Eichenbaum, *sjužet* is identical with artistic construction (in Todorov 1965, p. 55), though neither he nor any other Formalist specifies whether the *sjužet* in this sense is a prelinguistic element (like the *fabula*) or an artistic construction in language.

A third meaning of the term can be found in Shklovsky's writings. For him, the *sjužet* is "not merely the artistic arrangement of the story stuff, but the totality of 'devices' employed in the process of telling the story. This includes elements of esthetic structure like digressions irrelevant to the narration" (in Erlich 1969, p. 242). Unlike the first two senses, this meaning does not designate the narrative, whether prelinguistic or linguistic, but the techniques used to create it.

Further broadened, the term *sjužet* often becomes identical with the work as a whole, and the distinction between it and the *fabula* no longer differentiates between two aspects of the work, but rather between the whole (*sjužet*) and one of its parts or aspects (*fabula*).

In order to render the term useful and precise, a selection of one of the four meanings or a formulation of a new definition is necessary. But before we do so, let us examine the parallel French terms, *histoire* (or *récit*) and *discours*. These terms originated both in Todorov's translation of the Russian Formalists and in the application to literature of categories introduced into linguistics by E. Benveniste. Here is Todorov's definition in "Les categories du récit littéraire":

> Au niveau le plus général, l'oeuvre littéraire a deux
> aspects; elle est en même temps une histoire et un discours.
> Elle est histoire, dans ce sens qu'elle évoque une certaine
> réalité, des événements qui se seraient passés, des person-
> nages qui, de ce point de vue, se confondent avec ceux de la
> vie réelle. Cette même histoire aurait pu nous être rapportée
> par d'autres moyens; par un film, par exemple; on aurait
> pu l'apprendre par le récit oral d'un témoin, sans qu'elle soit
> incarnée dans un livre. Mais l'oeuvre est en même temps
> discours: il existe un narrateur qui relate l'histoire et il y a

en face de lui un lecteur qui en perçoit. A ce niveau ce ne sont pas les événements rapportés qui comptent mais la façon dont le narrateur nous les a faits connaître. [1966, p. 126]

Like the Russian *fabula*, the French *histoire* is the basic story stuff, governed by a chronological and logical order of its own, similar to that of "real life" and independent of its artistic shaping. The French *discours*, on the other hand, corresponds to the second of the four meanings of *sjužet*, namely the artistic construction into which the events are molded. Unlike the first meaning of *sjužet*, confined exclusively to the handling of time, the definition of *discours* deliberately refuses to give temporal "deformation" a place of honor in the distinction and classes it together with point of view, digressions, spatial construction (Todorov 1966, p. 139).[3]

Whereas the Formalists are not explicit about the linguistic or prelinguistic status of the *sjužet*, the Structuralists emphasize the medium of language. Having observed that the *histoire* is the constant element which can be abstracted from the different media and translated from one medium to another, Todorov and Bremond wished to be consistent and make the media themselves the variable component. The *discours*, then, is the telling of the *histoire* in language, addressed by a narrator to a reader or listener. The Russian *sjužet*, on the other hand, is distinguished from the *fabula* mainly by being molded into an artistic composition, not necessarily in a specific medium. Indeed, it will not be wrong to say (although the Formalists themselves have not made this point) that in every medium there can be both a *fabula* and a *sjužet*, and, on the other hand, in one and the same medium a *fabula* can be molded into different *sjužets*. Moreover, just as the same *fabula* can be abstracted from the different media, so can the same *sjužet* (if the term is taken to mean the prelinguistic "construction"). This, of course, does not mean that every device can be used in every medium. There are certainly devices which are medium-bound, but others are transferable from one medium to another, although their technical realization will be different in each. For example, a distortion of natural chronology in the form of a flashback can characterize a film as well as a story or a novel. The *fabula* in Jack Clayton's film *The Pumpkin Eater* begins with the heroine as an attractive young woman, whereas the *sjužet* begins with the same heroine as an elderly haggard woman, wandering like a ghost in her drawing room (Stephenson and Debrix 1965, pp. 101–2). In a narrative like Robbe-Grillet's *L'année dernière à Marienbad* not only the same *fabula* (or the same mutually exclusive *fabulas*) but also the same *sjužet* can be discerned in novel and film alike.

A third difference between the Formalist and Structuralist approaches is the hierarchy which they establish between the two aspects in their practical analyses of literary works. While most of the Russian Formalists see the *fabula* as a preartistic element and devote their studies to the *sjužet,* most of the French Structuralists are interested in the *histoire* itself, rather than in the way in which it is organized in the accomplished narrative. Todorov explicitly criticizes the Formalists' conscious disregard of the *fabula,* taking Shklovsky's polemical declarations as the epitome of what he considers the wrong approach.

> Chklovski declarait que l'histoire n'est pas un élément artistique mais un matériau prélittéraire; seul le discours était pour lui une construction esthétique. Il croyait pertinent pour la structure de l'oeuvre le fait que le dénouement soit placé avant le noeud de l'intrigue; mais non le fait que le héros accomplisse tel acte au lieu de tel autre (en pratique les formalistes étudiaient l'un et l'autre). Pourtant les deux aspects, l'histoire et le discours, sont tous deux également littéraires. La rhétorique classique se serait occupée des deux: l'histoire relèverait de l'*inventio,* le discours de la *dispositio.*
>
> Trente ans plus tard, dans un élan de repentir, le même Chklovski passait d'un extrême à l'autre, en affirmant: "Il est impossible et inutile de séparer la partie événementielle de son agencement compositionnel, car il s'agit toujours de la même chose: la connaissance du phénomène" . . . Cette affirmation nous paraît tout aussi inadmissible que la première: c'est oublier que l'oeuvre a deux aspects et non un seul. Il est vrai qu'il n'est pas toujours facile de les distinguer, mais nous croyons que, pour comprendre l'unité même de l'oeuvre, il faut d'abord isoler ces deux aspects.
> [1966, pp. 126–27]

Despite affirmations that a work of art has two aspects, not one, many Structuralist studies attempt to discover deep structures governing the *histoire*, in abstraction from their concrete manifestations as a *discours*. Todorov's own *Grammaire du Décaméron* belongs to this category. According to him, the book is a contribution to the nonexistent science of "narratology," rather than to literary criticism, although he hopes that his conclusions will not be devoid of interest to the student of literature. "Le système narratif que nous décrivons," he says, "est une abstraction par rapport au text réel: nous traitons des résumés des nouvelles plus que des nouvelles elles-mêmes" (1969, p. 16).

In view of the various definitions given by the Formalists and the differences between them and the parallel notions in French Structuralism, it seems necessary to make my own distinctions as explicit as possible, especially because I borrow most of the above terms, but give them a slant of my own. I propose a ternary rather than a binary classification, dividing narrative into (1) *fabula,* (2) *sjužet,* and (3) discourse.

1. I retain the term *fabula* for the totality of actions in their "natural" chronological and logical order. The *fabula* in this sense is a premedium and precomposition level. It can be conveyed in language, in cinematic shots, in mime, or in ballet, and it can be translated from one medium to another. In each medium, it can be molded into various *sjužets* by a change in the time sequence, in point of view, and the like.

2. The *sjužet* is defined in this study as an artistically shaped but prelinguistic (premedium) presentation of the *fabula*. It is thus on a higher level than the *fabula* itself because it is already subjected to artistic construction, but it is still abstracted from the system of signs in which it is finally communicated to us. The *sjužet* is a premedium but not a precompositional level. The main devices used to make a *sjužet* out of the *fabula* are the following:

a. The handling of time. While the time sequence in the *fabula* is linear, the *sjužet* can distort chronology. It can start from the end and delay the expositional material to the very last pages, as in detective stories; it can use flashbacks, as in James's "Madame de Mauves," or anticipations, as in Muriel Spark's *The Prime of Miss Jean Brodie.* By way of compression and expansion, the *sjužet* can assign to events a hierarchy of importance different from that which they have in life (in the *fabula*). In Joyce's "Eveline," the story of a lifetime is compressed into short bouts of reminiscence while the experiences of one day are conveyed in much greater detail.

b. The selection of point of view. In the *fabula* there is no point of view; there are simply events arranged in the order of occurrence. In the *sjužet* the same events can be narrated from the point of view of the main agent involved, as in Nabokov's *Lolita*, or rendered by a witness-observer, as in Fitzgerald's *The Great Gatsby*, or told by an authorial narrator, as in Fielding's *Tom Jones*. A change in point of view leaves the *fabula* unaltered, but it can radically transform the *sjužet*. What a different book *Lolita* would be if related from the point of view of the "nymphet" herself or from that of an authorial narrator!

c. The use of analogies. Analogies, like the one between Père Goriot's death and Mme de Beauséant's farewell party, establish spatial relations between elements which are merely linear in the *fabula*.

d. The use of digressions. Because it is a sequence of events, the *fabula* has no digressions, but in the *sjužet* digressions can become so central as to overshadow all action. *Tristram Shandy*, of course, is the classical example.

All these techniques can, at least theoretically, be used in different media, and the *sjužet* is, in a sense, medium-free. I say "in a sense" because in the actual work of art it is difficult to separate the *sjužet* itself and its manifestation in the medium. In literature, for example, it is the words that *create* the point of view or the shift in time or the analogies. And yet the compositional principles and the *sjužet* created by them are separable (at least for the sake of the analysis) from their manifestation in language, which is already a third level.

3. I shall refer to the actual manifestation in language as "discourse," in accordance with the meaning of the term in linguistics, not in French Structuralism, where it resembles the Russian *sjužet*. Although it is in language that the *sjužet* is conveyed to us, the two need not follow the same compositional principle. A character may, for example, be the grammatical

subject of a sentence but the logical object of the narrated situation, as in "I received a blow." *Fabula, sjužet,* and discourse, then, are three different though interrelated levels of literary narrative, and it is at all these levels that I wish to describe the workings of ambiguity. The level of discourse will be discussed in the section devoted to verbal ambiguity, while the preverbal levels of both *fabula* and *sjužet* are the subject of the present inquiry.

The Basic Units

Vladimir Propp, one of the pioneer students of the structure of the folktale (1928; reprint edition 1958), was the first to separate the actional structure from its artistic handling in the texture of the work. In an attempt to define the basic actional unit, Propp distinguishes between variable and constant components: The variable components are concrete elements of the individual narrative, while the constant components are analytical concepts, abstractions from the narrative. For example, a mother sends her son to look for his sister, a king sends his knight to pursue the Holy Grail, a student goes to some distant country to acquire knowledge—all these are concrete manifestations, variables of the constant "abstract" concept of quest. Propp's main interest is in the constant elements, in the "abstracted" actions which he calls *functions.* A function, then, is the basic narrative unit, perceived not from the point of view of the "variable" actions of the narrative as it is actually told, but from that of the "constant" action abstracted from its *fabula.* In fact, in order to qualify as function the abstracted unit must be one that advances the plot, and something approaching a basic *armature* is thus established by listing the functions one after the other. Propp's preoccupation, however, is not with the *armature* of individual tales, but with that of a whole genre. His main contention is that the number of the basic functions is limited (31 in the narrative *langue* of the Russian folktale) and so is the number of the possible combinations between them. From this small number of functions we can derive numerous variable manifestations by operating a fixed set of transformations characteristic of the given genre (Propp, in Todorov 1965, pp. 234–62).

Propp's analyses were taken up by some of the French Structuralists who, like him, are interested in structures under-lying the narrated world, rather than in the actual composition of the individual narration. Like Propp, whose method he violently criticizes (1964, pp. 10–12), Bremond calls the basic unit a function (*fonction*) and goes on to show how the func-tions are grouped in sequences and the sequences in higher sequences until the whole narrative is formed (1966, pp. 60–76).

Similar in approach is Todorov's *Grammaire du Décaméron.* The book purports to analyze the "syntactic aspect" of narra-tive, that is, the combination of the units among themselves, their mutual relations (1969, p. 18).[4] The basic syntactic unit is called a *proposition,* and an attempt is made to arrive at some calculus of propositions. According to Todorov, the proposition designates "une action 'indécomposable' " (p. 19), and although some of his initial examples make the impression that he is interested in variable texture manifestations ("Jean steals the money," "the king kills his grandson," [p. 19]), he is in fact concerned with abstract syntactic structures ("X pun-ishes Y," "X sins") which are then filled in at the semantic level (p. 24).

A strong emphasis on hierarchy between the units is put by Eugene Dorfman in *The Narreme in the Medieval Romance Epic.* Like Propp, Bremond, and Todorov, Dorfman deals with the actional structure, but he is more explicit than the others about the basic *armature* versus the totality of incidents.

For this reason, the incidents, as structural units, may be divided into two main classes: *central* or core *incidents,* whose function is to serve as the central focus or core of a larger episode, and *marginal incidents,* which cluster around the core, supporting it and filling out the episode. The structure of a narrative may thus be analyzed in two ways: as a chain, containing all the incidents, central and marginal, that form the complete story; and as a much smaller chain of functionally central incidents, linked to each other in an organic relationship. By reason of their special function as core incidents in the structure of the narrative, these central units will be called *narremes.* [1969, p. 5]

How can we determine whether a given incident is or is not a narreme?

> In each case, there is a simple but decisive question: can the incident under consideration be omitted from the inventory without interrupting the continuity of the story? Except for the initial narreme which serves as the necessary foundation for what is to follow, and the final narreme, which is the natural outcome of what has preceded, the test of a narreme is that it be the organic consequence of the preceding narreme and the effective cause of the following one. [p. 67]

The above studies are concerned with the abstracted actional structure. Tomashevsky, on the other hand, seems to be more concerned with the texture of the *sjužet* than with abstractions from the *fabula*, and this is so because his interest is mainly in the narrative *parole* and only by implication in the narrative *langue*. The basic narrative unit is called a *motif*, and it is defined semantically.

> After reducing a work to its thematic elements, we come to parts that are irreducible, the smallest particles of thematic material: "evening comes", "Raskolnikov kills the old woman", "the hero dies", "the letter is received", and so on. The theme of an irreducible part of a work is called the *motif;* each sentence, in fact, has its own motif. [Lemon and Reis 1965, p. 67]

Motifs like "Raskolnikov kills the old woman," "the hero dies," "the letter is received" would not be classed as functions or propositions in the Propp-Bremond-Todorov models. Raskolnikov, the old woman, the hero, the letter are lexical "fillers," or what Propp calls "variable elements," and therefore are less crucial to the narrative *langue* than the actions themselves. Moreover, even the actions as they appear in Tomashevsky's examples would be rephrased by Propp, Bremond, and Todorov according to their function in the advancement of the story (misdeed, reception of information, and so on). But it is murder, not simply a misdeed, that characterizes *Crime and Punishment,* and it is Raskolnikov, not simply a neutral agent, who committed the crime. In dealing with

concrete units, Tomashevsky is closer to the actual composition of the text than are Propp, Bremond, and Todorov (who,
of course, are not to be criticized for not doing what they did
not intend to do).[5]

Moreover, Tomashevsky's units are not confined to the
action. Digressions and retardatory devices are also classed as
motifs, but a distinction is made between free and bound
motifs. Bound motifs are those that cannot be omitted without
disturbing the whole causal-chronological course of events,
while free motifs can be dropped without causing such harm
(Lemon and Reis 1965, pp. 68–69).

Barthes makes a similar distinction between "cardinal
functions" (or "kernels") and *"catalyses"* (1966, p. 9), but
unlike Tomashevsky he does not define the cardinal functions
by their indispensability. His "kernels" are the moments of
choice in the story, and even when they are trivial, they remain
"cardinal" by virtue of the alternatives they open.

These, then, are the main attempts to define narrative units.
What contribution can they make toward the definition of the
constituent units of narrative ambiguity? In order to answer
this question we must distinguish between direct and indirect
contributions. The direct contributions are those devoted to
the study of ambiguity, while the indirect ones are possible
applications of what was said of narrative units in general to
the particular case of the constituent units of narrative
ambiguity.

The only direct contribution I know of can be found in
Todorov's *Grammaire du Décaméron* (1969, pp. 65–67). In
this book Todorov distinguishes between "ambiguity of proposition" and "ambiguity of sequence," the one defined in purely
"syntactic" terms, the other in terms of the *discours* as a whole.
Propositional ambiguity is the result of the inclusion of one
proposition in two or more sequences at the same time. Thus,
the proposition "X kills Y" can become an act of punishment
in one sequence and a misdeed in another. The source of
sequential ambiguity, on the other hand, is the existence of
several characters with whom the reader tends to identify.
When the angle of vision "passes successively from one character to another, it is highly possible that a sequential ambi-

guity will appear" (p. 67; my translation). And he concludes, "L'ambiguïté séquentielle consiste précisement dans la possibilité d'attribuer deux ou plusieurs structures à une même histoire" (p. 67). The attractiveness of these definitions for the modern theorist lies in their resemblance to Chomsky's description of grammatical ambiguity.

> Occasionally, a grammar may permit us to construct nonequivalent derivations for a given sentence. Under these circumstances we say that we have a case of "constructional homonymity", and if our grammar is correct, this sentence of the language should be ambiguous. [1957, p. 28]

If indeed one can establish this degree of similarity between linguistics and "trans-linguistic practices" (Kristeva, in Todorov, ed., 1968, p. 80) one's "systematic self" has every reason to rejoice. Nor is it only a matter of one's joy in system and symmetry per se. For there is no doubt that the contemporary study of linguistic structures is much more developed than the younger research into narrative structures, and if the analogy between the two is as perfect as Todorov's *Grammaire du Décaméron* wishes to imply, the way to advance the analysis of narrative is paved by the relatively easy application to it of knowledge acquired in linguistics. But the analogy is not perfect, and the application is quite problematic.

Todorov's definition of sequential ambiguity is two-fold, and I suspect that it is unconsciously so. On the one hand, he defines it as a matter of point of view, a definition which clearly belongs to the realm of texture and which, in Chomskian terminology, is a phenomenon of the surface. On the other hand, he speaks about the possibility of attributing two or more structures to the same story, a formulation which seems to refer to the actional structure itself and which recalls Chomsky's view of "constructional homonymity" as the existence of two or more deep structures underlying the same surface manifestation. If Todorov's double definition is wittingly or unwittingly intended to imply an analogy between actional structure and texture, it is an overly optimistic (and equally simplistic) view of things. For a novel may contain various shifts in point of view without being ambiguous (for example, Faulkner's *The Sound and the Fury*), and on the other hand it may derive from different deep structures without involving a change in point of view (for example, James's *The Turn of the Screw* and *The Sacred Fount,* Nathalie Sarraute's *Portrait d'un inconnu*).

The definition of propositional ambiguity raises another problem. It is hard to see why the inclusion of one proposition in two sequences must in itself be ambiguous. There is nothing ambiguous in a murder which is a punishment from one point of view (revenge, for example) and a crime from another ("Vengeance is mine"). The Chomskian analogy is here misleading. A narrative proposition becomes ambiguous only if it is incorporated in mutually exclusive sequences in which it plays mutually exclusive roles. Although out of context, in an isolated list or a dictionary of antonyms, *crime* and *punishment* may appear as opposites, in a given context they can become perfectly compatible. It is indeed possible to view murder as a punishment for a crime and yet to consider this retributive act as a crime in itself. The two are not mutually exclusive, and they do not create propositional ambiguity.

The analogy from transformational grammar is mainly valid at the macrostructural level of what I have called "finalized hypotheses." If we take the complete narrative to be analogous to a grammatical sentence, then narrative ambiguity can be described as the possibility of attributing two or more "deep structures" to the same narrative (and the term "deep structures" is used more or less metaphorically). This, in fact, is another way of describing the "conjunction" of mutually exclusive finalized hypotheses, which I have discussed in chapter one. We can even go further and define narrative ambiguity as the coexistence of mutually exclusive *fabulas* in one *sjužet,* a "constructional homonymity" whereby the same surface *sjužet* derives from exclusively disjunctive *fabulas.* But we cannot infer from this an analogous form of microstructural ambiguities, whether at the level of the proposition or at that of the sequence. In other words, the ambiguity of a given narrative need not imply the ambiguity of all or even some of its constituent units. Indeed, a narrative may be ambiguous even if it does not contain a single unit which is ambiguous in itself. This is so because narrative ambiguity is constructed around a central pivot which polarizes the data into two mutually exclusive systems. The "propositions" (to use Todorov's terminology) need not be locally integrated in mutually exclusive "sequences," provided that they are integrated in the generalized macrostructural sequences which I have called "finalized hypotheses." What I am trying to define are not the basic ambiguous units, but the basic units which contribute to the creation of the overall ambiguity of the narrative, and Todorov's distinctions are not sufficiently illuminating in this direction.

Perhaps we could derive additional light from an application of what has been said about narrative units in general to the definition of the constituent units of narrative ambiguity. Two main problems immediately arise.

1. Is the smallest unit really indivisible? Todorov is aware of this problem when he says of the 'proposition':

Elle correspond à une action "indécomposable" . . . Cependant cette action n'est pas indécomposable qu'à un certain niveau de généralité; à un niveau plus concret, une telle proposition serait représentée par une série de propositions. Autrement dit, une même histoire peut avoir des résumés plus ou moins succincts. Ainsi l'un posséderait la proposition "Le roi fait la cour à la marquise" là où dans un autre on aurait: "Le roi décide de partir", "Le roi voyage", "Le roi arrive à la maison de la marquise" etc. etc.
[1969, p. 19]

If the reducibility or irreducibility of a unit is to be determined by criteria derived from actions in reality, there is hardly any action which (at least theoretically) is not infinitely divisible. But even if the criteria are to be derived from the relatively closed world of the text before us, such units as "Raskolnikov kills the old woman" are clearly divisible into "Raskolnikov goes to the woman's house," "he opens the door quietly," "he lifts the axe," "he then lowers it on the woman's head," and the like. The limits of divisibility will be determined by the details given in the text, but many of these would be of the kind that the above studies would wish to group together under one generic name. This brings me to the tentative conclusion that objective irreducibility may not be a feasible condition for the demarcation of narrative units and that the boundaries of the units should perhaps be determined by the needs of the analysis rather than by a "myth" of indivisibility. What this implies is a flexible approach in which the units change as the object of the study changes. The limitedness of the object of study chosen by the above critics is my next point.

2. The main object of study in all the works surveyed above is action. Propp, Todorov, and Bremond define the basic units by their contribution to the advancement of the action, while Tomashevsky, Barthes, and Dorfman use this criterion to distinguish between core and marginal components. Critics concerned with the actional structure seem to identify "narrative" with "action," while critics interested in the texture of the work recognize the existence of nonactional (or only slightly actional) narrative units (digressions, for example), but class them as marginal elements, or as *free motifs,* or as *catalyses*—namely, as elements which do not enter into the basic *armature.* It is difficult to see how these approaches can account for novels like *Tristram Shandy,* in which the bulk of the "action" is composed of nonactional units, or to put it in more precise terminology, the main motifs in the *sjužet* are those that would be classed as "free" in the *fabula.* But even if we disregard for the moment such extreme examples, the fact remains that the concept of action in the studies discussed is very narrow. It applies to folktales and to thrillers like the James Bond series (Barthes 1966, pp. 7–11), but it is problematic even in the case of detective stories. The whole body of retardatory devices which bulk large in detective stories will be either completely ignored (in the actional-structure type of analysis) or relegated to the role of "free motifs" (in an analysis of texture). In detective stories the governing principle is not simply *action* in the sense of "deeds," but a series of attempts to solve an enigma, and the narrative units, it seems to me, should be defined in relation to this central enigma.[6] Such centripetal rather than linear segmentation is based on an internal "norm" rather than on an external actional *langue.* It divides the units according to their function in relation to the object of analysis,

which in this case is also the governing structural principle of the work.[7] It thus dispenses with the progression of the action as the crucial yardstick (unless it is precisely the progression of the action that constitutes the object of the analysis) and accounts for the centrality of delays, digressions, and other "nonprogressive" elements. It also dispenses with the criterion of irreducibility, since the boundaries of the units are determined according to their function (in the traditional, non-Proppian sense of the term), not according to objective divisibility.

The approach I suggest is even more useful for the kind of enigma stories in which the enigma remains unsolved even after the completion of the narrative. James's "The Figure in the Carpet" is a case in point. The first reading of such stories is directed toward the solution, but once we realize that no solution exists, we establish new relations between the data, based on their contribution to the definitive evasion of disclosure. The units in this case are determined according to their arresting rather than advancing function, and a new hierarchy (that is, a new governing principle) is thereby established. It is true that such a definition of units is retrospective, but so are the definitions suggested by Propp, Bremond, Todorov, Tomashevsky, and the others. Being based on an end result concept of action, the latter studies assume the completion of the action in order to be able to decide which units are responsible for its development. In any case, a definition of the basic units is not identical with the process of reading, and its retrospective character is almost a necessity.

A considerable contribution toward the definition of the constituent units of narrative enigmas is Barthes's "hermeneutic code." Barthes does not speak about enigma stories, but about the enigma element in every story. He defines the hermeneutic code as "l'ensemble des unités qui ont pour fonction d'articuler, des diverses manières, une question, sa réponse et les accidents variés qui peuvent ou préparer la question ou rétarder la réponse; ou encore: de formuler une énigme et d'amener son déchiffrement" (1970, p. 24).[8] The hermeneutic units are called *herméneutèmes* (pp. 215–16), and they include retardatory devices as well as devices which advance the narrative toward the desired solution.

The question of enigma stories is intimately connected with that of narrative ambiguity. For ambiguous works inevitably create a central enigma: Is there a 'figure' in Vereker's 'carpet'? Are there real ghosts at Bly? Are there vampirish relations between the guests at Newmarch? Did Mathias rape and kill the girl? Did the anonymous couple really meet at Marienbad in the previous year?[9] When the narrative is truly ambiguous, the enigma remains unsolved, not because the text provides no answer, but because it provides two mutually exclusive yet equally tenable answers. Searching for a solution, the reader gropes for clues and realizes that they balance each other in the deadlock of opposition. Everything (or almost everything) in an ambiguous work is functional for the "game" of fitting clues together, and it is from the point of view of this "game" that the constituent units are best determined. The basic unit is a *hermeneutic clue,* and it is determined by its function as evidence in relation to the central enigma, not by its objective indivisibility. The suggested division is according to relations, not according to inherent qualities. Thus, unlike Tomashevsky's motifs, each contained in a sentence, the hermeneutic clues vary in mode and in extent: they can take the form of a word, a sentence, a paragraph, an event, a conversation, a description, and so on.

Having defined the units in relation to the central enigma or gap, we must now proceed to a detailed description of gaps, followed by a "calculus" of possible links and combinations between the various gap-filling units.

The Glory of the Gap

In his 1914 essay entitled "The New Novel," Henry James praises Conrad's achievement in *Chance*:

> Mr. Conrad's first care on the other hand is expressly to posit or set up a reciter, a definite responsible intervening first person singular, possessed of infinite sources of references, who immediately proceeds to set up another, to the end that this other may conform again to the practice, and that even at that point the bridge over to the creature, or in other words to the situation or the subject, the thing 'produced' shall, if the fancy takes it, once more and yet once more glory in a gap [Shapira, ed., 1968, p. 381][10]

James is here describing an extreme instance of a narrative
gap and a specific technique used to create it. But the creation
of gaps of one kind or another is characteristic of almost all
literature. Indeed, it is one of the main ways in which the raw
material of the *fabula* is molded into an artistic composition
which constitutes the *sjužet*.

Gaps are a necessity because no narrative, not even an extended one like *War and Peace,* can render every detail of the
corresponding "reality." It is therefore imperative to select, to
decide which events, motives, thoughts, will be told or dramatized and which will be left untold or undramatized—a gap for
the reader to fill in. The principles of selection vary from period
to period, from artist to artist, and from work to work, but
selection always exists and so do the gaps which it entails. The
process of reading is therefore partly a process of filling in gaps,
of inferring the unsaid from the said. To my knowledge,
Monroe Beardsley was the first critic to call attention to this
phenomenon.

> The situation in a literary work, or its chain of events if it
> is a narrative, is always more than the work explicitly
> states. Certain actions are reported; from them we are to
> infer other events and states of affairs, including character
> and motives. Daisy Miller appears at the hotel; therefore,
> she must have been born. She goes out with men she has
> barely met; therefore she is careless of her reputation. Part
> of what is involved in coming to understand a literary work is
> this process of filling out our knowledge of what is going
> on, beyond what is overtly presented. I shall call this process,
> somewhat arbitrarily, the *elucidation* of the work.
> [1958, p. 242]

Elucidation, according to him, "is something we do intuitively and without conscious effort in our ordinary reading" (p.
242). This, however, is not always the case. We must distinguish between different kinds of gaps and, correspondingly,
between different ways of filling them in.

Gaps can be classified from different points of view, those
most relevant to my study being (1) centrality, (2) duration,
(3) the level at which the gap is situated, and (4) the manner
in which it is filled in. These four aspects are usually inter-

related, but the connections between them are neither automatic nor "deterministic."

Centrality. It is possible to establish a scale of the importance or centrality of gaps in the narratives in which they appear, ranging from the most trivial gaps, through various degrees of importance, to gaps which are so crucial and central in the work as to become its very subject. Unimportant or trivial gaps are often not intended to be filled in. The Bible frequently creates gaps of this kind when the communication of information is not relevant to its purpose.[11] Other trivial gaps, on the other hand, are automatically filled in and are consequently hardly grasped as gaps. Beardsley's example from *Daisy Miller* is a case in point. It is obvious that if Daisy appears at the hotel, she must have been born, so obvious that we hardly think of it as an inference drawn by the reader, as an act of 'elucidation'. At the other end of the scale there are gaps which are so crucial and so central as to become the very pivot of the work in which they appear. The central gap in detective stories, usually the identity of the murderer, is the object of the search with which the whole novel is concerned, and the minute it is discovered, the novel cannot but come to an end. Similarly, the crucial gap in Henry James's *The Turn of the Screw* or *The Sacred Fount* is the object of the quest and the subject of conversation of all the characters, and to read these novels at all is to engage in the attempt to fill it in.

Duration. The aspect of duration is usually in direct proportion to that of centrality. Unimportant or noncentral gaps are, as a rule, filled in a short time after they are opened (if they are not of the type which is not intended to be filled in). For example, Nick Carraway, the narrator of *The Great Gatsby,* visits his friend, Tom Buchanan, where, on an enormous couch, he sees "two young women . . . buoyed up as though upon an anchored balloon." One of them he recognizes as his second cousin, Daisy, but "the younger of the two was a stranger to me" (Penguin Modern Classics Edition, p. 14). The question thus arises, "who is the younger woman?" but we have to wait no longer than half a page to hear from Daisy's murmuring lips "that the surname of the balancing girl was Baker," and later we are given much more information about the same young woman. This, of course, does not mean that Miss Baker herself is unimportant in the novel, but only that the recognition of her identity is not made a central mystery in it. Gaps which do constitute central mysteries are generally kept open until the end of the narrative, as in detective stories, or even beyond the end, as in "The Figure in the Carpet," *The Turn of the Screw*, and *The Sacred Fount*. We can thus distinguish between temporary and permanent gaps. Temporary gaps are opened at some point in the story in order to be filled in at a later stage. Permanent gaps, on the other hand, remain open even after the book is closed. As we have seen above, some gaps are permanent simply because they are not intended to be filled in. While permanent gaps of this kind do not call for 'elucidation', in Beardsley's sense of the term, there are central and crucial gaps which simultaneously call for 'elucidatory' efforts and frustrate them.[12]

The level at which the gap is situated. Whether a gap is temporary or permanent corresponds to the level at which it is situated. Temporary gaps are opened at the level of the *sjužet* alone, whereas permanent gaps exist in *fabula* and *sjužet* alike. In "The Sign of Four," as in most detective stories, the gap relating to the Agra treasure remains open until the last part of the story, but it is finally filled in by Jonathan Small's report. In the *fabula* there is no gap—the identity of Jonathan Small as well as the whole story of the treasure are included in it and antedate events which precede them in the *sjužet*. The gap in such stories is an element of the composition, not of the narrated world. Nor are detective novels unique in this respect. Nabokov's *The Real Life of Sebastian Knight* hinges on a central gap, announced by its very title: What *is* the real life of Sebastian Knight? Who is the real Sebastian Knight? The narrator, Knight's half-brother, sets out on a quest for his deceased brother's real personality and real life story. A complex system of retardatory devices withholds the desired information, but because this information constitutes a part of the *fabula*, it is finally disclosed in the narrator's concluding sentence, "I am

Sebastian, or Sebastian is I, or perhaps we both are someone whom neither of us knows." This solution differs from the standard revelation in detective stories in that it is only metaphorical. The narrator has not unveiled the object of his quest, he has only discovered that by setting out on a quest, one becomes the object one is looking for. Although at the literal level we still know nothing about the real Sebastian Knight, we have learned that every search is ultimately a subjective search for oneself, and the gap has been filled in at least at the figurative level.

A similar literary search, Henry James's "The Figure in the Carpet," refuses to solve the central enigma (what is the 'figure' in Vereker's 'carpet'?) whether at the literal or at the figurative level. The retardatory devices operate here in much the same way as they do in *The Real Life of Sebastian Knight*, but whereas in Nabokov's novel a solution exists in the *fabula* —no matter how late it appears in the *sjužet* (and, in fact, also in the *fabula* itself)—in "The Figure in the Carpet" the delay does not lead to a revelation. The gap in this story is permanent, and it is situated in both *fabula* and *sjužet*. A gap in the *fabula* necessarily entails a gap in the *sjužet*, while a gap in the *sjužet* need not entail a corresponding gap in the *fabula*. This is why permanent gaps in the *fabula* are the most radical type of gaps.

The manner in which the gap is filled in. The last aspect, the manner in which the gap is filled in, is again related to the other aspects, and we have already hinted at some possibilities. Some gaps are filled in almost automatically, others with varying degrees of intellectual effort, and still others are deliberately prevented from being filled in. The filling in of the gaps is based both on "laws of probability," deriving from our knowledge of life and of accepted social and cultural conventions and on explicit or implicit indications within the text itself. "External probabilities" usually determine an automatic or almost automatic filling in, as in the assumption that in order to be able to appear at the hotel Daisy Miller must have been born. But when probabilities are less universal than birth, death, and marriage, and when the cultural background of the narrative is either chronologically or geographically remote from ours, this external 'elucidation' may become highly problematic and may require a great deal of knowledge (Kermode 1969, pp. 891–915). Internal indicators can take the form of explicit telling by the narrator or by one of the other characters at some point succeeding the creation of the gap, or of implicit suggestions derived from the internal logic of the work, its genre, its language, its structure. When the explicit telling is close enough to the creation of the gap, the reader is spared the 'elucidatory' effort. On the other hand, when this telling comes late in the narrative or does not come at all, the reader has to rely on implicit suggestions in an attempt to construct hypotheses which will fill in the gap. This process often requires a laborious search for clues and for links between the clues, and, further, a choice among the various emergent hypotheses of the one which accounts for the maximum of data in the text in the most consistent and coherent way. But sometimes the text deliberately frustrates our attempts to fill in the gap, either by providing no clues or by providing contradictory clues or, in an even more complex way, by yielding two (or more) mutually exclusive yet equally plenary, consistent, and coherent sets of clues, thus rendering impossible the choice between the alternative hypotheses. In these perplexing cases, we can discern two mutually exclusive *fabulas* in the same *sjužet*, and the story is an example of narrative ambiguity.

The gaps with which the present study is concerned are central, permanent, located at the level of both *fabula* and *sjužet*, and prevented from being filled in by the existence of mutually exclusive sets of clues.

Gaps are perceptible either in advance or in retrospect. We may be made aware of a gap at a relatively early stage of the *sjužet*, and if it is of the central type, the whole reading of the story will be an attempt to fill it in. But the novel or short story can also be constructed in a way which prevents us from perceiving the gap until the very end of our first reading. Only when we reach the end are we made aware of the existence of a gap, and the result is a twist which forces us to change our interpretation retrospectively. Both types of gaps can be used for the creation of narrative ambiguity. Henry James's *The*

Sacred Fount is an example of ambiguity created by the con-
tinuous fitting of clues designed to fill in a gap which was
opened in the second chapter of the novel. "The Lesson of
the Master," on the other hand, is an example of a gap perceptible in retrospect. Only at the end does the disquieting
question arise: "Was it a plan?" The question forces us to
reconsider the story, and we are then bound to discover evidence confirming the possibility of a plan. But because the
story is ambiguous, these clues are balanced by the innocent
no-plan reading, and the question of whether the story is or is
not "inverted" remains open.

"The Labyrinth of Linkages" (Tolstoy's phrase; see Erlich
1969, p. 241)

Narrative ambiguity, we have seen, is constructed around a
central informational gap, in relation to which all the narrative
units can be defined.[13] The reader relates the units to each
other with a view to forming a hypothesis which will fill in the
gap. But the logic of the story is such that two, rather than
one, hypotheses emerge, and the two are mutually exclusive. The
links among the units are thus conditioned by their relation to
the mutually exclusive hypotheses, the units assuming the role
of hermeneutic clues which confirm or refute each of the conflicting possibilities. Or, to start the other way round, the
hypotheses emerge because of the mutually exclusive sets of
possible links between the units. In any case, the result is two
(or more) mutually exclusive systems of gap-filling clues, a
phenomenon which can be seen as the realization of what I
have previously called the coexistence of mutually exclusive
fabulas in one *sjužet*. The object of this section is to examine
the links established among the units so as to construct the
mutually exclusive systems of gap-filling clues,[14] or,—in terms
of the previous definition—to trace the relations which the
sjužet establishes between the units so as to dovetail two mutually exclusive *fabulas* within one narrative.

The possibilities of combinations between units are, at least
theoretically, infinite, and they vary from text to text. It is
impossible in this study to give an exhaustive account of all
the linkages ever used to create narrative ambiguity. All I can

do is offer a general outline of the modes of combination under which individual variations can be subsumed.

Todorov distinguishes between three orders of "syntactic" relations among units: logical, temporal, and spatial (1969, p. 20). In chapter one I have defined ambiguity as the logical relation of the "conjunction" of exclusive disjuncts, and I have specified that in narrative ambiguity the exclusive disjuncts are the "finalized hypotheses." But logical relations are not confined to the "abstract" level of "finalized hypotheses." They also obtain between each hypothesis and the units which constitute it.[15] At this level the relation is one of confirmation or repudiation of the hypothesis by the hermeneutic clue, and if the narrative is ambiguous, there will be complete balance between the two opposed relations. Let a and b stand for mutually exclusive hypotheses, and let confirmation and repudiation be represented by $+$ and $-$ respectively. It is possible to make a and b equitenable in two major ways: either by the balance of evidence for (or against) one hypothesis by counterevidence for (or against) the other ($a+$, $b+$; or $a-$, $b-$), or by the creation of equilibrium between confirmation and repudiation of the same alternative ($a+$, $a-$; or $b+$, $b-$). The two methods are closely related, for a detail which refutes one hypothesis automatically strengthens the other, and vice versa ($a- \diagup\!b+$; and $b+\diagup\!a-$). The narrator of James's *The Sacred Fount* acutely points out this relation to his opponent, Mrs. Brissenden: "It *is* the weakness of my case . . . ," he says, "that any particular thing you don't grant me becomes straightaway the strength of yours" (pp. 215–16). These two techniques correspond to the two kinds of opposites in logic; $a+$, $b+$ is an example of contraries, while $a+$, $a-$ is an instance of contradictories. The connection which the narrator of *The Sacred Fount* discerns between the two again recalls the presuppository relation I have pointed out between contradictories and contraries.

Both in the case of contraries and in that of contradictories, the balance can be effected in two ways:

The equilibrium of singly directed clues. Every scene, conversation, or verbal expression which supports only one hypothesis is balanced somewhere else in the narrative by another scene, conversation, or verbal expression which supports exclusively the opposite hypothesis. In the linear process of reading, such singly directed evidence momentarily seems to offer the comfort of definitively turning the scale in favor of one of the mutually exclusive possibilities. But they soon recede to the background, and the comfort they seemed to offer is frustrated when other pieces of evidence, supporting with equal definitiveness the other alternative, come to the fore.

Doubly directed clues, that is, scenes, conversations, or verbal expressions which are open to a double interpretation, supporting simultaneously the two alternatives.

How are these logical relations manifested in the temporal rendering of the story? At the local level of the combination of units into segments, the two principles of organization are (1) the enchainment of homogeneous clues, for example, $a+a+a+a+$ or $b-b-b-b-$ or $\begin{smallmatrix}a&a&a&a\\b&b&b&b\end{smallmatrix}$ (doubly directed); (2) the alternation of heterogeneous clues, for example, $a+b+a+b+$ or $a+a-a+a-$ or $a+{}^a_b a-{}^a_b a+{}^a_b a-{}^a_b$. There are seven possible combinations of the homogeneous type and twenty-one of the heterogeneous type, but the above examples will suffice.

The same principles that apply to the combination of single units into segments can also apply to the combination of segments into the complete narrative. The possibilities here are even more numerous, depending both on the composition of each segment and on the various modes of combination among the segments. Indeed, a narrative can (and usually does) combine the principle of homogeneous enchainment with that of heterogeneous alternation, and the variety of possibilities is thereby multiplied. The range of the various segments, that is, the number of clues they contain, is not uniform: it changes from story to story and within the same story, thus further enriching the variety of possible combinations. There is only one constraint on the combination of units in an ambiguous narrative: the units cannot all be homogeneous unless they are also doubly directed.

To make the foregoing discussion more concrete, I propose to give examples of a few modes of combination actually used in ambiguous narratives. Akira Kurosawa's film *Rashomon*

(1950) first presents a bulk of $a+$ clues ranging over the whole story and then, from the point of view of another character, a bulk of $b+$ clues ranging over the same story and excluding possibility a. It is in fact only after b is presented that we suspect the existence of ambiguity. While *Rashomon* combines the complete *fabula a* with the complete *fabula b* by way of linear succession, Robbe-Grillet's novel, *Le Voyeur*, intermingles the two *fabulas* and creates an alternating sequence of clues, whereby the authorial narrator intermittently affirms and denies the occurrence of the central events. The major technique in *Le Voyeur* is $a+a-a+a-$ . . . , or a double movement of confirming and negating. Henry James's *The Turn of the Screw* and *The Sacred Fount*, as well as his other ambiguous works, manifest a variety of combinations of both the enchainment of homogeneous clues and the alternation of heterogeneous ones, a variety which I hope will emerge from the second part of my study.

As a result of these various modes of clue distribution, the opposing clues can either appear in linear succession or be scattered over various parts of the narrative. Thus there can be a sequence of $a+a-$ or of $a+b+$, but there can also be a "suspended" $a+$ "waiting for" its negation $(a-)$ or for its counterpart $(b+)$, which will appear at a later stage of the story. What this means for the three orders of "syntactic" relations (the logical, the temporal, and the spatial) is the establishment of spatial links above and beyond the temporal ones. The reading of ambiguous narratives in fact proceeds on two planes: on the one hand, the linear progression from sentence to sentence, paragraph to paragraph, and scene to scene; on the other hand, the supralinear grouping of the data into two sets of clues governed by the mutually exclusive hypotheses. But because the supralinear grouping is governed by the mutually exclusive hypotheses, and the mutually exclusive hypotheses on their part are created by the supralinear grouping of the data, the problem of a double reading arises. In a discussion of the fantastic story which, according to him, is a subclass of narrative ambiguity, Tzvetan Todorov says: "De là que la première et la seconde lecture d'un conte fantastique donnent des impressions très différentes (beaucoup plus que pour un autre type de récit); en fait, à la seconde lecture, l'identification [avec le personnage ou le narrateur] n'est plus possible, la lecture devient inévitablement méta-lecture: on relève les procédés du fantastique au lieu d'en subir les charmes" (1970, p. 95).

Can we claim that narrative ambiguity is perceived only retrospectively, in a rereading or a mental reshaping, rather than in a first reading? If this is the case, the first reading is guided by the belief that the central gap will finally be filled in either by the text itself or by the reader's inferences. Only when we reach the end do we realize that, instead of one unequivocal solution, there are two mutually exclusive but equitable alternatives. We then go over the story again, grouping clues "spatially" according to the two hypotheses. This process is somewhat analogous to the reading of detectives stories. In detective stories we are first engaged in the attempt to fill in the gap and to construct the complete *fabula* on the basis of clues that seem central. But the end reveals the correct solution, which almost invariably differs from the one we have been expecting, and we then establish a new, retrospective hierarchy among the clues. The final *fabula*, presented in the climactic revelation, entails a retrospective reorganization of clues both from the point of view of their truth or falsity and from that of their centrality. Clues that seemed to be pointing the way to the truth are now perceived as misleading hints, and others that seemed positively false now become the carriers of truth. Similarly, clues that seemed negligible become central, and those that seemed central are rendered insignificant. One linear reading is completely replaced by another, and clues are eliminated as soon as the correct hypothesis is "finalized."

In reading an ambiguous narrative, we also start by expecting a "finalization" of one hypothesis in a way which will render the other emergent possibilities either incorrect or marginal. But such unequivocal finalization does not occur; two (or more) hypotheses prove equally correct and equally central. There is therefore no possibility of eliminating clues and substituting one *fabula* for another. The clues remain foci in themselves, and a new hierarchy is created in which everything is crucial in its contribution to the "spatial" coexistence of mutual exclusives.

Is this "spatial" coexistence only retrospective? Is the analogy with detective stories preserved at least from the point of view of retrospective rearrangement, even though in detective stories one arrangement replaces the other, whereas in ambiguous narratives both are retained? It is true that some ambiguous narratives, like Henry James's "The Lesson of the Master," for example, are so constructed as to make the reader perceive the ambiguity (and the gap on which it hinges) only retrospectively.[16] But other ambiguous narratives, like *The Turn of the Screw* and *The Sacred Fount,* distribute conflicting clues from an early stage of the *sjužet* and do not deliberately screen one of the possibilities, as does "The Lesson of the Master." It is probably impossible to determine at what point the reader becomes aware of the ambiguity of a novel like James's *The Sacred Fount* or Robbe-Grillet's *L'année dernière à Marienbad* in a first reading of the text, although it is quite possible to determine in retrospective analysis where the polarization of clues objectively starts in these narratives. Perception of the ambiguity and the rate at which it is reached is ultimately a relative matter, conditioned by a variety of factors in the reader's personal make-up, as well as in his experience of literature. Many readers are perfectly capable of a passionate perusal of *The Turn of the Screw* or *The Sacred Fount* without ever realizing their ambiguity; others may become aware of the ambiguity only in retrospect, once their search for a final solution lands them with equipollent "candidates" or once they have read an Edmund Wilson article on the ambiguity of Henry James; and still others grasp the very first shadow of a hint and start grouping clues in contrasted sets as they go along. The reader is more likely to remain unaware of the ambiguity if *The Turn of the Screw* or *The Sacred Fount* is the first Jamesian novel or the first ambiguous novel he has ever read. On the other hand, a reader accustomed to ambiguous narratives will be rather quick in spotting the ambiguity of any new narrative he reads; he may even be overly quick in spotting ambiguities where none exist. To sum up: the heuristic process as well as the passage from reading to "metareading" are to a large extent a relative matter which cannot be determined for all readers and need not be identified with a first and second reading. What can be objectively determined is the composition of the narrative, including the point at which the reader is potentially made aware of the ambiguity, or, to put it differently, the point at which spatial and logical links are projectable onto the linear unfolding of the narrative.

To conclude these theoretical considerations of narrative ambiguity, I would like to turn once more to the question of plurality and closedness. I have described narrative ambiguity as a relatively closed phenomenon, subordinating most of the data to mutually exclusive systems of gap-filling clues. The gap and the clues on which I have concentrated belong to what Barthes calls "the hermeneutic code," and within this code the freedom of interpretation is severely restricted, all potential hypotheses being logically classifiable either under category a or under category $\bar{a}$ (the various bs, I have already remarked, are ultimately subsumable under $\bar{a}$). But this limitation of plurality may be somewhat alleviated by the activation of other codes which are often generated by the hermeneutic. In a discussion of Bentley's enigmatic *Trent's Last Case,* Professor Kermode correctly observes, "So the hermeneutic spawns the cultural. It also spawns the symbolic" (1972, p. 15). In other words, even when the hermeneutic code predominates, the narrative may activate other systems of reading or interpretation, thus calling for multiple coding and opening the "horizontal" closedness of the hermeneutic code by the "vertical" plurality of the interplay among the various codes. This is certainly true of ambiguous narratives, and the various symbolic interpretations given to the four Jamesian narratives under discussion seem to support this contention. And yet, it is not by chance that I have described such multiple coding as only *somewhat* alleviating the closedness of ambiguous narratives. For it seems to me that works which belong to the narrow category I have defined as ambiguous establish a hierarchy which makes all the codes depend on the basic hermeneutic polarity. Without finding out what is happening, it is hardly possible to offer any coherent interpretation—be it cultural, symbolic, or other. And since the answer to the question of happenings remains conclusively inconclusive and definitively ambiguous, interpretations deriving from other codes also tend to contradict each other, thus indirectly (and sometimes even directly) confirming the basic hermeneutic ambiguity. In the works I am about to analyze, the reader is induced to subject multiple coding to the polarity of mutually exclusive hermeneutic hypotheses. Of course, the reader may choose not to be docile, to ignore the hierarchy implied by the structure of the work, and to let multiple coding operate independently (as many readers and critics in fact do). The question of legitimacy then arises, and I am not sure that a reading which ignores the hierarchy implicit in a text can be called an adequate interpretation. But the problems of adequacy and hierarchy are too involved to be properly treated here.

VERBAL AMBIGUITY

The problem of verbal ambiguity has been recurrently studied by linguists, especially since the development of transformational grammar. Since verbal ambiguity plays a subordinate role in my study, being examined mainly for its contribution to the creation of the overall ambiguity of the narrative, I shall not go beyond a sketchy and eclectic account of the subject. However, I refer the reader to a recent book which discusses the problem in a thorough and stimulating way, J.G. Kooij's *Ambiguity in Natural Language* (1971), a study on which my own comments draw rather heavily.

Preliminary Comments and Distinctions

It will be remembered that in the analysis of narrative ambiguity, the narrative itself was taken as the superordinate ambiguous unit, and the subordinate units which constitute it —some ambiguous in themselves, some unambiguous—were identified as the hermeneutic clues in their various forms. In verbal ambiguity, the superordinate ambiguous unit is the sentence, and the subordinate elements of which it is composed are phonemes, morphemes, words, syntactic structures. The reasons for positing the sentence, and not its constituent elements, as the *locus* of ambiguity are stated by Kooij in the following way:

Finally, I wish to point out that the term 'ambiguous' will
be used for sentences, and not, if it can be avoided, for all
kinds of individual linguistic elements. In the literature, the
same term 'ambiguous' and the related terms 'homonymous',
'homophonous' and 'polysemous' are sometimes used both
for sentences and phrases, and also for words and morphemes
taken as isolated elements, or studied as members of a
grammatical paradigm. Terminologically this is unfortunate,
nor is it merely a matter of terminology. If the term
'ambiguous' is used both for sentences that can have more
than one interpretation and for segmental elements in the
sense of their being able to have more than one function
within the same paradigm, the term will eventually be
applied also in cases where the potential ambiguity of such
an element, let us say an affix in an inflectional language,
will never be realized on the level of the constructions in
which these elements obligatorily occur. [Pp. 6–7]

But the analogy between the sentence and the narrative as
loci of ambiguity immediately raises the problem of context.
While the narrative is both the superordinate ambiguous unit
and the context within which the ambiguity is determined,
developed, and sometimes even resolved, the sentence is the
superordinate unit of verbal ambiguity, but not its final context, and the context can have a drastic impact on the ambiguity of previously isolated sentences.[17] Consider, for example,
the following sentences:

The soldiers took the port at night.
They are flying planes.

Taken in isolation, these sentences are ambiguous. The first
can mean either that the soldiers conquered the harbor or that
they had an alcoholic drink. The second sentence can be taken
to refer either to some people ("they") who are engaged in
flying planes or to some aircraft defined as "flying planes,"
as distinguished from "standing planes," for example. But
sentences are seldom said in isolation. They usually appear in
a context that is either linguistic or situational or both, and the
context usually acts as a disambiguating factor. If in a conversation about the frivolous life of soldiers somebody says that
the soldiers drank whiskey at night, and another member of

the company corrects him by saying that it was actually port, not whiskey, that the soldiers took, the sentence, "The soldiers took the port at night" is automatically disambiguated. Indeed, it is very likely that in such a context disambiguation precedes our perception of the ambiguity, for the latent ambiguity is not even grasped when everything in the conversation clearly points in one direction. To use an analogy from the visual arts: it is equally likely that if we draw a duck pond or a rabbit warren around Gombrich's rabbit-or-duck figure, that figure will be grasped unambiguously as either a rabbit or a duck, depending on the visual context in which it appears (Gombrich 1969b, p. 235).

But the relevance of the context is not confined to disambiguation. Our very recognition of ambiguities can also be accounted for by our capacity to "dream up" mutually exclusive "communication settings" conveyed by the message. Here is Rommetveit about "they are flying planes":

> A subject can hardly be said to have discovered the syntactic ambiguity unless he can specify at least two distinctively different messages. The moment he does so, we would also conclude that he is in possession of a particular syntactic competence. The actual procedures employed may nevertheless conform very well to the steps described above: He may first visualize a situation in which a person is wondering what is up there in the sky, and a second situation in which a person is wondering what his copilots during the war are now doing. Or he may work his way from two equally available meaning potentialities of a single word: "flying" is first attended to in isolation, as different from "on the ground". Then he attends to "are flying" as distinct from "are walking" etc., and the two different event structures emerge via chain reactions. [1968, p. 235]

The context can also create an ambiguity in cases where the isolated sentence is perfectly univocal. A sentence like "He is leaving London today" is not ambiguous in itself, but it may become so if the pronoun *he* can be made to refer to two different men.

Because a sentence in isolation and the same sentence in a context are not always identical as far as ambiguity is concerned, "one needs a distinction between the ambiguity of sentences that, in abstraction from context and situation also, inherently have more than one meaning . . . and the ambiguity of sentences that do not have two meanings inherently but could still, in actual use, have more than one interpretation" (Kooij 1971, pp. 5–6). Let us call the first type "inherent ambiguity" and the second "contextual ambiguity" (Kooij calls them "inherent" and "noninherent"). For a linguist, the primary object of analysis is the former, because, unlike the latter, it is amenable to a description of invariable properties of language. From the contextual point of view, a sentence can be ambiguous in one context and unambiguous in another, thus making it virtually impossible to describe the ambiguity of sentences themselves. A study of the language system can perhaps afford to ignore the context (though even this is now questioned), but a study of the operation of language in literary texts certainly cannot. Indeed, an analysis of verbal ambiguity in a given literary text is an analysis of contextual rather than of inherent ambiguity; it must also point out the inherent properties which made the ambiguity possible, but it is primarily concerned with those ambiguities that are realized in the text.

A distinction between potential and realized ambiguity should thus be added to the inherent vs. contextual dichotomy. The relation between these two distinctions is easy to perceive: inherent ambiguity can be seen as a potential which may or may not be realized in the particular context; contextual ambiguity, on the other hand, can be either an inherent ambiguity maintained by the context (hence "realized ambiguity") or a noninherent ambiguity created by the context alone. The most a linguistic description can achieve, says Kooij, "is to indicate the conditions under which a sentence is *potentially* ambiguous inasfar as its grammatical structure is involved. The actual decision as to whether a sentence *does* or *does not* have two meanings for native speakers, depends on factors that are outside the domain of a description of sentences in isolation" (p. 115; Kooij's italics). It is precisely these factors that predominate in the creation of verbal ambiguities in literary texts, and an analysis of these ambiguities must indicate not only the inherent conditions for potential ambiguity but also the contextual conditions which either realize or create an actual ambiguity.

A description of verbal ambiguity in literature thus moves on the borderline between language and language use. The language aspect can afford an explanation of the conditions governing inherent ambiguity. These are regarded as potentialities from the point of view of language use, and the operation of the context is investigated in order to find out if and how it maintains the inherent ambiguities and creates noninherent ones.

Sources of Inherent Ambiguity

A description of inherent ambiguity involves three levels of representation: the phonological, the lexical, and the grammatical. Taking these levels as his starting point, Kooij says that a sentence can be defined as inherently ambiguous when it is "same" at the level of phonological representation but "different" at that of lexical or grammatical representation (p. 8). The notions "same" and "different" are rather problematic, as Kooij himself admits (p. 8), but for the purposes of this study they need not be pursued to their furthest limits. On the other hand, it is important to recall at this point that my own definition of ambiguity requires mutual exclusiveness of meanings, not simply a difference between them. However, since mutual exclusiveness is more often a result of the context than an inherent quality of sentences themselves, the adoption of Kooij's definition of inherent ambiguity does not imply, as it may seem to do, a broadening of my initial definition of ambiguity.

Ambiguity and phonology. Of the three levels giving rise to ambiguity, the phonological is the most easily disambiguated in actual use. This is why many linguists are reluctant to treat it as a genuine case of ambiguity, but it seems to me that a discussion which treats inherent ambiguity as potential ambiguity should not overlook this source.

There are two main types of phonological ambiguity, the one confined to speech, the other to writing. In speech, the most common type of potential phonological ambiguity are homophones, namely, words that sound the same but have different meanings, like *dear* and *deer, pause* and *paws, sight, cite,* and *site.* However, once these words are orthographically transcribed, the ambiguity disappears and the homophones remain a fecund source for puns—all too often for feeble ones. While homophones preserve the boundaries of the segmental elements of which they consist, other phonological ambiguities may result from the capacity of the same segmental elements to form more than one morphemic sequence. Examples of this phenomenon abound in discussions of *juncture,* that is, "any manifestation of those features which it has been claimed distinguish utterances that are equivocal as to the division of the sequence into morphemes" (Kooij 1971, p. 14). The English *a name* and *an aim,* the American-English *he's a bee feeder* and *he's a beef eater,* the French *celui qui l'aime* and *celui qu'il aime* are all cases in point. Perhaps the most spectacular example of the derivation of various morphemic sequences from the same phonological segments is the often quoted couplet by Marc Monier.

> Gal, amant de la reine, alla, tour magnanime
> Galamment de l'Arène à la Tour Magne à Nîmes. [Ullmann 1962, p. 40]

But are the phonological segments really the same? There is a disagreement among linguists on the question of whether examples like the above are same at the level of phonological representation and different only at the lexical and grammatical levels, or whether they are also different at the level of phonology. The argument for a phonological difference rests on the assumption that there exist acoustically manifest breaks or marked prosodic features that correspond to the alternative structures (Kooij 1971, pp. 9–10, 51). According to Kooij, the argument against a disambiguating phonological difference rests on two main points. "(i) That the role of prosody in this respect is of necessity limited and therefore, the claim that sentences of the kind discussed above are not 'really' ambiguous in linguistic description is unwarranted. (ii) That the viewpoint that, in actual speech, the linguistic context or the situation in general will 'trigger' the intended prosodic realization or interpretation is simplistic inasmuch as context may very well have the opposite results" (p. 55).

Prosody, in fact, is the second source of potential phonological ambiguity. Whereas the foregoing examples of ambiguity are confined to speech, those which derive from a double possibility of prosodic realization are confined to written sentences and are usually disambiguated once the sentences are spoken or read aloud. In isolation, the Shakespearean line "Shall I compare thee to a summer's day?" (Sonnet XVIII) can have two different stress patterns, our choice of one rather than the other assigning a different meaning to the sentence. If we stress the word "shall" (*"Shall* I compare thee . . . ?") the question is simply whether it is desirable or possible to compare the addressee to a summer's day. If, on the other hand, we stress the "I," the question becomes, "Shall *I,* or will somebody else, compare thee . . . ?" When we speak the line, we must choose between the two stress patterns (that is, we disambiguate the verse), and the only record of the ambiguity is the fact that we can say the line twice, with the stress falling on a different word each time.

Ambiguity and lexis.   The lexical ambiguity of a sentence is a result of the potential ambiguity of one (or more) of its constituent words and of some "solidarity" in the selection and combination of the other words which confers equal plausibility on both meanings of the potentially ambiguous element. There is thus even within the sentence itself an interplay between the inherently ambiguous word (or words) and the internal context formed by the other elements of the sentence.

As Kooij observes, following Reichling, a prerequisite of a linguistic description of inherent (potential) ambiguity is the distinction between the content of a sentence and its interpretation. The term *content* refers to the inherent semantic structure of a sentence, whereas *interpretation* designates "the various ways in which one and the same sentence can be understood in each unique case of language use" (p. 117). The mere fact that a word can be understood in different ways on different occasions does not mean that it has inherently more than one meaning, for the different interpretations it receives may simply be different contextual specializations of one and the same meaning. The example given by Kooij is the word *hate*, which will be understood differently in the sentences "I hate soup," "I hate Kathy," and "I hate lies," and yet cannot be taken to have three distinct inherent meanings (p. 118). Only those words which have various inherent meanings belong in a discussion of inherent lexical ambiguity.

Such words may be instances of either homonymy or polysemy. In homonymy different words have the same form and sound; in polysemy the same word has different meanings. In practice, the distinction is not easy to make because the only available criterion for deciding whether given meaning units are different words or different senses of the same word is the degree of relatedness between the meanings. This, in turn, presupposes an infallible awareness of the relatedness or unrelatedness of word meanings—an awareness which, unfortunately, human beings do not possess. Because of the obvious absence of relatedness between the two meanings, it is easy enough to affirm that *bank* of a river and *bank* in the sense of "a place where money is deposited" are homonyms, but it can be disputed whether *beat*, "to hit," and *beat*, "to defeat," are unrelated senses or not (Kooij 1971, p. 124; Ullmann 1957, pp. 159, 180–81).

In fact, the situation is even more complicated, for in addition to related meanings like "go after" and "understand" for *follow*, and unrelated meanings like "a small animal" and "a spot on the skin" for *mole*, there are also diametrically opposed meanings like "high" and "low" for the Latin *altus* or "hinder" and "allow" for the English *let*. Is opposition a manifestation of unrelatedness, or is it rather a particular form of relatedness? Nor is this merely a theoretical problem. Words characterized by an antithesis between their inherent meanings acutely pose the problem of the mutual exclusiveness of meanings and constitute a particular category as far as ambiguity is concerned (especially ambiguity in my narrow sense). Ullmann is undoubtedly right in suggesting that, "When two homonyms belong to different and non-related spheres of discourse there is little danger of ambiguity (e.g., the two "seals"). But, on the other hand, it is highly inconvenient to have the same name for the senses 'hinder' and 'allow' (the word is 'let')" (1957, p. 133).

He is also right in stating that words like *let* most strongly call for disambiguation. We must choose between "blessed" and "accursed" for the Latin *sacer*, between "protect" and "forbid" for the French *défendre*, and we usually do so on the basis of the context—whether the limited sentence-internal context or the wider context of the discourse or of the situation. One could, perhaps, conclude from this that words whose meanings are antithetical are seldom ambiguous in actual use. But the truth of the matter is that when the context provides no clues for disambiguation, these words become the most radical type of ambiguity because their meanings exclude each other most forcefully. The ambiguity of the German word *aufheben*, based as it is on the antithesis between its inherent meanings— to lift up, to preserve, to cancel—is said to enhance the persuasiveness of Hegel's central theme, the dialectic (Ullmann 1962, pp. 172–73). The ambiguity of the Greek word *p^cvios* meaning both "the brutal violence of a grasp" and "the sweet persuasion of a deliverance" (Vernant 1969, p. 114), enacts one of the major themes of Aeschylus's *The Suppliants,* the theme of the nature of *cratos.* "Is *cratos* based on law, that is to say, on mutual accord, on sweet persuasion, *peitho?* Or is it, on the contrary, based on domination, pure force, brutal violence, *bia?*" (Vernant 1969, pp. 114–15). Sigmund Freud observes that ancient Egyptian abounds in words which have antithetical meanings, and relates this kind of potential ambiguity to a complete *Weltanschauung.* "The essential relativity of all knowledge, thought, or consciousness cannot but show itself in language. If everything that we know is viewed as a transition from something else, every experience must have two sides; and either every name must have a double meaning, or else for every meaning there must be two names" (1925, 4:189; Freud here quotes Abel, who quotes Bain).

Inherent homonymy and polysemy, with their various degrees of relatedness between meanings, are only one source of lexical ambiguity. The other main source is the context—whether sentence-internal or sentence-external—but discussion of this important source must be left to a separate section.

Ambiguity and grammar. Grammatical ambiguity differs from lexical ambiguity in that in the former the ambiguity resides not in the meanings of the words themselves but in the syntactic relations among them. In practice, the two types often (though not always) overlap, for on the one hand lexical ambiguity is made possible by the structure of the sentence, and on the other hand many grammatical ambiguities would be nonexistent without the individual words giving rise to mutually exclusive meanings (Stanford 1939, p. 10).

What do we mean by an ambiguity which resides in the syntactic relations among the words? Commenting on the sentence "Old men and women were left at the village," in which "old" can modify either "men" alone or both "men" and "women," Kooij says:

> It is not the meaning of (4) [the above sentence] in the sense of the speaker's intention or the hearer's interpretation, that determines its grammatical structure: sentences such as (4) have two different 'hierarchical structures' and therefore can be understood in more than one way. In particular, sentences such as (4) do not have at the same time *both* structure A *and* structure B; from the viewpoint of a grammatical description they have *either* structure A *or* structure B. But since these two disjoint grammatical structures are represented by a sentence that is 'same' as far as the words and morphemes it contains is concerned and its linear arrangement, it also follows that there may be instances of language use where such sentences are meant or understood to be 'ambiguous' in the sense that they do mean two things 'at the same time'. [Kooij 1971, p. 66; Kooij's italics]

This description of ambiguity as "grammatical homonymy" or as the coexistence of two disjoint structures in one and the same sentence corresponds to my own definition, summed up in the formula $a \wedge b$. It is impossible to enumerate here all the relations between the constituents which can give rise to grammatical ambiguity, and I shall content myself with a few examples from the vast literature on the subject.

Sentences like "Old men and women were left at the village" can be assigned to two different structures owing to the "double-directedness" of "old." As was pointed out above, "old" can attach either to "men" alone or to both "men" and "women," thus giving rise to two structures:

1. *N (Phr) + and + N (Phr)*
2. *Mod + N (Phr)*

These structures reflect two interpretations that can be paraphrased as follows:

1. Women were left at the village, and old men were left at the village
2. Old men were left at the village, and old women were left at the village (Kooij 1971, p. 64).[18]

Similar to this is Ullmann's example from Romain Rolland: "Sophie quitte Anna rassurée," where "rassurée" can refer either to Sophie or to Anna (1962, p. 158).

Prepositional phrases that can relate to different elements in the sentence are another source of grammatical ambiguity. Take, for example, "He hit the man with the stick," where the phrase "with the stick" is ambiguous between an adjectival and an adverbial function. In its adjectival function it is related to "the man" and acts as an adjunct in the noun phrase "the man with the stick." In its adverbial function it describes the manner of hitting, thus acting as complement to the predicate phrase "hit the man" (Kooij 1971, p. 67).

In Leech's example from Yeats's poem "A Coat," the ambiguity is created by the double function of the two objects. "I made my song a coat" can have either the structure of *subject + verb + indirect object + direct object,* meaning "I made a coat for my song," or that of *subject + verb + direct object + object complement,* meaning "I made my song into a coat" (1969, p. 207). And in the oracle-like line from the second part of Shakespeare's *Henry VI,* the double structure arises from the interchangeability of subject and object. The line is "The

Duke yet lives that Henry shall depose" (1, 2, 30), and it can mean either that Henry will depose the Duke or that the Duke will depose Henry.

The famous "They are flying planes" as well as Leech's equivalent example, "I like moving gates," can be construed either as *nominal constituent* ("they") + *verb phrase* ("are flying") + *nominal constituent* ("planes"), or as a nominal constituent ("flying planes") within the predicate phrase ("are flying planes"). This difference in constituent structure corresponds to a difference in grammatical function. In the first structure, "planes" is object to the predicator "are flying"; in the second "flying planes" is a predicate complement to the predicator "are." "They" is subject in both. The alternative interpretations of the sentence are, "Certain people are engaged in flying certain objects" and "Certain objects are planes that fly" (Kooij 1971, p. 57). This and similar examples have often been adduced by transformationalists to point out the shortcomings of phrase structure grammars and to drive home the advantages of transformational grammar which can account for grammatical homonymy by the difference in deep structures and/or in the transformational process (see Chomsky 1965, p. 21 and passim; Lees 1960, pp. 207–21).

If the foregoing examples seem artificial, almost created for the sake of linguistic studies, it is because they are somehow too neat (which, of course, they should be in a linguistic description of isolated sentences) and too detached from "living" contexts. It is to the problem of the context that we must turn now.

The Role of the Context

As I have pointed out above, the context often acts as filter, eliminating potential ambiguities through "isotopy." The term is borrowed from structural semantics, where it means "the establishment of discourse at a homogeneous level of sense" (Ricoeur 1969, p. 77). To put the same principle in the language of lexical semantics, the context can be said to operate by uniformity of utterance, reducing the potentiality of sense, "thanks to a play of affinities and reinforcements of all analogous dimensions in the other lexical terms" (p. 72). This delimiting operation of the context can occur at all the levels of representation. At the phonological level, the potentially ambiguous stress pattern in Shakespeare's "Shall I compare thee to a summer's day?" is resolved by the univocal meaning of the contiguous sentences. The second line of the sonnet—"Thou art more lovely and more temperate"—makes it quite clear that the pivot of the opening question is the possibility of comparison, not the identity of the comparer, and that the stress should therefore fall on "Shall" and not on "I."

A well-known biblical injunction can serve to illustrate the contextual resolution of lexical ambiguity. The original Hebrew version is, "*Zedek, zedek tirdof*" (Deut. 16:20). While the word *Zedek* unambiguously denotes "justice," the meanings of the verb *lirdof* are characterized by the polarity of contraries; it can mean either "to pursue," "to follow," "to seek," or "to chase," "to persecute," "to drive away." Thus, if we take the biblical injunction in isolation, we can construe it either as "Justice, justice, shall you pursue" or as "You should chase out (drive away) justice." Anyone who is acquainted with the Bible would intuitively feel that the first rendering is more in keeping with the biblical world view. But such a conclusion in fact takes a context, albeit broad and generic, into account. When severed from its immediate context and from the broad framework of the Bible, the sentence contains no indication as to which reading is correct, thus becoming a perfect example of inherent lexical ambiguity. Reverting back to the contiguous verses in chapter 16, the intuition of the Bible-conscious reader is immediately confirmed. For the context is one in which justice is a supreme value, and instructions are given as to the ways of pursuing it, "Thou [the judge] shalt not wrest judgement; thou shalt not respect persons, neither take a gift: for a gift doth blind the eyes of the wise, and pervert the words of the righteous" (16:19). The principle of isotopy forcibly suggests the correctness of the first reading. And indeed the English translation is entirely unambiguous, "That which is altogether just shalt thou follow, that thou mayest live, and inherit the land which the Lord thy God giveth thee" (verse 20). The potential ambiguity thus disappears in the context and remains merely a source of witticisms.

The following stanza from W.B. Yeats's "When You Are Old" resolves the *grammatical* ambiguity contained in *posse* in the first line.

> How many loved your moments of glad grace,
> And loved your beauty with love false or true,
> But one man loved the pilgrim soul in you,
> And loved the sorrows of your changing face;

In isolation, the first line is grammatically ambiguous, for "your moments of glad grace" can be taken either as the subject or as the direct object of "loved," and the sentence can mean either "How many people loved your moments of glad grace?" or "How many people did your moments of glad grace (that is, you) love?" (The synecdochic nature of "moments of glad grace" is stronger in the second interpretation than in the first). But the meaning and structure of the other lines of the stanza give the first interpretation a degree of probability which approaches conclusiveness. While the second line may still be construed in two ways (though less convincingly than the first), the third and fourth lines are unambiguous. Their subject is "one man" who "loved" (predicate) "the pilgrim soul in you" (direct object) and "the sorrows of your changing face" (direct object). In itself, this evidence is not conclusive, for there is no constraint that all the lines of a stanza should have the same sentence structure. But other features of the last two lines also suggest an analogy between their structure and that of the first two. Line three starts with "But one man," thus encouraging the reader to establish a contrast between this "one man" and the "many [men]" of the first line, just as "the pilgrim soul in you" and "the sorrows of your changing face" are grasped in opposition to "your moments of glad grace." It is therefore very probable that the structure of the first two lines is similar to that of the last two lines. Thus, "How many [men]" is the subject, "loved," a word which recurs in all the lines, is the predicate, and both "your moments of glad grace" and "your beauty" are direct objects.

The foregoing examples of the contextual resolution of potential ambiguities at the phonological, the lexical, and the grammatical levels were confined to what may be called the linguistic context. But there may also be an extralinguistic context of the situation which can resolve a potential ambiguity, as it were, "without saying a word." For example, the sentence "We shall have to take action" will naturally mean "legal action" to a lawyer and "a military operation" to a soldier, without any need for linguistic disambiguation (Ullmann 1962, p. 161).

But the context, whether linguistic or situational, does not always resolve a potential ambiguity. As a result of either inadequate control or deliberate compositional devices, the context sometimes

> maintains or even creates a concurrence between several "places" of signification. By diverse procedures, discourse can realize the *ambiguity* which thus appears as the combination of a lexical fact—the polyseme—and a contextual fact—the permission allowed to several distinct or even opposed values of the same name to be realized in the same sequence. [Ricoeur 1969, p. 72. His italics]

The permission given to discordant isotopies (to speak the language of structural semantics again) to unfold concurrently has a negative and a positive aspect. The negative aspect is the absence (or active omission) from the context of directives which will reduce ambiguity to univocality. The positive aspect is the implicit presence in the context of mutually exclusive directives, assigning the sentence to disjunctive sets of relationships (see also Nowottny 1962, p. 156). The technique is thus similar to that employed in the creation of narrative ambiguity, namely the opening of a central gap (that is, omission) and the supplying of mutually exclusive clues for filling it in. To illustrate the realization of potential ambiguity in a context which allows the coexistence of discordant isotopies, let me borrow Winifred Nowottny's example from Marvell's "Mourning":

> How wide they dream! The Indian Slaves
> That sink for Pearl through Seas profound,
> Would find her Tears yet deeper Waves
> And not of one the bottom sound.
>
> I yet my silent Judgement Keep,
> Disputing not what they believe;

> But sure as oft as Women weep
> It is to be suppos'd they grieve.

In these stanzas Nowottny detects two ambiguities, the one grammatical and the other lexical.

> If 'sound' is taken as a verb, the quatrain says that the waters of Chlora's tears are so deep that even the Indian pearl-divers could not sound their depths; if however it is taken as an adjective, then the quatrain says that if one were to procure divers experienced enough to get to the bottom of these waves, it would be found that none had any solid ground beneath. Similarly with 'It is to be suppos'd they grieve'; this may be taken to mean either that when women weep, the obvious explanation is that they are really grieving —or that when women weep, everybody is expected to make a polite pretence of believing that they have properly demonstrated a proper amount of concern. [P. 158]

Both sentences are inherently ambiguous, and their ambiguity is realized in the context owing to the mutually exclusive directives it contains. Thus, for example, we are encouraged to take "sound" as an adjective because of the analogy with its rhyme-word "profound," an adjective postposed to its noun. On the other hand, the structure of lines three and four encourages us to relate "sound" to "would find" and, seeing it as a verb, to interpret the stanza as, "The Indian slaves . . . would find her tears yet deeper waves and would not sound (would not be capable of sounding) the bottom of any of them." Similarly, the lexical ambiguity of "It is to be suppos'd they grieve" is maintained and reinforced by the fluctuation between reservation and affirmation in the speaker's attitude: he keeps his silent judgment; he refrains from disputing what "they" believe—and he probably does not—and then goes on to affirm, "But sure . . . ." Is this his own opinion or a free indirect quotation of what "they" believe? The uncertainty concerning attitudes facilitates the opposed readings of the last line.

In addition to disambiguation on the one hand and the realization of potential ambiguities on the other, the context can also create ambiguity in cases where the isolated sentence is not ambiguous in itself. This is usually made possible by the absence or vagueness of an element or elements in the originally isolated sentence. The most common source of such purely contextual ambiguity is pronoun reference.

Linguists distinguish three types of pronouns according to their position in relation to the noun they replace. (1) An *anaphoric* pronoun is one postposed to its antecedent, for example, "John said he would come. *He* didn't though." (2) A *cataphoric* pronoun is one preposed to its referent, for example, "*He* came, my son, but he was so different now." Both anaphoric and cataphoric pronouns are textual in the sense that their referent can be found either before or after them in the text. In other words, the referential function of both anaphoric and cataphoric pronouns depends on the linguistic context in which they appear. It is precisely in this respect that the third type differs from the first two. (3) An *exophoric* pronoun is one whose referent is not in the 'text', that is, not in the linguistic context, but in the extralinguistic situation. If in a discussion someone says, "Have you seen him lately?" and no one has been mentioned in the preceding sentences or is to be mentioned presently, the pronoun is exophoric. More than any other pronouns, exophoric ones assume the existence of a common focus between speaker and addressee because it is only their common knowledge of the situation that can supply the missing referent.

All three types can give rise to ambiguity. Anaphoric and cataphoric pronouns can make a sentence ambiguous if they refer to more than one antecedent in a context which gives no indication as to which is the intended referent. An amusing example of an unintended ambiguity of this kind is the following advertisement for washing machines: "Don't let hard work kill your wife. Let electricity do it." Ambiguity also results from pronouns which can refer both backward and forward. The *it* in the following sentences from James's *The Wings of the Dove* can be both anaphoric and cataphoric, and the context makes both possibilities equally tenable. "Nothing was so odd as that she should have to recognize so quickly in each of these glimpses of an instant the various signs of a relation; and this anomaly itself, had she had more time to give to it, might well, might almost terribly have suggested to her that her doom was to live fast. *It* was clearly a question of the short run and the consciousness proportionately crowded" (see Chatman's comment on this passage, 1972, pp. 56–58).

Exophoric pronouns, on the other hand, have no referent in the linguistic context, and when the situational context supplies two different referents an ambiguity is created. Think, for example, of a conversation in which someone reports his impressions of the last football match, saying admiringly "They have done it again." If "they" can refer to either team, the sentence becomes ambiguous unless further information is supplied as to the speaker's intention or the results of the game. A classical example of a double situational referent, this time not of an exophoric pronoun but of an exophoric substitution, is the prediction of the Delphic oracle: "Croesus by crossing the Halys will ruin a mighty realm," where the "mighty realm" can be either his enemies' or his own.

In the two foregoing chapters I have discussed the formative principle of ambiguity and described its realization at the narrative and verbal levels. First I suggested that ambiguity be defined as the "conjunction" of exclusive disjuncts, and expressed this definition with the help of an ad hoc formula, $a \wedge b$. Then I specified what the exclusive disjuncts are in narrative and verbal ambiguity. In narrative, the a and b represent the "finalized hypotheses," and the ambiguity is created by the coexistence of mutually exclusive hypotheses. In language, the exclusive disjuncts are the meanings of the given expression, and it is again their coexistence that creates ambiguity. On the basis of these definitions, I distinguished between ambiguity and cognate phenomena, among others: double and multiple meaning, openness, ambivalence, vagueness, irony, and symbolism.

Passing from this abstract macrostructural level to its realization in the literary text, I have attempted a definition of the "concrete" microstructural units which constitute the ambiguity, and of the linkages among them. Thus I redefined narrative ambiguity as the coexistence of mutually exclusive *fabulas* in one *sjužet*, or—at a more concrete level—the coexistence of two (or more) mutually exclusive systems of gap-filling clues. Subsequently I described verbal ambiguity as a combination of inherent (potential) ambiguity arising from various phonological, lexical, and grammatical factors, and the contextual permission given to discordant isotopies to unfold concurrently.

The second part of this study will apply the tools evolved in the theoretical part to an analysis of four ambiguous works by Henry James. All these works manifest some of the principles described in the first part, but they do so in varying degrees and varying combinations, so that the final network is different in each case. The interest of the analysis will be in the differences as much as in the similarities, and I shall try to relate the *differentia specifica* of the ambiguity in each work to its other thematic, structural, and functional aspects. The works will be discussed chronologically, and some kind of an increase in complexity will be pointed out, although I shall not make development my main concern.

2   The Ambiguity of
Henry James

3   "The Lesson of the Master"

"The Lesson of the Master" (1888) is James's first ambiguous story. There are all kinds of uncertainties and indeterminacies in earlier works,[1] but this is his first fully ambiguous story. Its technique, both in the selection of the ambiguous elements and in the composition of the narrative, is less daring than that of later "impossible objects" like "The Figure in the Carpet" (1896), *The Turn of the Screw* (1898), and *The Sacred Fount* (1901). But the reliance of this story on well-established Jamesian techniques should not blind us to the differences within the similarities, to the new and almost subversive use it makes of old techniques in order to create ambiguity.

Two conflicting *fabulas* can be abstracted from "The Lesson of the Master." The first is a story of rivalry between the famous middle-aged novelist, Henry St. George, and his young and naive disciple, Paul Overt, both of whom are interested in Miss Marian Fancourt. Hoping or half hoping to win the girl, St. George preaches to Paul the doctrine of renunciation, eloquently telling him that "one's children interfere with perfection. One's wife interferes. Marriage interferes" (p. 264). The talented young novelist, who instinctively rebels against this "arraignment of art" (p. 269), is so overpowered by the Master's austere lesson that he leaves England for a long period and devotes himself to the religion of art. Paul's absence makes things easier for St. George, and when the older man's wife dies he succeeds in winning Marian's heart. The two are on the point of getting married when Paul returns to England, bitter and disappointed, feeling completely "sold."

But we can also abstract a diametrically opposed *fabula*, according to which "The Lesson of the Master" becomes a story of salvation. Henry St. George, a best-selling novelist who has never really attained perfection, believes his failure to be due to his marriage and all the material obligations which it entails. He therefore preaches the doctrine of renunciation to Paul Overt, whose talent and growing infatuation with Marian Fancourt are evident to the older man. St. George himself likes and appreciates Marian, but he knows that even a woman with her passion for literature must interfere with an artist's pursuit of perfection. After his wife's death he decides to marry Miss Fancourt, thinking (among other things) that this would save Paul from the dangers of matrimony and knowing that he himself is no longer in danger, having ceased to count as a real writer.

The point of divergence between the two *fabulas* is the causal relation between the doctrine of renunciation and the Master's decision to marry Miss Fancourt. Is the doctrine preached in order to drive away a rival in love and facilitate St. George's courting of Marian (*fabula* 1)? Or is it spoken out of deeply felt belief, and is the Master's behavior then consistent with the idea of saving the real artist from marriage (*fabula* 2)? The major statement to be abstracted from the first *fabula* is "St. George tricks Paul," while the second *fabula* yields "St. George does not trick Paul." Or, phrased so as to answer Paul's crucial question, hypothesis a is "It was a plan"; and hypothesis b, "It was not a plan" ($\wedge b = \bar{a}$). Put together, these two statements are a classical case of contradiction: $a.\bar{a}$. If one reformulates $\bar{a}$ in positive rather than negative terms (as indeed I have done in telling the second *fabula*), the clashing statements—now contraries rather than contradictories—become: a, "St. George tricks Paul"; b, "St. George saves Paul," and their combination yields the basic formula of narrative ambiguity, namely $a \wedge b$.

The gap which gives rise to these mutually exclusive hypotheses is perceptible only in retrospect. No question about causality and motivation can arise before Paul and the reader learn about St. George's impending marriage to Marian, and this information is disclosed in the last section of the story (chap. 6).

Before this information is imparted, the text encourages us to take the confession as sincere and to rely on the Master's own words for an interpretation of his motives. "Look at me well and take my lesson to heart, for it *is* a lesson. Let that good come of it at least that you shudder with your pitiful impression and that this may help to keep you straight in the future. Don't become in your old age what I am in mine—the depressing, the deplorable illustration of the worship of false gods!" (pp. 238–39).

As we shall see later, the two main features which encourage us to take the Master's confessions at face value are the pitch and eloquence of his speeches and his married state. It is true that James prepares us for Mrs. St. George's death by dropping hints about her illness, but these are not allowed to carry enough weight to arouse suspicions as to the nature of her husband's interest in Miss Fancourt. Indeed, St. George's married state is such a predominant presence (and predominant theme) in the story that one is almost likely to forget his wife's illness and to recall it only in retrospect when she dies.

It is only when we reach the last section of the story, St. George's impending marriage and Paul's bitter "Was it a plan?", that our view of causality and motivation is reversed. We no longer take the Master at his word, and all his past actions are now tinted with the sinister color of deception. But the reversal is deliberately rendered inconclusive. Rather than canceling out the first reading, the new "inverted" interpretation coexists with it, and there is no way of choosing between these mutually exclusive alternatives.

What all this means is that the ambiguity of "The Lesson of the Master" is based on the well-established technique of the "inverted story," from which it deviates by making both readings equally tenable, instead of substituting the one for the other.

The defining properties of an inverted story are:

1. The sequel or end of the inverted story cancels out the meaning the reader has attached to the first part of the story.

2. The *implications* of the new interpretation are diametrically opposed to those of the former.

3. The inverted story actively leads the reader astray, and the devices employed for misleading the reader can be pointed out.

4. On the other hand, the author subtly hints at the real subject of the inverted story *from the very beginning*.

5. The inversion that takes place organizes the composition of the *whole* of the story, and is not to be regarded merely as a local technique (Perry 1969, p. 261).[2]

The inverted story is a species of the well-known category of *pointe* stories. In fact, every inverted story is also a *pointe* story, though not every *pointe* story is inverted. The difference lies in the relation between the interpretations: In *pointe* stories the interpretations need not exclude each other, nor does the one necessarily supplant the other. The new interpretation may qualify, modify, or enrich the previous interpretation without neutralizing it altogether. However, both inverted stories and the more general category of *pointe* stories share the same basic structure, namely that of a narrative which encourages us to take it one way until it reaches a surprising twist (the "reversal scene," let us call it) and then compels us to revert to earlier parts of the story and interpret them differently—though how differently depends on the type of *pointe* story concerned.

The Jamesian canon abounds in *pointe* stories of all kinds, the degree of modification effected by the surprising twist varying from work to work. In "A Tragedy of Errors" (1864), "Gabrielle de Bergerac" (1869), "The Siege of London" (1883), and "The Solution" (1889) the surprising twist, which turns the character's action against his own intention, does not force us to interpret the earlier parts differently, although (I should add) some modification is an inevitable condition of the "serves-him-right" feeling aroused by these stories. "Master Eustace" (1871), "A New England Winter" (1884), and "Sir Dominick Ferrand" (1891), on the other hand, force us, through new information about a character's behavior, to carry out a retrospective patterning, but this reconstruction results in a clarification, qualification, or modification of the initial reading, not in its replacement by a virtually new interpretation. Such a retrospective replacement of the initial interpretation by a new reading, a reading which, moreover, is diametrically opposed to the first, occurs in "Osborne's Revenge" (1868), "A Landscape Painter" (1866), "The Marriages" (1891), and even more clearly in "Madame de Mauves" (1874) and "The Path of Duty" (1884).

"The Lesson of the Master" seems to belong to the same category of inverted stories, with the discreditable interpretation of St. George's behavior being substituted for the creditable one. But, in fact, the supplanting reading is fully balanced by the interpretation which it is supposed to supplant, and perpetual oscillation is imposed upon the reader. "The Lesson of the Master" is an ambiguous story, and its ambiguity turns precisely on the insoluble question of whether it is or is not inverted.

In order to see how the inversion of this story is rendered ambiguous, I propose to examine James's treatment of the two main stages constituting an inverted story, namely the reversal scene and the retrospective patterning of the parts which precede it.

THE REVERSAL SCENE

The reversal scene in "The Lesson of the Master" coincides with the last section of the story, and it is, in fact, an ambiguous reversal, yielding two mutually exclusive interpretations of the motives of both Henry St. George and Marian Fancourt. This final section can be read both as a reversal and as a non-reversal of the whole story, owing to the zigzag sequence in which creditable and discreditable explanations alternate, as well as to double-edged statements giving rise to both possibilities and making choice impossible. These two techniques, the balance of singly directed clues and the presence of doubly directed ones, become much more elaborate in "The Figure in the Carpet," *The Turn of the Screw,* and *The Sacred Fount,* but they are already present in "The Lesson of the Master."

Let us start with the oscillating treatment of St. George's motives in the reversal scene. Paul's first reaction upon hearing about Marian's and St. George's impending marriage is a feeling of complete loss, "He didn't understand what had happened to him, what trick had been played him, what treachery practised" (p. 277). Although he tries to talk himself into believing that the marriage has nothing to do with him, the possibility of a cunning plan to which he, the dupe, had fallen prey keeps nagging at him relentlessly. Later the same evening he meets St. George at Marian's party, and the tormenting "uncertainty

as to whether he had the right . . . to regard himself as his
victim" (p. 280) momentarily gives way to the feeling "that
the author of *Shadowmere* had now definitively ceased to count
—ceased to count as a writer" (p. 280). If St. George is no
longer a writer, it is implied, his marriage does not contradict
his doctrine, and Paul may have no reason to consider himself
"sold." Suspicion, however, is again uppermost in Paul's mind
during his conversation with the Master. Recalling their talk
in St. George's house two years earlier, Paul bitterly says: "Yes
—no wonder you said what you did" (p. 281), thus bringing
up the idea of a plan. To this St. George answers that he could
not have foreseen the death of his wife (an answer which the
reader does not wholeheartedly accept, having been informed of
her illness) and proceeds to present his own version of the
events. Unwittingly echoing Paul's momentary idea that "the
author of *Shadowmere* had now definitively ceased to count,"
St. George reiterates his disapproval of a writer's marrying,
and adds, "But you don't call me a writer?" (p. 282). The real
writer is Paul, and St. George did not tell him about his intention to marry Marian because "I wanted to save you, rare and
precious as you are" (p. 282). This then is the other, the
creditable interpretation of the Master's behavior: he was
sincere in his doctrine, and, knowing that he himself could
afford marriage because he was no longer an artist, he decided
to save Paul from the dangers of matrimony, thereby facili-
tating Paul's lonely pursuit of perfection. This creditable
interpretation, however, is inconclusive, being offered by the
Master himself, and being subject to immediate attenuation in
St. George's answer to Paul's direct question whether he is
marrying Miss Fancourt to save him. "Not absolutely," says
the Master, "but it adds to the pleasure" (p. 282). So the
marriage is not devoid of self-interest (and why should it be?),
and the creditable interpretation is somewhat shaken. Nevertheless, the sequence immediately operates to reestablish its
validity. It is Paul who now reflects that "the strange thing was
that he [St. George] appeared sincere—not a mocking fiend"
(p. 282), and because this assertion comes from Paul it carries
more weight than the Master's own declaration of sincerity.
But this possibility is also prevented from becoming definitive

by the double-edged nature of Paul's statement. Paul does not say that St. George *was* sincere; he only says that he "appeared" sincere, and appearance may or may not correspond to reality. The very negation of the Master's fiendishness simultaneously serves to arouse the converse affirmation in the reader's mind, if not also in Paul's. And indeed, the negative is soon enough converted into the positive: "This was too much— he *was* the mocking fiend." What was too much was St. George's preceding remark: "Don't you remember the moral I offered myself to you—that night—as pointing? . . . Consider, at any rate, the warning I am at present" (p. 283).

Paul sees this as the comment of a mocking fiend because he takes "the warning" to refer to the Master's cunning appropriation of the woman they both love. But the statement is doubly directed, and St. George can also be pointing out his own decline as a living warning to Paul, showing him what the result of "all the domestic and social initiations and complications" (pp. 265–66) can be for the intrinsic value of one's art. Yet even the dangers of marital life are put in doubt when Paul meditates that "there would have been mockery indeed if now, on his new foundation, at the end of a year, St. George should put forth something with his early quality—something of the type of *Shadowmere* and finer than his finest" (p. 284). This contingency is particularly painful because it would undermine Paul's faith not only in the Master himself but in the whole doctrine of renunciation. The epilogue-like statement with which the story ends gives no answer to this excruciating problem and eschews even the communication of actual information as to St. George's literary career. "The former still has published nothing, but Paul Overt does not even yet feel safe. I may say for him, however, that if the event were to befall he would really be the first to appreciate it: which is perhaps a proof that St. George was essentially right and that Nature dedicated him to intellectual, not to personal passion" (p. 284).

Several critics cite these last sentences of the story as an indication that the Master's real motives no longer matter, and that, whether he was cynical or sincere, he was essentially right about Paul's natural propensity to Art rather than Life (Blackmur 1945, p. 220; Andreas 1948, p. 88). But James characteristically leaves the end open. His last sentence contains a *perhaps* which most critics omit and which intensifies the sense of inconclusiveness, of an inability to choose between the two possibilities. The reader's position corresponds to Paul's own perplexity, described in a metaphor which aptly conveys the presence of a gap. He feels "as if some of the elements of a hard sum had been given him and the others were wanting: he couldn't do his sum till he was in possession of them all" (p. 278).[3]

Nor is Paul or the reader in possession of all the elements needed to account for Marian's behavior, and the last section again allows for conflicting interpretations. Paul's tacit questions, upon noticing her somewhat aggressive and (as he feels) almost stupid happiness, give rise to a double discreditable interpretation. "Why to *him*," thinks Paul, "Why not to youth, to strength, to ambition, to a future? Why, in her rich young capacity, to failure, to abdication, to superannuation? . . . Didn't she know how bad St. George could be, hadn't she perceived the deplorable thinness—? If she didn't she was nothing, and if she did why such an insolence of serenity?" (p. 279).

Thus, one possible explanation of Marian's marriage is that she does not see St. George's deterioration,[4] in which case she is not as intelligent as Paul thought she was, and would not have done as his wife. But there is another possibility, partly hinted at by Paul's "and if she did." Perhaps Marian does see the literary decline of her future husband but does not really care about perfection. All she cares about are literary men, not literature itself, and she wishes to marry a successful rather than a perfect author. Both interpretations are discreditable, attributing to Marian either imperceptiveness or superficiality and cynicism. A creditable interpretation, on the other hand, emerges not from anything actually said about Marian, or by her, but from St. George's defense of his own behavior. If St. George marries Miss Fancourt partly in order to save Paul, can we not see her as marrying St. George for the same purpose? Marian may have realized that Paul will be saved by remaining a bachelor, whereas St. George, having ceased to pursue perfection, can afford to get married.[5]

Thus the reversal scene in this story is rendered ambiguous, and we cannot tell whether the story is or is not inverted. Feeling uneasy with conflicting interpretations of the same happenings, we are urged to do what we always do in inverted stories, namely, to revert to earlier parts of the narrative and repattern them retrospectively. But whereas in inverted stories the aim of our rereading is a projection of the reversal onto the rest of the story and a correction of our initial erroneous interpretation in its light, in "The Lesson of the Master" the retrospective perusal is motivated by the hope of solving the ambiguity of the would-be reversal, of discovering clues which will turn the scales in favor of one of the mutually exclusive interpretations. But these expectations are ingeniously frustrated. As opposed to what happens in inverted stories, a rereading of "The Lesson of the Master" allows no neutralization of the first reading, for what we discover is an equal number of clues supporting the two conflicting hypotheses.

RETROSPECTIVE AMBIGUITY

Let us begin again with the motives behind St. George's surprising action. A retrospective perusal reveals a complete balance between creditable and discreditable clues. The creditable clues are those which in the first reading encouraged us to take the Master at his word, and which in a purely inverted story are retrospectively assigned the role of "devices employed for misleading the reader" (property 3). The discreditable clues, on the other hand, are those subtly hinting devices which exist in an inverted story from the start but are prevented from becoming prominent until the actual reversal (property 4). "The Lesson of the Master" being an ambiguous story, this account is true only of a first reading. In retrospect it is impossible to say which clues are screening devices, deliberately misleading the reader, and which are disclosing devices, subtly hinting in the right direction.

A creditable view of the Master is encouraged by the two confession scenes. We tend to take St. George's realization of the declining quality of his work and the courage he shows in admitting it as evidence of integrity, of something in his personality which rebels against the prostitution of his creative gifts for the sake of financial gain. The seemingly gratuitous nature of the whole confession strengthens our inclination to see it as sincere, an inclination which we have no reason to check until we learn about St. George's decision to marry Marian. The Master's choice of Paul as someone who deserves to be made privy to his innermost feelings, based as it is on a realization of the quality of the young man's work, as well as St. George's high-pitched offer, "Ask me anything in all the world. I'd turn myself inside out to save you" (p. 262) inevitably strike the note of sincerity.

Jarring notes, however, are not absent, arousing some suspicion even in the first reading and completely balancing the creditable ones in retrospect. It is by means of contradiction that the discreditable possibility is suggested: contradiction between what the Master says and what he does or between what he says on one occasion and what he says on another. Meeting St. George with Marian at an exhibition, Paul reflects that the novelist's "manner of conducting himself toward her appeared not exactly in harmony with such a conviction" (p. 249), the conviction expressed earlier by St. George that "She's not for me!" Going back to this earlier conversation, we discover that it is in fact doubly directed. The Master and Paul are discussing the beauty of Marian's personality, and Paul says, "One would like to paint a girl like that" (p. 242). To this St. George answers: "Ah, there it is—there's nothing like life! When you're finished, squeezed dry and used up and you think the sack's empty, you're still spoken to, you still get touches and thrills, the idea springs up—out of the lap of the actual— and shows you there's always something to be done. But I shan't do it—she's not for me!" Paul now asks, "How do you mean, not for you?" And St. George replies, "Oh, it's all over —she's for you, if you like." But Paul modestly explains, "She's not for a dingy little man of letters; she's for the world, the bright rich world of bribes and rewards. And the world will take hold of her—it will carry her away" (p. 242). In the context of this conversation, "She's not for me" can be taken either as "She's not for me as a literary subject" or as "She's not for me as a woman." The first reading does not contradict the Master's subsequent demeanor toward Marian, the second reading does.

The two other contradictions do not even have the potentially "redeeming" quality of double-edgedness. On Paul's first visit to Manchester Square, Marian informs him that St. George has decided not to come: "He said it wasn't fair to you [to Paul]" (p. 254), but the minute Paul leaves the house, he sees Henry St. George stepping out of another hansom. Thus, what first seemed an act of generosity on the Master's part now becomes a possible trick devised to enable St. George to be alone with Miss Fancourt.

Equally perplexing is St. George's attitude toward his wife. This time, the contradiction is between what he says about her on different occasions. Whereas in the confession scene St. George describes his wife as an interference with his art, as a person whose good worldly intentions pave the way to an artistic hell, after her death he writes to Paul: "She took everything off my hands—off my mind. She carried on our life with the greatest art, the rarest devotion, and I was free, as few men can have been, to drive my pen, to shut myself up with my trade. This was a rare service—the highest she could have rendered me. Would I could have acknowledged it more fitly!" (p. 273).

These remarks strike Paul "as a contradiction, a retraction" and arouse doubt in his mind about the validity of St. George's doctrine of renunciation. While understanding the soreness and sorrow expressed in St. George's letter and seeing its fitness, Paul still wonders: "if she was such a benefactress as that, what in the name of consistency had St. George meant by turning *him* upside down that night—by dosing him to that degree, at the most sensitive hour of his life, with the doctrine of renunciation? If Mrs. St. George was an irreparable loss, then her husband's inspired advice had been a bad joke and renunciation was a mistake" (p. 273). These contradictions point to a possible insincerity on the part of Henry St. George, an insincerity which anticipates his final act, but they are never allowed to become definitive, fully balanced as they are by suggestions of integrity and genuine concern about Paul's career.

A similar coexistence of creditable and discreditable clues emerges from a retrospective scrutiny of the genuineness of Marian's interest in literature and perfection. But whereas the ambiguity of the Master is achieved mainly by the balance of singly directed clues (with one example of a doubly directed conversation), in the case of Marian doubly directed clues become more prominent, although not so prominent as to outweigh the balance of singly directed clues, which remains the central technique employed in "The Lesson of the Master" to create narrative ambiguity.

Singly Directed Clues

The creditable view of Marian emerges from what is said about her, while the discreditable possibility is dramatized by her own actions and speeches. Those speeches which are "shown" in the text arouse our suspicion, while those speeches that are said to shine with the superb beauty of her spirit are left undramatized. We are told that in the conversation with Paul about St. George's fiction, Marian said things that struck her interlocutor as bold, intelligent, and first-rate (p. 251), but none of these things is "quoted," and consequently we cannot verify her intelligence and sincerity for ourselves and are compelled to rely on judgments expressed by the other characters or by the undramatized narrator. St. George sees Marian's passion for literature as genuine: "Her interest in literature is touching—something quite peculiar to herself; she takes it all so seriously. She feels the arts and she wants to feel them more. To those who practise them it's almost humiliating—her curiosity, her sympathy, her good faith" (p. 242). Paul also describes her as "an angel from heaven" (p. 242), and in the second nocturnal conversation with St. George he confidently mentions Marian as the one woman capable of "seeing further" and of collaborating in her husband's pursuit of perfection (p. 268). But both St. George and Paul may be blinded by their love, and their view of Marian may consequently be biased and unreliable. Indeed, this possibility is directly suggested by the narrator. "She sat there smiling at him [Paul], and he never asked himself which book she meant; . . . That seemed a vulgar detail . . ." (p. 225).

We must therefore look for additional confirmation from a

different quarter, and we find it in the narrator's words. Meeting Paul at the exhibition, Marian tells him about St. George's presence, and the narrator comments that her face "expressed no cheap coquetry, but simply affirmed a happy fact" (p. 246). And later, when Paul and Marian discuss "with extreme seriousness, the high theme of perfection" (p. 252), the narrator finds their seriousness amusing, but not, for that, any less sincere. "And it must be said, in extenuation of this eccentricity, that they were interested in the business: their tone was genuine, their emotion real; they were not posturing for each other or for some one else" (p. 252).

Balancing these five singly directed creditable clues is an equal number of discreditable clues, but—as I have already pointed out—whereas the creditable suggestions are all made by the other characters, the discreditable ones are dramatized mainly through Marian's own behavior and words. This is a necessary consequence of the narrative data. If the predicament is to be poignant and the doctrine of renunciation really exacting, it is necessary for both Paul and St. George to be charmed by Marian. As a result, neither of them can serve as a direct vehicle of criticism. Nor can the narrator criticize too profusely without damaging the surprising effect of the *pointe*. This is why the possibility of Marian's superficiality has to be dramatized rather than talked about. "It's so interesting, meeting so many celebrated people" (p. 228); "I should like so to hear you talk together" (p. 228); "How momentous—how magnificent! . . . How delicious to bring you together!" (p. 229); and "You shall meet in Manchester Square; you shall talk—you shall be wonderful!" (p. 247)—all may have more than a touch of the superficial pleasure derived from socializing with celebrities. At one point the "diplomatic" touch in her behavior is felt even by the admiring Paul, although he sees it as an asset rather than a defect. Miss Fancourt, says the narrator, "translating" Paul's perceptions, "evidently had the habit of saying the things that, by her quick calculation, would give people pleasure" (p. 227).

The juxtaposition of real interest in art and superficial socializing with artists—the lion-hunting so often satirized by James—is underscored on several occasions by the sequence of statements. Marian's own words in the conversation with Paul abruptly pass from the one to the other: "But what is art but a life—if it be real? . . . I think it's the only one—everything else is so clumsy! . . . It's so interesting, meeting so many celebrated people" (p. 228).

Paul's thoughts about Miss Fancourt also waver from one possibility to the other.

> He could not get used to her interest in the arts he cared for; it seemed too good to be real—it was so unlikely an adventure to tumble into such a well of sympathy. One might stray into the desert easily—that was on the cards and that was the law of life; but it was too rare an accident to stumble on a crystal well. Yet if her aspirations seemed at one moment too extravagant to be real, they struck him at the next as too intelligent to be false. They were both noble and crude, and whims for whims, he liked them better than any he had met. It was probable enough she would leave them behind—exchange them for politics, or "smartness", or mere prolific maternity, as was the custom of scribbling, daubing, educated, flattered girls, in an age of luxury and a society of leisure. [P. 253]

But the oscillation ends with a statement of its ultimate insignificance for Paul's attitude because "meanwhile he had fallen in love with her" (p. 253). Earlier in the story, Paul's vacillation fell into the opposite sequence, starting with an accusation and then retracting it (although the linguistic realization of this narrative sequence is reversed, announcing the retraction before the accusation). "Above all she was natural—that was indubitable now—more natural than he had supposed at first, perhaps on account of her aesthetic drapery, which was conventionally unconventional, suggesting a tortuous spontaneity" (p. 226).

Doubly Directed Clues

In addition to the balance of singly directed clues, there are three doubly directed statements, two made by other characters, one by Marian herself. This is how General Fancourt describes his daughter: "She's very fond of art and music and literature and all that kind of thing" (p. 217). The generality of "all that kind of thing" lends itself to a double interpretation: it indicates either the superficiality of Marian's interest in the arts or the General's vagueness about and lighthearted contempt for them.

When Marian is introduced to Paul, the impression she makes on him is "of an enthusiasm which, unlike many enthusiasms, was not all manner" (pp. 223–24). "All manner" is related to both parts of the comparison, and a shift of emphasis can therefore make it yield two distinct meanings. If we stress the link with "many enthusiasms," the sentence will primarily mean that whereas other enthusiasms are all manner, Marian's is all sincerity. But if we emphasize the restrictive qualification of Marian's enthusiasm by "all manner," the suggestion will be that her enthusiasm is not, perhaps, *all* manner, but that it is at least partly so.

The ambiguity of the third doubly directed statement is not caused by the vagueness or the syntax of the language, but by the interpretation of the "psychology" behind it. Marian's "Ah, perfection, perfection—how one ought to go in for it! I wish I could" (p. 251) may be an indication of her serious concern with perfection, but it may also be taken as a gushing adolescent exclamation with little practical weight. The last part of the exclamation, "I wish I could," can be seen as profound regret that, being a woman (see p. 252), or being someone who is not engaged in creative writing, she cannot herself achieve perfection, but it can also be taken as a warning that she may not be able "to go in for it" as an artist's wife (and, if we accept the Master's words, this is another consequence of her being a woman).

Thus, the genuineness of Marian's interest in the arts is as ambiguous as St. George's sincerity, but it is less central in its own right and more instrumental to the main issue of the Master and the "lesson" he teaches Paul. Marian's intelligence and her interest in art are necessary to make plausible the love of both men for her, to make Paul's sacrifice as difficult and as painful as possible, and to support a creditable view of the final marriage. Her superficial attraction to successful rather than perfect men of letters, on the other hand, is needed for the *vraisemblance* of her marriage to a best-selling novelist who has failed the intrinsic test of perfection. In this sense, there is a similarity between the ambiguity of Marian's candidness and that of Milly Theale's illness in *The Wings of the Dove*. The prospect of a mortal disease is necessary for the flowering of Kate's design, while the possibility of a "psychological" illness is essential for the impact of Milly's tragedy, of her turning her face to the wall as a result of the betrayal. Hence an ambiguity, "resolved" only by the postulation of a psychosomatic disease *avant la lettre*.

"The Lesson of the Master" is less daring than later ambiguous works in four main respects: the choice of motives rather than actual happenings as the central ambiguous issue; the reliance on the inverted story technique, resulting in retrospective rather than prospective ambiguity; the relative simplicity of the network of conflicting clues; and the limited role played by linguistic ambiguity in the creation of the overall ambiguity of the narrative. It is perhaps this apparent orthodoxy that conceals from most critics the element of novelty in the tale. (For brief mentions of the ambiguity see Swan 1952, p. 26; Matthiessen and Murdock 1961, p. 87; Geismar 1963, p. 114; Segal 1967, p. 141.) Nevertheless, I have argued that, like St. George's own work, the story about him contains "a bottomless ambiguity" (p. 250), but whereas the ambiguities in the Master's novels are "inequalities, superficialities" (p. 250), artistic weaknesses, in "The Lesson of the Master" they are the governing structural principle, turning what may seem an orthodox James story into a deadlock of opposites. Inverted or uninverted? Both. Ambiguous.

4   "The Figure in the Carpet"

Like "The Lesson of the Master," "The Figure in the Carpet" (1896) yields mutually exclusive "finalized" hypotheses: *a,* "There is a figure in Vereker's carpet; and *b* (or *ā*), "There is no figure in Vereker's carpet." Each of these contradictory propositions is the major statement abstracted from a more detailed hypothesis in order to render with the utmost conciseness the main point of divergence between the two *fabulas* summed up in the finalized hypotheses. In fact, each of the contradictory *fabulas* has various contrary ramifications, as I have pointed out in the first chapter, and the basic formulas of the story are both *a.ā* and *a*∧*b*.

But whereas in "The Lesson of the Master" it is the structure of the inverted story that "hovers" as an implicit norm from which the narrative deviates, "The Figure in the Carpet" is modeled on enigma narratives. Consequently, the gap in this tale appears at an early stage, and the whole story is an attempt to fill in the missing information, an attempt which (contrary to accepted practice in enigma stories) yields mutually exclusive systems of gap-filling clues. Thus, the ambiguity of "The Figure in the Carpet," unlike that of "The Lesson of the Master," is prospective rather than retrospective.

In order to see how this ambiguity is created, I propose to consider one after the other three aspects which are often coeval in the actual continuum of the text: the permanent central gap, the awakening of suspicion, and the mutually exclusive systems of gap-filling clues.

THE PERMANENT CENTRAL GAP

In a crucial nocturnal conversation, Hugh Vereker tells the narrator that there is a hidden unifying principle in all his works, a principle which Vereker describes as the "heart" (p.

284), the "organ of life" of his whole creative endeavor, an "exquisite scheme" (p. 282), the string on which his pearls are strung (p. 289) or, in the narrator's own words, the "figure in the carpet" (p. 289). Although this "little point" is "the finest, fullest intention of the lot" (p. 281), critics have always missed it with an admirable perfection, and their reviews, according to Vereker, have therefore never surpassed the level of "the usual twaddle" (p. 278). The enthusiastic and puzzled narrator now formulates the question which the whole story sets out to answer: "What then may your 'little point' happen to be?" (p. 281). With extreme eloquence and zest, Vereker offers a further description of the features of his "secret," but does not disclose its identity. "By my little point I mean—what shall I call it?—the particular thing I've written my books most *for*. Isn't there for every writer a particular thing of that sort, the thing that most makes him apply himself, the thing without the effort to achieve which he wouldn't write at all, the very passion of his passion, the part of the business in which, for him, the flame of art burns most intensely? Well, it's that!" (p. 281).

In addition to creating an informational gap, this enigmatic confession also functions to arouse in narrator and reader alike the desire to fathom the "secret" and unveil the "idol" (p. 305). If the very passion of Vereker's passion is "naturally the thing for the critic to look for" and even "the thing for the critic to find" (p. 282), if Vereker "live[s] almost to see if it will ever be detected" (p. 283), no wonder that the narrator is fired as he has never been before and determines "to do or die" (p. 283).

Thus, the whole story is a search for the "buried treasure" (p. 285), but it is an unresolved search, and leaves the gap permanently open. To achieve this unresolvedness James uses two main techniques. The first technique is the creation of ancillary gaps or, put differently, the omission of information which could act as univocal evidence. Not a single passage from Vereker's work is "quoted," and even if it were, it would not be enough, since the 'figure' runs throughout the Master's *oeuvre;* not a single description of his novels is given—nothing to enable us to judge independently what the figure might be. Similarly, we never hear Vereker's approval of Corvick's theory. We have only Corvick's word for the Master's confirmation, but no independent dramatization of the scene. The second technique James uses is the "planting" of retardatory devices behind every apparent move toward a solution.

But the technical viability of the permanent gap is not enough. It is also necessary to make it thematically plausible. The thematic justification of elements which are primarily technical devices has been intensively studied under the heading of "motivation" by the Russian Formalists (Lemon and Reis 1965, pp. 78–87). In a separate article I have discussed the retardatory devices in "The Figure in the Carpet" from a point of view combining Barthes's hermeneutic code and the Formalists' notion of motivation (Rimmon 1973, pp. 183–207). I shall only repeat here that in this story the motivation of the delay takes two forms, implying two degrees of mediation: (1) an unmediated manipulation of the events, introducing into the action obstacles which motivate either a temporary delay (departures) or a final blocking of information (deaths), and (2) a mediated manipulation through the characters' categorical refusals or partial evasions which, in turn, are further motivated by professional, personal, or technical reasons put forward by the characters themselves to explain their behavior. Although these are also finally attributable to the discourse, they are less directly so, and we are primarily aware of their relevance to the character speaking and to the subject discussed.

THE AWAKENING OF SUSPICION

In spite of the realistic motivation of the consistent evasion of a solution, the evasion's very existence also serves to arouse the suspicion that there may be no figure in Vereker's carpet. In the beginning, the reader is carried away by the confession scene and led to expect what he always expects in enigma stories, namely, the resolution of the mystery. But the recurrent frustration of these expectations may gradually decrease their pressure and suggest to the reader that the desired information will perhaps never be disclosed. However, it is only at the end that nondisclosure becomes an irrevocable fact, and it is therefore only at the end that a suspicion founded on the permanent gap can become substantial.

A similar cumulative effect is created by the series of departures and deaths (in particular the deaths) which constitute the "unmediated motivation" of the delay. What happens is that the reader becomes gradually aware of the instrumental character of these occurrences and consequently suspects that James's main concern may be to prevent the revelation of the secret. The rapid and convenient succession of deaths does not even pretend to be more than the equivalent of "exit, pursued by a bear" when a Shakespearean character is no longer needed in the play (*The Winter's Tale*, 3. 3. 59). No deep emotions are expressed in the story upon the deaths of the admired author and the narrator's best friends. The reports are brief, matter-of-fact, and completely subordinate to the issue of the quest. The resulting effect is mechanical and funny, and attracts attention to the device as such. The device is, as it were, laid bare, "denuded" (Tomashevsky's term, Lemon and Reis 1965, p. 84), presented and accepted for what it is, thus deliberately leaving the much expected and much delayed revelation unprotected against the reader's skepticism.

But, like the effect of the delay itself, the suspicion based on the artificiality of the deaths becomes substantial only at the end. Before the end, these devices gain artistic plausibility (as distinct from realistic plausibility) from James's skillful exploitation of the reader's curiosity and state of suspense. The reader is, like the narrator, so curious to know what the secret is that he hardly pauses to reflect, as the action proceeds and he participates in the quest, on the plausibility or implausibility of each successive death. For him, too, the deaths are subordinate to the issue of the quest, and he cares about them as little as does the narrator. He easily resigns himself to each setback as it occurs and presses on, with the narrator, hoping to find the secret round the next corner. From time to time he may doubt the likelihood of revelation, but it is only at the end, when he reviews the whole quest he has participated in and the unresolved enigma it leaves on his hands, that he fully recognizes the artificiality of the deaths.[1]

Nor is the reader's suspicion based solely on such a largely retrospective recognition of the evasion. It is also provoked by occasional declarations on the narrator's part, distributed throughout the story, that "the buried treasure was a bad joke, the general intention a monstrous *pose*" (p. 286). As we shall see in a later section, these declarations by no means carry definitive weight, but they are enough to cast the shadow of a doubt over the existence of the figure in the carpet and make us read the story with two conflicting hypotheses in mind.

But the main technique employed to put the reader on his guard at various points of the narrative continuum is the contradiction between data. The conflict between pieces of evidence is particularly salient in Vereker's changing attitude toward the discovery of the secret and in the seemingly subsidiary theme of marriage and its relation to the unearthing of the "treasure."

On the one hand, Vereker sees the figure in the carpet as "the thing for the critic to look for," even as "the thing for the critic to find" (p. 282), and waits impatiently for his secret to be detected. On the other hand, in the very sentence expressing the desire to witness the detection of his involuntary secret, he adds, "But I needn't worry—it won't!" (p. 283). If he lives in the hope of seeing the discovery of his inmost intention, why does he find the unlikelihood of revelation reassuring? The possibility of amused irony in this sentence should not escape us, but straightforward discouragements reinforce our perplexity. "Give it up, give it up!" Vereker says to the narrator on two occasions (p. 285; p. 289), and, "Good-night, my dear boy—don't bother about it" (p. 284). He even goes to the length of writing a letter to the narrator, exhorting him both to forget the challenge and not to transmit it to others. How are we to explain this apparent contradiction?

Even more perplexing is the opposition of statements regarding the impending marriage between Corvick and Gwendolen. Whereas in Vereker's case the contradictions are between various statements he himself makes, and could perhaps be explained by the ambivalence in his attitude toward the discovery of the secret, the engagement between Corvick and Gwendolen is subject to conflicting assertions made by the two

lovers, and these concern facts, not only attitudes. Before
going to India, Corvick explains to the narrator, who is worried
about the latter's lengthy separation from his fiancée, "Ah, I'm
not a bit engaged to her, you know!" and "Well, there *was* one
["a private understanding"]. But there isn't now" (p. 295).
Taking the liberty of thinking "that the girl might in some
way have estranged him" (p. 295), the narrator is understand-
ably astonished when Corvick's letter contains the promise to
tell Gwendolen everything once they are married. Gwendolen's
spontaneous reaction, "It's tantamount to saying . . . that I
must marry him straight off!" (p. 300), seems so to take for
granted the betrothal that the narrator feels compelled to clarify the disparity between it and Corvick's statement by asking
her directly whether she is engaged to him. "Of course I am!"
(p. 300), she declares in flat (unwitting) contradiction to Corvick's previous denial. Whose account are we to trust, and
how can we reconcile the two?

These two contradictions put in doubt the veracity of statements made by the main vessels of information, namely
Vereker and Corvick. Vereker's changing attitude toward the
discovery of the secret gives rise to the uneasy feeling that
there may perhaps be no 'figure' in his 'carpet' and that the
distinguished author is sometimes seized by an understandable
desire to prevent such a negative discovery.

If there is no figure in Vereker's carpet, we ask ourselves,
how does Corvick discover it? The answer to this question
establishes one possible connection between the two striking
contradictions outlined above. For the impression gathered
from the contradiction between Corvick's and Gwendolen's
statements on the subject of their impending marriage is that
perhaps Corvick does not really see the light. Is it not possible
to maintain that, knowing Gwendolen's eagerness to fathom
Vereker's "general intention," Corvick simply lies about his
momentous discovery in order to trick her into marriage?
(Westbrook 1953, pp. 134–40, Vaid 1964, pp. 85–87). After
all, Vereker's confirmation of the discovery is never dramatized,
and there is room for doubting Corvick's account. This indeed
is a possible connection, but it is by no means the only possible
connection. It is true that there is enough reason to question

Corvick's account, yet there isn't enough reason to denounce it as unambiguously unreliable, and the issue remains open.

The original question, "What is the figure in Vereker's carpet?" thus triggers a more radical question, "Is there a figure in Vereker's carpet?" and it is this question that can be answered in two contradictory yet equally tenable ways.

The Mutually Exclusive Systems of Gap-Filling Clues

As in "The Lesson of the Master," the two methods of clue balancing are the equilibrium of singly directed clues and the presence of doubly directed clues. But whereas in "The Lesson of the Master" singly directed clues predominate, in "The Figure in the Carpet" they are outweighed by doubly directed ones. This, together with the fact that the contradictory singly directed clues in "The Figure in the Carpet" always appear one after the other in the narrative sequence, effects a *rapprochement* between the linear and the supralinear readings of the text. In this story, the reader's grouping of clues runs parallel to the sequential unfolding of the narrative, whereas when $a+$ and $a-$ are separated by a block of other clues—as they often are in *The Sacred Fount*—the conflicting systems established in a "metareading" form a "superstructure" which ignores or "distorts" the linear sequence. In short, reading and metareading are closer to each other in "The Figure in the Carpet" than they are in "The Lesson of the Master" on the one hand and in *The Sacred Fount* on the other.

Singly Directed Clues

The singly directed clues in "The Figure in the Carpet" are of the $a+$ $a-$ type, and they fall into two categories: divergences between the narrator and the other characters, and oscillation in the narrator's own view.

If this classification creates the impression that the narrator is the pivot of the ambiguity in this story, the following point should be taken as a corrective. Whereas in later works, like *The Turn of the Screw* and *The Sacred Fount*, it is the validity of the narrator's view that is tested against the other characters' confirmation and repudiation, what is tested in "The Figure in the Carpet" is the validity of Vereker's and later also of Corvick's claims, and the narrator is used as one of the testing figures. It is true that his statements are perhaps more prominent than those of the other characters, the whole story being told by him and filtered through his consciousness, but it is equally true that it is not *his* views that are put in doubt by the ambiguity. This seems to me an important point to make because of the prevalent tendency in James criticism to identify all ambiguity with the problem of the reliability or unreliability of the narrator. In "The Figure in the Carpet," I submit, the ambiguity has little to do with the narrator's reliability, and even in later works the problem of reliability is by no means the only source of the ambiguity.

Let us start the discussion of singly directed clues with the divergences between the narrator and other characters. Conflicting opinions appear in several dialogues, the narrator taking the view that the "secret" is a bad joke, the other characters firmly asserting its significance. Denial and affirmation follow each other in the conversational sequence. Thus, after the narrator's feverish but unsuccessful month with Vereker's novels, he tells Corvick about the author's confession. The anecdote has an "immense effect" upon Corvick, as "it fell in so completely with the sense he had had from the first that there was more in Vereker than met the eye" (pp. 286–87). The unsuccessful narrator ventures a cynical, disbelieving remark that "the eye seemed what the printed page had been expressly invented to meet," but Corvick is not in the least disconcerted by this denigrating statement. Instead, he administers to the narrator's comment a "psychological twist" intended to invalidate it by pointing out the motives underlying it. The narrator, he says, denies the existence of the secret only because he himself has failed in discovering it. "He immediately accused me of being spiteful because I had been foiled" (p. 287). The same zigzag sequence appears in the next conversation between the two. "He [Corvick] was like nothing, I told him, but the maniacs who embrace some bedlematical theory of the cryptic character of Shakespeare. To this he replied that if he had had Shakespeare's own word for his being cryptic he would immediately have accepted it" (pp. 291–92). The narrator thereupon expresses surprise at the importance

Corvick attaches to Vereker's word, and the former bluntly inquires "whether I [narrator] treated Mr. Vereker's word as a lie," an extreme position that the narrator is not prepared to take (p. 292).

Another brief sequence of singly directed clues appears in the conversation between the narrator and Gwendolen after Corvick's alleged discovery of the secret. Gwendolen, anticipating an unenlightening letter from her fiancé says, "Perhaps it won't go in a letter if it's 'immense'," to which the narrator answers in the language of suspicion, "Perhaps not if it's immense bosh" (p. 297). The opposite sequence occurs in the dialogue between the two after Corvick's death and Gwendolen's refusal to disclose the secret. The narrator begins with a negation, "I know what to think then; it's nothing!" and Gwendolen retorts, "It's my life!" and "You've insulted him!" (p. 307).

In addition to these conflicts between the narrator's views and the opinions of other characters, the narrator's own attitude is subject to constant oscillation. Whereas sometimes he expresses an unqualified suspicion, like "This general levity [of Vereker] helped me to believe that, so far as the subject of the tip went, there wasn't much in it" (p. 289), he more often concludes a negation with some reservation, some explanation of the possible psychological motive behind it. Thus, for example, the narrator expresses his irritation with Corvick's and Gwendolen's enthusiasm: "hadn't I even made up my mind that it [the secret] was hollow, wouldn't stand the test? The importance they [Corvick and Gwendolen] attached to it was irritating—it rather envenomed my dissent." He then immediately adds, "That statement looks unamiable, and what probably happened was that I felt humiliated at seeing other persons derive a daily joy from an experiment which had brought me only chagrin" (p. 291).

Similarly, when Corvick asks him whether he treats Vereker's words as a lie, the narrator meditates that he "wasn't perhaps prepared, in my unhappy rebound, to go as far as that, but I insisted that till the contrary was proved I should view it as too fond an imagination" (p. 292). This statement is followed by the attenuating glimmering, "the sharpness of a

sense that Corvick would at last probably come out somewhere" (p. 292), implying that there is something to be discovered. Perhaps more difficult to perceive is the alternation
of doubt and its attenuation in the passage describing the
narrator's confusion after a maddening month of what he
now calls his "ridiculous attempt," his "vain preoccupation."
"I accounted for my confusion—perversely, I confess—
by the idea that Vereker had made a fool of me. The
buried treasure was a bad joke, the general intention a monstrous *pose*" (p. 286). The reservation is inserted within the
denigrating statements, not succeeding them as in the other examples, but its parenthetical nature should not blind us to the
suggestion it makes, namely, that the narrator's dismissal of
"the general intention" may simply be a rationalization of his
personal failure. Another parenthetical reservation, with the
opposite effect, appears in the narrator's explanation of Gwendolen's refusal to tell him the secret after the death of her
husband. "Certainly that reserve was something of a shock to
me—certainly it puzzled me the more I thought of it, though I
tried to explain it, with moments of success, by the supposition
of exalted sentiments, of superstitious scruples, of a refinement
of loyalty" (p. 306). Both the conscious attempt ("I tried")
and the "moments of success," implying the other moments of
failure, attenuate the plausibility of these noble motives and
arouse our suspicion. I have called this "the opposite effect"
because, as a rule, the sequential or parenthetical reservations
attenuate the narrator's suspicions and doubts, whereas here
they provoke them in the midst of a favorable interpretation of
another character's motives.

Doubly Directed Clues

As I have pointed out above, doubly directed clues are more
dominant in "The Figure in the Carpet" than singly directed
ones, thus contributing to the *rapprochement* of the linear and
the supralinear. The doubly directed clues in this story are of
the psychological and the linguistic kinds.

What is open to two interpretations in the psychological
clues in "The Figure in the Carpet" are the reasons underlying
a character's action, decision, or assertion. The actions, deci-

sions, or assertions themselves constitute the apparatus of "mediated motivation," and they are all characterized by an omission of a link from the expository chain. A fully explicit chain contains the cause, the effect, and the link between them. For example, in "He could not work at home because a cable was being repaired in the street, and the workers were making a lot of noise," the effect ("he couldn't work at home") and the cause ("a cable was being repaired in the street") are linked by the explanation that "the workers were making a lot of noise." Without this explanation, the connection between cause and effect remains merely implicit. Frequently the connection is so obvious that the explanation can be omitted, as in "He could not come to the meeting because he was ill." James, however, omits the explanatory link when its identification is far from obvious and in situations which provide at least two possible completions.[2]

When Vereker first discourages the narrator's quest, all he says is, "Good night, my dear boy—don't bother about it. After all, you do like a fellow" (p. 284). The connection between the two parts is unclear, not to say recondite. Why should one's liking of "a fellow" counsel one to abandon the pursuit of the secret which that fellow "live[s] almost" to see discovered? The context offers two interpretations, depending on whether we relate Vereker's words anaphorically or cataphorically. If we establish an anaphoric connection, Vereker's words will be taken as a reaction to the narrator's stupid question, "Is it something in the style or something in the thought?" and the suppressed implication will be that the narrator will do Vereker a favor by not letting his imperceptive mind interfere with his friend's work. But we can also relate Vereker's words cataphorically and see them in the light of the narrator's subsequent question, "And a little intelligence might spoil it?" This question is itself doubly directed, for it may imply either Vereker's fear ("translated" by the narrator) that a little intelligence might spoil his secret by exposing the fraud behind it, or his apprehension that there is an ineffable "something" in the secret which must be spoiled, murdered, when unearthed by intelligence alone (see also p. 276). The grammatical ambiguity of *it* adds yet another variation, one which I shall discuss in the section devoted to doubly directed linguistic clues.

The conversation between Vereker and the narrator ends on another anxiously warning note. "Give it up—give it up!" Vereker says, and the narrator feels that "This wasn't a challenge—it was fatherly advice" (p. 285). But why fatherly advice? Is it because the narrator is not "intellectually equipped for the adventure," as he later believes Vereker to think (p. 289), or is it because Vereker wants to spare the young critic a fruitless search for a nonexistent secret?

Vereker's subsequent letter to the narrator is equally perplexing. In it the novelist says that he has read another of the narrator's articles, an article which gave him great pleasure. "The consequence of this has been that I begin to measure the temerity of my having saddled you with a knowledge that you may find something of a burden" (p. 287). In what sense is the one a consequence of the other? Why will the narrator find the knowledge "something of a burden"? If his article is intelligent and promising, perhaps he will find this knowledge the first step to further knowledge, to the actual discovery of the figure in the carpet? There are again two ways of supplying the missing link in this nonsequitur or even self-contradictory explanation. Both hypotheses are formed by the reader (not by the narrator or any other character in the story) on the basis of evidence prior to or contained in this letter. Remembering the narrator's preceding suspicion that "the general intention was a monstrous *pose*" (p. 286), the reader may want to infer that the knowledge will become a burden because it will make him seek something which does not exist. On the other hand, the reader may draw an inference from the rest of the letter and conclude that the knowledge will become a burden because the narrator will find difficulty in keeping it to himself, and Vereker desires to prevent the expansion of the information. His confession to the narrator has already spoiled a part of his fun, and "I really don't want to give anybody what I believe you clever young men call the tip" (p. 288). This is also the explanation Vereker offers in the meeting with the narrator. "The reason of his note to me has been that he really didn't want to give us a grain of succour—our density was a thing too perfect in its way to touch" (pp. 289–290). But there is no reason why we should accept this explanation as conclusive.[3]

Vereker, however, is not the only character whose statements are often incomplete and doubly directed. Corvick's letter to the narrator after the alleged discovery is not less tantalizing. "Have patience," he writes, "I want to see, as it breaks on you, the face you'll make! *'Tellement envie de voir ta tête.'* " (pp. 298–99). This is sufficiently suggestive to make us feel that there is something unexpected about the secret, but it says nothing about the kind of unexpectedness or—the other side of the coin—about the type of facial reaction anticipated on the part of the narrator. Would that reaction be amazement at the beauty of the secret, surprise at its simplicity, shame at not having seen it before, or humorous acceptance of the trick?

Equally enigmatic is his letter to Gwendolen, promising to tell her everything when they are married, but not before. Why does Corvick insist on waiting until after the wedding? What is the connection between marriage and the secret? On the basis of cultural conventions as well as of Vereker's preceding words about marriage and the secret, the reader forms the hypothesis that Corvick wishes to wait until their union is complete, a hypothesis which gains support from the narrator's retrospective meditations after Corvick's death. "Corvick had kept his information from his young friend till after the removal of the last barrier to their intimacy" (p. 306). But this is not the only possibility, and James suggests that it isn't by making the narrator qualify Corvick's words as a "remarkable statement" (p. 300). The other possibility is suggested, although unwittingly, by Gwendolen's reaction to this condition: "It's tantamount to saying—isn't it?—that I must marry him straight off!" (p. 300). Is it possible, we ask ourselves, that Corvick is playing a foul trick in order to force Gwendolen into marriage?

Closely connected to this is Gwendolen's mystifying explanation of the contradiction between hers and Corvick's statements about the imminence of their wedding. "What the state of things has been," she says, "is that we felt of course bound to do nothing in mamma's lifetime" (p. 301). But Mrs. Erme is still alive when this is said, and the invocation of her opposition to the engagement does nothing to clarify the cause of the changed decision. The narrator asks for clarification, "But now you think you'll just dispense with your mother's consent?" (p. 301). Now, says Gwendolen, opening yet another gap, her mother will simply have to "swallow the dose" (p. 301). Why now more than before? (For a similar phenomenon in James's style, see Chatman 1972, p. 87.)

After Corvick's death the narrator attempts to extract the secret from Gwendolen, but she expresses a firm resolution not to make him privy to the precious knowledge. Her "justification" of the resolution amounts to a tautology: She will not tell because she means to keep the secret to herself (p. 305). But why does she mean to keep it to herself when the opposite course of action would be creditable to the memory of both Vereker and Corvick? We may assume with the narrator that she is moved by "exalted sentiments," "superstitious scruples," "a refinement of loyalty" (p. 306), but we may also agree with his later statement, "I know what to think then; it's nothing!" (p. 307).

If Gwendolen is not in possession of the secret, the reader may rightly ask, "How are we to explain the improvement of her second novel and her newly gained beauty and dignity?" (pp. 305–6). The improvement of the novel (if it is not only the narrator's subjective impression) can be explained by her past intimacy with Corvick, by "the better company she had kept" (p. 308), just as the inferior quality of her third novel is accounted for by her marriage to Drayton Deane: "Was it worse because she had been keeping worse company?" (p. 311). As for her personal flowering after her husband's death, we must remember that the narrator's observation of this strange phenomenon is by no means unqualified. The sequence of his statements as well as the verb *to fancy* are worth noticing. "I couldn't help fancying after I had seen her a few times that I caught a glimpse of some such oddity. I hasten to add that there had been other things I couldn't help fancying" (p. 305). The suggestion, then, is attenuated both by the last sentence and by the verb used in the description itself. Perhaps we can also explain the new sense of beauty and dignity in Gwendolen as a rationalization on the part of the narrator, who is contemplating marrying her for the sake of the secret. This will recall the similar ambiguous motif toward the end of "The Aspern Papers," where the narrator suddenly perceives or imagines "a sort of phantasmagoric brightness" beautifying Miss Tita, whom he was thinking of marrying for the sake of the precious letters (*The Complete Tales of Henry James*, 6:381). Both the literary and the personal improvement of Gwendolen are, of course, easily explained on the opposite assumption, the assumption that it is the knowledge of the secret that is "discernible in her increasing bloom" (p. 311), and the issue remains perfectly ambiguous.

The last episode in the story, Drayton Deane's confession of ignorance, is again doubly directed. It may even be doubly doubly directed. Deane's ignorance (if it is real) clearly means that Gwendolen told him nothing about Vereker's "general intention," but the motives behind her silence can be interpreted in two ways, one suggested by the narrator and one implied by Deane. What the narrator concludes is that Gwendolen had not "thought him [Deane] worth enlightening" (p. 314), and this naturally makes the secret appear even more precious. Deane's words, on the other hand, may suggest that Gwendolen had told him nothing because there was nothing to be told. In three irritated outbursts, Deane says, "I don't know what you're talking about" (p. 314); "What the devil's the matter with you?" (p. 314); and "I think you must be mistaken as to Mrs. Drayton Deane's having had any unmentioned, and still less any unmentionable, knowledge about Hugh Vereker" (pp. 314–15). So perhaps the narrator has been thoroughly misled, and there is, in fact, nothing to know about Hugh Vereker. But, of course, Deane's denial may also be an attempt to cover the shame of having had no glimpse of the very thing on which his wife lived.

But what if the whole confession of ignorance is a lie? The possibility was brought up by the narrator, and although he later retracts it, expresses belief in Deane, and starts telling him the whole history of the figure in the carpet, the reader may want to retain this possibility side by side with the diametrically opposed alternative. The potential motives behind such a lie are again two: either Deane is "amiably amused at [the narrator's] impotence" (p. 312) and is rather cruelly "playing with [him]" (p. 313), as the narrator himself originally suspected, or—upon the assumption that Deane knows that there is no secret—he is trying to protect the honor of all the dead by turning the objective blanks into personal blankness on his part.[4]

Against the background of all these ambiguous psychological clues, the paucity of doubly directed linguistic clues in this story is conspicuous. In "The Figure in the Carpet" there are several doubly directed pronouns, one ambiguity arising out of an elliptical construction, and a few ambiguous images.

Of the six potentially ambiguous pronouns in "The Figure in the Carpet," one is a momentary misapprehension, two are immediately resolved, and three remain fully ambiguous. I shall discuss only the three unresolvedly ambiguous pronouns because the others contribute nothing or very little to the central narrative ambiguity. Even the three pronouns to be discussed do more to distinguish subtly the narrative possibilities than to make them mutually exclusive, and in this they differ from ambiguous pronouns in later works, like *The Turn of the Screw* and *The Sacred Fount*.

All the fully ambiguous pronouns occur in the late-night conversation between Vereker and the narrator about the figure in the carpet. The following passage, beginning with Vereker's statement, contains two ambiguous pronouns which, for convenience, I shall underline in the text.

"If my great affair's a secret, that's only because it's a secret in spite of itself—the amazing event has made it one. I not only never took the smallest precaution to do so, but never dreamed of any such accident. If I had I shouldn't in advance have had the heart to go on. As it was I only became aware little by little, and meanwhile I had done my work."

"And now you quite like *it?*" I risked.

"My work?"

"Your secret. It's the same thing."

"Your guessing *that*", Vereker replied, "is a proof that you're as clever as I say!" [P. 283]

The "it" in the narrator's question can have two anaphoric antecedents: either the last noun preceding it, namely "work," or the main subject of the discussion, namely the secret. The first possibility is brought up by Vereker, the second by the narrator, who then proceeds to dissolve (rather than resolve) the ambiguity by equating the two alternatives. But the equation itself is doubly directed. Vereker's secret and his work may be "the same thing" in the sense that once the secret is discovered, once the figure in the carpet is deciphered, it is seen to embrace the whole of Vereker's work and shed a new light upon it, a light which is then recognized as the only true one. But the two may also be identical in another sense. Rather than taking the word "secret" to refer to the essence underlying it, we may regard it as designating only the presence of the secret, the secret as a phenomenon. Vereker's work will then be identical with the existence of a secret, not with its content, and such a secret, Todorov rightly says, "is by definition inviolable, as it resides in its own existence" (1971, p. 183). Vereker's answer to the narrator's conjecture is also grammatically ambiguous. "Your guessing that," Vereker replies, "is a proof that you're as clever as I say." Is Vereker complimenting the narrator for the realization that "now [he] quite like[s] it" ("it" being either the work or the secret or both), or is he praising him for grasping the identity of the work and the secret?

The third fully ambiguous pronoun is another "it" with a double anaphoric referent, which occurs in a passage I have already discussed from a different point of view. Let me quote again the relevant bit, beginning with Vereker's words.

> "Good night, my dear boy—don't bother about it. After all, you do like a fellow".
> "And a little intelligence might spoil *it*?" I still detained him. [P. 284; my italics]

We have previously seen that the narrator's question is doubly directed, meaning either that a little intelligence might spoil the secret by exposing the fraud behind it, or that intelligence might ruin the ineffable element in the secret. Both these interpretations take the "it" to replace "the secret," but "it" can also be taken to substitute for "one's liking of a fellow." This possibility is again doubly directed, suggesting that a little intelligence may spoil one's liking for Vereker either because it will expose him or because it is insufficient for the discovery of the figure and will therefore only irritate the critic (which is indeed what happens).

In addition to pronouns with two referents, elliptical constructions can also give rise to linguistic ambiguity, but there is only one such example in "The Figure in the Carpet." Drayton Deane is trying to "prove" that his wife could not have been in possession of Vereker's secret. Had she had knowledge about Vereker, he argues, "She would certainly have wished it—if it bore on his literary character—to be used." The inconsiderate narrator, pursuing only his own end, answers, "It *was* used. She used it herself. She told me with her own lips that she 'lived' on it." At this, Deane grows pale and murmurs the incomplete, "Ah, 'lived'—!" (p. 315). Two completions are again possible. Deane's ejaculation can be read as an abridgment of the tacit realization that his wife "lived without admitting [him] to the very essence of her life," but it may also be a sigh of grief, inwardly completed by something like, "Ah, she lived then, but now, alas, she is dead." The first possibility indirectly confirms the existence of the secret through Deane's painful acceptance of his *anagnorisis*. The second reading, on the other hand, leaves intact Deane's assertion that the narrator must be mistaken, thus passively maintaining (if not actively supporting) the discreditable interpretation.

More frequent in this tale are doubly directed images. In describing the secret figure, Vereker employs a series of closed similes which can be interpreted in one way on the basis of the explicitly mentioned common quality and in another on the basis of semantic collocation. "The thing's as concrete there as a bird in a cage, a bait on a hook, a piece of cheese in a mousetrap. It's stuck into every volume as your foot is stuck into your shoe. It governs every line, it chooses every word, it dots every i, it places every comma" (pp. 283–84). The common quality between tenor and vehicle in the first three similes is said to be concreteness, and the rest of the passage adds the notions of centrality and obviousness which can be easily projected back to the first images. The bird, the implied fish, and the suggested mouse are not only "concrete" or "palpable" (to cite an adjective from a passage on p. 282); they are also the end for which the cage, the hook, and the trap were designed. In the same way, the figure in the carpet is the center, the core, the *raison d'être* of the whole of Vereker's creative endeavor—it is indeed "the finest, fullest intention of the lot" (p. 281). But, owing to their collocation, the range of the similes is enlarged beyond the explicitly mentioned qualities. The three images belong to the same semantic field, and this establishes another link between them, namely, the unifying quality of imprisoning, catching, ensnaring, trapping. But this unifying quality can be interpreted in two opposed ways, the images being related to different aspects of the phenomenon and consequently pulling in contrasted directions. The first simile compares the secret to the bird in the cage, the caught creature, whereas the other two compare it to the "instruments" of catching, the bait on the hook and the piece of cheese in the mousetrap. One interpretation of the passage projects the meaning of the first simile onto the others and sees the 'secret' as something which has to be caught by the eager 'hunter.' The second interpretation, on the other hand, focuses on the two other images and suggests that the figure in the carpet, like the bait on the hook and the piece of cheese in the mousetrap, is a trick used to lure the victim and ensnare him under false pretenses of being the real thing (food, the whole cheese, the "general intention"). The caught creature, in this view, is not Vereker's secret but, ironically, Vereker's reader.

Other images of hunt in the story support both possibilities. On the one hand, the pursuit of the secret is frequently described as a hunt. Corvick and Gwendolen "followed *the chase* for which I myself [narrator] had *sounded the horn*" (p. 291). Corvick wants to *"bring down the animal* with his own rifle" (p. 293) and will not knock at Vereker's door before he has *"run him to earth"* (p. 293; my italics). On the other hand, the narrator's unsuccessful pursuit amounts to self-imprisonment rather than an imprisonment of the secret. "I was *shut up* in my obsession for ever—my gaolers had gone off with the key. I find myself quite as vague as a *captive* in a *dungeon* about the time that further elapsed before Mrs. Corvick became the wife of Drayton Deane. I had foreseen, through my *bars,* this end of the business" (p. 310; my italics). The tantalizing secret has proved a bait on a hook, a piece of cheese in a mousetrap, and now the fish, the mouse, the narrator rather than the secret, is forever shut up in captivity.

Being by nature associated with violence, the hunt images ironically suggest, behind the speaker's back, that bringing down the animal "with [one's] own rifle" is actually killing the animal. Does this mean that the discovery of the secret equals its murder, or does it only imply that the figure in the carpet has to come out of its own accord, as another animal image (to be fully developed in a later story, "The Beast in the Jungle") intimates? "He [Corvick] hasn't gone into it, I know; it's the thing itself, let severely alone for six months, that has simply sprung out at him like a tigress out of the jungle" (p. 297). The tigress in the jungle is in its own natural element. The bird in the cage, the fish on the hook, and the mouse in the trap are not. Is the figure in the carpet organic to the whole, as the image of the heart also suggests (p. 284), or is it only "stuck into" it by the hunter, put into the textual cage by an act of imposition, of "reading into"? Is it the very "organ of life" of the text (p. 284), or is it life imprisoned and doomed to die—a bird in a cage, a mouse in a trap, a fish on a hook? One can hardly think of images more opposed to each other than a heart and a cage, and it is difficult to see how the same figure can be both.

The images describing the figure, we have seen, are either doubly directed or opposed to each other, and consequently they cannot tell us whether the characters are engaged in a commendable and feasible quest or whether they are merely trapped by a trick designed to catch the unwary. The story being, in a sense, metaliterary, it duplicates itself in the inevitable interplay with the implied reader. Just as the characters search for the figure in Vereker's carpet, so does the reader look for the parallel figure in James's. Is such an attempt to fathom the secret of "The Figure in the Carpet" implicitly encouraged by the text, or is it parodied, ironically classified with the wild-goose chase of the fictional critics? Like everything else in the story, James's implicit attitude toward the implied reader is ambiguous, and we can conclude nothing definitive on the basis of the tale itself.

And yet, most critical interpretations of the story are completely unambiguous, and can be neatly divided into those which affirm the existence of the figure (for example, Anderson 1957, p. 149; Lainoff 1961, pp. 122–28; Levy 1962a, pp. 457–65) and those which deny it (Westbrook 1953, pp. 137–39; Finch 1968, pp. 98–101). Several critics grapple with the insolubility of the enigma (for example, Powers 1961, p. 226; Cixous 1970, p. 47; Todorov 1971, p. 183), but very few mention the ambiguity (Blackmur 1954, p. 214; Sollers 1968, p. 121; Segal 1969, p. 151), and no one analyzes it in detail. Therefore, I would like to hope that the foregoing analysis has contributed not only toward the establishment of "The Figure in the Carpet" in the canon of James's ambiguous works, but also toward an understanding of the techniques employed to create the ambiguity of this metaliterary enigma story.

5   *The Turn of the Screw*

    The ambiguity of "The Lesson of the Master" and "The Figure in the Carpet" has not been adequately analyzed by the critics. At best, it has been mentioned in passing, sometimes accompanied by a derogatory or a laudatory comment, but never described in detail. At worst, it has been completely ignored, resulting in one-sided interpretations (and this, in the rare cases where an interpretation, and not simply a cursory remark, has been attempted). With *The Turn of the Screw* (1898) the situation is completely different. The sheer quantity of books and articles dealing with this nouvelle is astounding. It is true that many of these still offer univocal interpretations, but it is hardly possible to do so today without relating to the phenomenon of ambiguity, be it only by way of rejection. Indeed, *The Turn of the Screw* has been so firmly linked with ambiguity that even people who have not read it know that it is somehow supposed to be ambiguous.

    My task in this chapter is, therefore, different from the one I have undertaken in the two previous analyses. There is no need to establish this profusely examined nouvelle in the canon of James's ambiguous works, although there is still need to insist that one of the implications of such a statement is the impossibility of choice between the mutually exclusive interpretations. There is also no need to show what is ambiguous in the various episodes of which *The Turn of the Screw* consists, for this too has been done before. In fact, most of the evidence for and against the governess's account has been pointed out in the endless debates on this narrative, and to demonstrate the ambiguity it would almost suffice to extract and juxtapose quotations from the diametrically opposed "camps" of critics. The degree of originality I can claim for this chapter is therefore rather limited, consisting mainly in the application of my own system to what has been said and done before. However, such an application has a three-fold advantage: the challenge of grappling with a work so famous for its ambiguity provides a good test case for the tools and categories proposed; an analysis based on categories of clues rather than on narrative episodes is capable of a higher degree of systematization of the various findings; and the perspective gained by the application of the *same* system to various ambiguous works allows us to see where and how each work differs from the others. A substantial part of this chapter will therefore approach *The Turn of the Screw* by way of comparing its ambiguity with that of "The Lesson of the Master" and "The Figure in the Carpet," a dimension that has not been discussed by other critics.

THE TURN OF THE SCREW AGAINST THE BACKGROUND OF "THE LESSON OF THE MASTER" AND "THE FIGURE IN THE CARPET"

The Turn of the Screw differs from "The Lesson of the Master" and "The Figure in the Carpet" in several respects, pertaining to theme, genre, and technique.

The theme of this nouvelle is not the conflict between Art and Life, but conflicts within Life itself. It is true that the governess is said to have written her story, but she is not a professional novelist, nor is she concerned with the predicament of the creative imagination. What she is mainly concerned with is the stuff that life is made of: love, fear, good and evil, salvation, pride, possessiveness, gnawing doubt. The major problems in *The Turn of the Screw* are moral and epistomological, and the emphasis on the metaliterary (which, of course, had moral and epistemological aspects of its own) has here given room to an emphasis on the purely human.

The Turn of the Screw is the only work among those selected for discussion which contains supernatural agents. The introduction of the supernatural into a world that is indeed purely human is likely to provoke an embarrassed reaction on the part of the reader. To quote Tzvetan Todorov:

> Dans un monde qui est bien le nôtre, celui que nous connaissons, sans diables, sylphides, ni vampires, se produit un événement qui ne peut s'expliquer par les lois de ce

même monde familier. Celui qui perçoit l'événement doit
opter pour l'une des deux solutions possibles: ou bien il
s'agit d'une illusion des sens, d'un produit de l'imagination
et les lois du monde restent alors ce qu'elles sont; ou bien
l'événement a véritablement eu lieu, il est partie intégrante
de la réalité, mais alors cette réalité est régie par des lois
inconnues de nous. Ou bien le diable est une illusion, un être
imaginaire: ou bien il existe réellement, tout comme les
autres êtres vivants: avec cette réserve qu'on le rencontre
rarement. [1970, p. 29]

If the work encourages the reader to take the first view, it
belongs to the genre that Todorov calls *l'étrange,* which leaves
the laws of the universe unchanged and explains the "strange"
phenomenon "realistically," by asserting that dream, madness,
the influence of drugs, hallucinations, can account for them.
On the other hand, if the work encourages us to take the
second view, it belongs to the genre of the *merveilleux,* which
admits of new laws of nature by which the unexpected phenomenon can be explained, new laws which provide for the
existence of supernatural beings like devils, fairies, ghosts (p.
46). Between these two extremes there is a third genre, the
fantastique, defined by a "hesitation" as to which of the contrary categories can best account for the uncommon happenings
in the story. According to Todorov, this genre

exige que trois conditions soient remplies. D'abord, il faut
que le texte oblige le lecteur à considérer le monde des
personnages comme un monde de personnes vivantes et à
hésiter entre une explication naturelle et une explication
surnaturelle des événements évoqués. Ensuite, cette hésitation peut être ressentie également par un personnage: ainsi le
rôle de lecteur est pour ainsi dire confié à un personnage et
dans le même temps l'hésitation se trouve représentée, elle
devient un des thèmes de l'oeuvre; dans le cas d'une lecture
naïve, le lecteur réel s'identifie avec le personnage. Enfin il
importe que le lecteur adopte une certaine attitude à l'égard
du texte: il refusera aussi bien l'interprétation allégorique
que l'interprétation "poétique". Ces trois exigences n'ont pas
une valeur égale. La première et la troisième constituent
véritablement le genre; la seconde peut ne pas être satisfaite.
Toutefois, la plupart des exemples remplissent les trois
conditions. [Pp. 37–38]

The "fantastic," then, is "un cas particulier de la catégorie plus générale de la 'vision ambiguë.' " (p. 38); and it can be resolved in the text by finally opting either for the "strange" or for the "marvellous." When a resolution occurs, the fantastic becomes a phase of reading rather than an autonomous genre (p. 46). On the other hand, when there is no resolution, the work remains in the realm of the *fantastique pur,* and the only thing it definitively affirms is the ambiguity.

With these notions in mind, we can return to the superhuman element in *The Turn of the Screw* and define the genre to which it belongs. The endless debates as to whether the ghosts are objective supernatural evil beings which appear to governess and children alike or whether they are hallucinations of the governess's deranged mind can now be said to hinge on whether we classify the story as *merveilleux* or as *étrange*. Or, in fact, the other way round: the genre to which the story belongs is determined by the degree and kind of substantiality attached to the ghosts. The debates are bound to be endless because it is impossible to choose between the two opposed alternatives, representing the two contrary genres. And this is so because *The Turn of the Screw* is written in the "pure fantastic" mode, maintaining the ambiguity to the very end.

Technically, also, the nouvelle differs greatly from the ambiguous tales of the literary life. One of the salient differences is the handling of point of view. "The Lesson of the Master" is told by an undramatized narrator, and its ambiguity turns on the motives behind St. George's surprising action, not on the reliability or unreliability of the narrator. "The Figure in the Carpet," on the other hand, is told in the first person by a dramatized narrator, but nevertheless the reliability questioned by the ambiguity is not that of the narrator, but that of Vereker and Corvick. It is in *The Turn of the Screw* that the reliability of the first-person narrator becomes a central issue. Take the governess as a reliable interpreter of events, and you have one story. Take her as an unreliable neurotic fabricator of nonexistent "ghosts of the mind" and you are reading a diametrically opposed narrative. The ambiguous status of a report given by a first-person narrator is a feature that *The Turn of the Screw* shares with most fantastic stories, according to Todorov (1970, pp. 88–91). It also shares this feature with another ambiguous work by Henry James, a work without supernatural or fantastic elements: *The Sacred Fount*.[1] This is perhaps the place to reiterate what I said in the previous chapter, namely that even when the problem of the reliability or unreliability of the narrator is central, it is by no means the only technique used to create the ambiguity. In fact, it can be seen as concomitant with the central informational gap and the mutually exclusive systems of clues designed to fill it in. Whether the reliability problem is considered one of the devices which "motivate" the other two elements or one of their causes depends mainly on where we start from—the *fabula* or the accomplished discourse—and is finally an unprofitable point to debate.

The differences in technique between the ambiguity of "The Lesson of the Master," "The Figure in the Carpet," and *The Turn of the Screw* are not limited to the handling of point of view. Another important difference can be grasped with the help of Barthes's proairetic and hermeneutic codes. The proairetic is the code in charge of sequences of actions, while the hermeneutic is the one which regulates the formulation, delay, and solution of enigmas (1970). The relations that each of the texts in question establishes between these two aspects corresponds to the way its ambiguity is constructed. As we have seen, the ambiguity of "The Lesson of the Master" is perceptible only in retrospect. Before reaching Paul's crucial question ("Was it a plan?"), the reader is not aware of an informational gap or of an enigma. He consequently reads the story as one reads a sequence of proaireticisms (without, of course, thinking of the term or even of the concept which it conveys). It is only when he reaches the final "twist" that he becomes aware of the enigma and projects it back on the narrative as a whole. A retrospective patterning of the story is, in fact, an attempt to solve the enigma, and hence the proairetic sequences are subjected to (or seen as) hermeneutic ones, although there are always "free" elements which are not enigma-bound or even action-bound and serve as transitions from one bound element to another or as means of characterization, or perform other functions that I cannot enumerate here.

Unlike the central gap in "The Lesson of the Master," that

in "The Figure in the Carpet" is perceptible from an early stage of the narrative. The question of what the figure in Vereker's carpet may be is posed in the nocturnal conversations between the famous author and his ardent disciple, and the whole story can be seen as an attempt to fill in the missing information. Most of the proaireticisms (again allowing for free elements) are related to the search for a solution, thereby becoming hermeneutic activities. Thus the *rapprochement* between the proairetic and the hermeneutic is effected in the progressive linearity of the narrative, not in retrospective perusal, as in "The Lesson of the Master."

Another characteristic of the hermeneutic aspect of "The Figure in the Carpet" is that the quest situation is reproduced in five consecutive "mirror scenes" (Rimmon 1973, pp. 183–207). Thus the central search is, as it were, distributed in installments—each has its own variable elements, but all five installments are concerned with the same focal question.

The Turn of the Screw takes this "distributional" technique one step further. The question concerning the reality of the ghosts arises in the sixth out of the twenty-four chapters of the nouvelle. From this point on, reading is imbued with a strong enigma-solving element, trying to answer the unanswerable question of whether there are or there are not real ghosts at Bly, seen by governess and children alike. But the narrative continuum divides this general question into a series of "local" questions, each forming the focus of a relatively self-contained section of the story. The reader is successively concerned with local questions like, Does Flora see Miss Jessel across the lake? Why does Miles go out in the middle of the night? Why does Miles insist on going back to school? Who blows the candle? It is clear, of course, that all these questions are part and parcel of the central enigma, but unlike the repetition of the selfsame question in five different installments in "The Figure in the Carpet," the local questions in *The Turn of the Screw* are distinct from one another, although they are all subdivisions of the central enigma. Moreover, the scenes that give rise to these local questions are full of proairetic material that is more directly relevant to the local issue than to the central one. The various scenes are felt to be there not only as further unfolding and illustration of one central enigma, but also in their own dramatic right. There is thus a double relationship between the proairetic and the hermeneutic material in *The Turn of the Screw*. On the one hand, it shares with the retrospective perusal of "The Lesson of the Master" and the linear reading of "The Figure in the Carpet" a teleological subjection of most proairetic material to the attempt of filling in the main hermeneutic gap. On the other hand, it shares with an "innocent" linear reading of "The Lesson of the Master" a high degree of independence of the proairetic material (though this is more restricted in *The Turn of the Screw* than in a prereversal reading of "The Lesson of the Master"). The various installments of or variations on the enigma in *The Turn of the Screw* have so much dramatic substance that they tend to become narrative *foci* in themselves, drawing attention to what is happening now and what is going to happen next at least as much as to the central enigma. This is one of the reasons why most critics analyze *The Turn of the Screw* according to narrative episodes, scenes, or sections, discerning (when they do) the ambiguity lodged in each, rather than the principles governing the overall organization into two mutually exclusive systems. The main narrative sections into which *The Turn of the Screw* falls are the prologue; the headmaster's letter; the governess's first "encounter" with the stranger; Mrs. Grose's "identification" of the stranger as Peter Quint; the first lake scene in which Flora is supposed to be communicating with a strange lady; the "identification" of the lady as Miss Jessel; the governess's third "encounter" with Quint and her realization that Flora is outside very late at night; the governess's "encounter" with Miss Jessel on the steps; the children's nocturnal escapade; the conversation between Miles and the governess on the way to church; the governess's schoolroom "encounter" with Miss Jessel; the second lake scene with Flora, her boat rowing and her "communication" with Miss Jessel; Flora's breakdown; Miles's confession and death. As against the usual analysis in terms of these focal narrative units, I prefer here an examination of the underlying organizational principles of the ambiguity. Since my method does not always conform to the scenic installments, it is doubly important to point out the "distribu-

tional" technique practiced in this nouvelle and the interesting
relations that it creates between the proairetic and the hermeneutic aspects.

Some of the sections listed, such as the prologue, the headmaster's letter, and the governess's first and second "encoun-
ters" with the stranger, precede the moment at which the
central ambiguity is first perceptible, but they are not irrelevant
to its analysis, as they point to another interesting compositional feature in *The Turn of the Screw*, the nouvelle's combination of prospective and retrospective ambiguity. The former
begins in chapter 6, developing with the linear progression of
the narrative, but once evident it is projected back to the preceding sections, having a local effect that resembles the total
one in "The Lesson of the Master." In other words, the retrospective ambiguity of the first four installments in *The Turn of
the Screw*, like the retrospective ambiguity of "The Lesson of
the Master" as a whole, is based on the technique of the inverted story, from which it deviates by making both readings
equally tenable, instead of substituting the one for the other.
Let us take the prologue as an example. A first reading arouses
suspense, an anticipation of a grim ghost story, and a predisposition in favor of the governess. The framework is a Christ-
mas eve fireside social gathering in which people appropriately
tell gruesome ghost stories. One of the guests has just finished
the story of a boy who saw a ghost and in his fear woke up his
mother, who immediately encountered the same apparition and
could not soothe her son, being terrified herself. The *I* who
narrates the prologue remarks, "I remember no comment
uttered till somebody happened to say that it was the only case
he had met in which such a visitation had fallen on a child. The
case, I may mention, was that of an apparition in just such an
old house as has gathered us for the occasion" (p. 15). This
story draws a somewhat belated observation from Douglas:
"I quite agree—in regard to Griffin's ghost, or whatever it was
—that its appearing first to the little boy, at so tender an age,
adds a particular touch" (p. 15). Douglas then promises to tell a
story that is "beyond everything . . . For general uncanny ugliness and horror and pain" (p. 16), and creates further suspense
by comparing the promised story with the one just completed.

"If the child gives the effect another turn of the screw, what do you say to *two* children—?" (p. 15).

All this arouses in the reader, as well as in the fictional audience, an expectation to hear from Douglas a real ghost story, a story of the genre of the *merveilleux*, about the appearance of supernatural beings to two little children. The reality of the ghost in the Griffin story is confirmed by the fact that it is seen by mother and child alike. Words like *visitation* and *apparition* reinforce the impression of the *merveilleux* and lead one to assume that Douglas's tale, a tale which is said to surpass Griffin's in its horror and in the number of children afflicted, will belong to the same genre. It is only after the possibility of reading *The Turn of the Screw* in two opposed ways is established that many of these assumptions—assumptions actively encouraged by the text—may be inverted. In retrospect, the reader may recall Douglas's "I quite agree—in regard to Griffin's ghost, or whatever it was—" and take "or whatever it was" as a reservation concerning the reality of the ghost; it may have been a ghost, but it may also have been mere hallucination. The qualification "or whatever it was" may indeed be a suggestion of doubt, but its suggestive character is deliberately concealed in a first reading. Its position is parenthetical, giving it less prominence than the centrally located "visitation" and "apparition" and the confirmation provided by the mother. Even if the reader does not overlook the parenthetical "or whatever it was," he probably makes it conform to the rest of the context by supposing that if it was not exactly a ghost, it may have been another kind of supernatural being: elf, incubus, succubus, goblin, what not. Only after the narrative gives us enough reason to think of hallucinations can we project this possibility back to the vague "or whatever it was"— though the uninverted original reading remains equally valid. Douglas's description of his tale as "beyond everything . . . For general uncanny ugliness and horror and pain" is again taken to refer to the effect of the ghosts, until the hallucination possibility makes us retrospectively realize that James's vague and inclusive "*general* uncanny ugliness" (my italics) allows for more than ghosts—for the governess's hallucinations and harassment of the children, for example.

The retrospective ambiguity of the prologue is not confined to the nature of the ghosts. The statements establishing the governess's amiable character can also be read either as inverted or as uninverted. In a first reading the picture that emerges from Douglas's description is very engaging: "She was a most charming person"; "She was the most agreeable woman I've ever known in her position; she would have been worthy of any whatever" (p. 17). This character testimonial clashes violently with the governess's behavior as it emerges from a reading in the light of the hallucination hypothesis. The perplexed reader then goes back to the prologue and discovers that while it does indeed encourage his initial favorable view of the governess, it also sows some seeds of doubt. Two points in particular attract his attention in retrospect: the lapse of time and Douglas's love for the governess. Immediately after the enthusiastic praise quoted above, Douglas says, "It was long ago, and this episode was long before" (p. 17). While in an "innocent" linear reading this sentence is taken only as a specification of chronology, in retrospect it can be seen as attenuating the applicability of Douglas's description to the Bly episode. After all, the reader may say, Douglas knew the governess a long time after her traumatic experience at Bly, and, for all we know, she might have spent the intervening time in a lunatic asylum (see Cranfill and Clark 1965, p. 23).[2] The second element in the prologue that can be inverted in retrospect is Douglas's love for the governess. Whereas originally it reinforces her worth, in retrospect it can undermine the validity of Douglas's judgment. After all, he was only a young man, she was ten years older, and this is precisely the kind of love that tends to deification rather than to a more or less objective view of the person toward whom it is directed. Thus the character testimonial of the prologue can be inverted, but we should not forget that rather than canceling out the initial view, the inverting elements balance them, thus rendering the evidence of the prologue ambiguous.

A similar retrospective ambiguity can be demonstrated with regard to the other sections that precede chapter 6, but I shall now proceed to a detailed description of the prospective ambiguity which occupies the bulk of *The Turn of the Screw*.

THE CREATION OF THE AMBIGUITY

The Turn of the Screw shares with the other ambiguous works the existence of a central permanent gap and of mutually exclusive systems of clues designed to fill it in. But the order in which the reader perceives these two components (as distinct from the logical order abstracted by the analyst and perhaps also from the creative order conceived by the author) varies from work to work. The order of perception depends, of course, on the order of presentation in the *sjužet*. In "The Figure in the Carpet" the reader is first made aware of the existence of an enigma, and only in following the characters' attempts to solve it does he come across conflicting clues which gradually form the mutually exclusive hypotheses of which the ambiguity consists. In *The Sacred Fount*, the next chapter will show, the narrator's theory with its symmetrical equations and its informational gap is gradually formed in the first two chapters and henceforth becomes the focus of all the conversations between the fictional characters as well as of the reader's clue-grouping activity, which makes him aware of the ambiguity. *The Turn of the Screw*, on the other hand, follows the reverse procedure: the reader is first faced with conflicting accounts, and it is this incompatibility that makes him perceive the central gap. On two occasions the governess sees a terrifying stranger who looks at her intently. In a conversation with Mrs. Grose, it transpires that the governess's description of the stranger recalls the master's valet, Peter Quint, and that Peter Quint is dead (p. 48). The figure, then, must be a ghost. Mrs. Grose herself "has seen nothing, not a shadow of a shadow, and nobody in the house but the governess was in the governess's plight" (p. 48). Who is right—the governess or everyone else in the house? the reader is likely to ask himself. A similar disagreement occurs when the governess expresses her conviction that Quint "was looking for little Miles," and Mrs. Grose challenges her: "But how do you know?" (p. 49). Trying to make up his mind whether the situation at Bly corresponds to the governess's ghost-ridden account or to Mrs. Grose's sealed-eye description, the reader is bound to realize that James gives him no independent information on which to base his decision. There is no independent dramatization of an encounter between either of the ghosts with any other member of the household, particularly the children, whom the governess believes to be in constant touch with the evil apparitions. Everything we hear about the ghosts (and for that matter, about everything else) comes from the governess, and there is no external source which could help us to decide whether the communications she attributes to the children are real or merely a figment of her own imagination. The reader is thus made aware of an informational gap at the core of the narrative.

The permanent gap is realistically "motivated" in various ways. The isolation of Bly explains both why the governess has hardly anyone to talk to in order to ascertain the facts and why nobody detects her madness (if madness it is). The uncle's injunction that she should never bother him with questions or information again explains why no gap-filling hint can be gleaned from that quarter (Goddard 1970, p. 73). As for the children, the governess is often tempted to ask them whether they see, or rather to prove to them that she knows they do, but she is deterred "by the very chance that such an injury might prove greater than the injury to be averted" (p. 87). In her room she often plans how she would start the crucial conversation, but she invariably breaks down "in the monstrous utterance of names" (p. 88). It is her own uncertainty, horror of the facts, and lack of experience, as well as her dread of communicating to the children a consciousness of something they know not that makes silence the best solution.

> "As they [the names] died away on my lips I said to myself that I should indeed help them [the children] to represent something infamous if, by pronouncing them, I should violate as rare a little case of instinctive delicacy as any school-room, probably, had ever known" (p. 88).[3]

So the governess's discretion provides psychological justification for not obtaining information from the children. However, the neutralization of the children as a possible source of information is temporary. The governess finally succumbs to the temptation, asks the fatal question, and the result is disastrous. Disastrous, but not enigma-solving. The last scenes with both

Flora and Miles are ambiguous (as I hope to show later), and the gap remains open.

Like the central gap, ancillary or local gaps are also realistically motivated. The reader is not, for example, given the wording of the headmaster's letter. He is only told by the governess that "The child's dismissed his school" (p. 28) and that "They go into no particulars. They simply express their regret that it should be impossible to keep him" (p. 29). "They go into no particulars" is, of course, built-in motivation, logically precluding the disclosure of nonexistent information. But perhaps something can be inferred from the laconic phrasing of the letter? To prevent this, James exploits Mrs. Grose's illiteracy. The governess offers Mrs. Grose the headmaster's letter, but the housekeeper obliquely and shyly intimates that she cannot read. The governess then decides to read the letter to her, but since the reader must on no account be in possession of the exact contents, James makes her have second thoughts; thus "faltering in the act and folding it up once more, I put it back in my pocket" (p. 28). Later, discretion is added to make plausible the governess's reluctance to obtain the desired information from Miles himself. "He never spoke of his school, never mentioned a comrade or a master; and I, for my part, was quite too much disgusted to allude to them" (p. 41).

Thus, both the central gap and the ancillary or local gaps are fully motivated. Having become aware of the gap by a confrontation with mutually exclusive visions of the state of affairs at Bly, the reader hopes that further information will clarify which of the two views corresponds to reality. Hence, he goes on reading with an eye to potential clues, discovering again and again a balance which forces him to realize afresh the ubiquity of the gap and of the ambiguity. As in the other ambiguous works, the deadlock-producing balance is created both by the equilibrium of singly directed clues and by the presence of doubly directed ones. But unlike the other works, in which the difference between the two methods is clearly felt, in *The Turn of the Screw* the difference is not so neat, for reasons which will become apparent in the course of my description of how both methods operate.

Singly Directed Clues

As the previous chapter has shown, the singly directed clues in "The Figure in the Carpet" fall into two categories: divergences between the narrator and other characters, and oscillation in the narrator's own view. The same categories (with a slight variation) apply to *The Turn of the Screw*. The difference, however, is significant, for in "The Figure in the Carpet" it is not the narrator's view that is the pivot of the ambiguity, and the narrator is therefore one of the testing factors whose statements can be balanced with those of the other characters. In *The Turn of the Screw*, on the other hand, the narrator's view is the pivot of the ambiguity, being thus in an analogous position to Vereker's and Corvick's statements in "The Figure in the Carpet." Had the clue-balancing technique been identical with that of "The Figure in the Carpet," it would have required a juxtaposition of confirmations and repudiations of the pivotal view (here the narrator's) by the other characters. This is the technique used in *The Sacred Fount,* where the balance of singly directed clues is partly obtained by a juxtaposition of the various interlocutors' confirmations of the narrator's view with their repudiations of it. In *The Turn of the Screw*, on the other hand, the narrator is, so to speak, both the tested and the tester, and it is the divergence between her views and those of the other characters that creates one kind of balance between singly directed clues. In addition (and almost as a consequence), the opposed clues follow each other in the dialogue continuum. The result is that the sequence of singly directed clues renders the scene in which they appear doubly directed. The clues themselves are not doubly directed, but because they are sequential and because they are focused on a well-defined situation every time, they render the situation doubly directed. This in turn is related to a phenomenon I have already pointed out, namely the prominence of relatively self-contained scenes or installments in *The Turn of the Screw*. Each installment is felt to be ambiguous, and this sense of the double-directedness of the unit is often stronger than the recognition of the sequential singly directed clues of which it is composed.

The first kind of balance between singly directed clues, namely the divergences between the narrator and the other characters, takes two forms, described in the theoretical part as $a+a-$ and $a+b+$ respectively. In *The Turn of the Screw*, the $a+a-$ technique is the creation of equilibrium between the governess's confirmations and the other characters' repudiations of the same hypothesis, resulting in a clash of contradictories (even when they are not verbally formulated as such). On the other hand, the $a+b+$ technique, or the use of contraries, is the balance between the governess's interpretation in the light of one hypothesis and a character's counterinterpretation in support of the other.

Let us begin with the equilibrium between the governess's confirmations and the other characters' repudiations of the same hypothesis. Up to a very late point in the narrative, Mrs. Grose is the only character in whom the governess confides. It is therefore mainly her reactions that counterbalance the governess's hypotheses, hypotheses which she often formulates as certainties. Only in the last parts of the story does she break the conspiracy of silence with the children, and her theories are then further checked by their objections.

When the governess first tells Mrs. Grose about the stranger, in the so-called identification scene, the housekeeper answers in questions and negations:

> "Do you mean he's a stranger?"
> "Oh, very much!"
> "Yet you didn't tell me?"
> "No—for reasons. But now that you've guessed—"
> Mrs. Grose's round eyes encountered this charge.
> "Ah, I haven't guessed!" she said very simply. "How can I if *you* don't imagine?" (pp. 44–45).

This tone of doubt and unwillingness to be talked into a position which she does not fully support persists throughout. The governess frankly reports that Mrs. Grose "herself had seen nothing, not a shadow of a shadow" (p. 48), and that when she [the governess] expressed her conviction of the children's knowledge, she could not help sensing the housekeeper's disbelief, "I felt her incredulity as she held me" (p.

56). Making her theory more specific, the governess explains, "Two hours ago, in the garden . . . Flora *saw!*" (p. 56), and Mrs. Grose asks with what is probably a mixture of horror and suspicion, "She has told you?" No, Flora has said nothing. But according to the governess, this is precisely the horror, Flora's silence being a clear symptom of dissimulation. The conclusion does not necessarily follow, of course, and it is again Mrs. Grose who brings this home with a simple question, "Then how do you know?" (p. 56). Thereupon the governess develops her theory one step further, announcing to her stupefied interlocutor that the person across the lake was her predecessor, to which Mrs. Grose replies in distress, "How can you be sure?" (p. 57). Short irritated questions or statements, implying a denial or a near denial, characterize Mrs. Grose's reactions throughout this installment: "Ah, how *can* you?" (p. 57); "Tell me how you know" (p. 58); and so on. In later sections she becomes more directly critical of the governess. "Lord, you do change!" (p. 81) she says when the governess once more changes her mind about Miles's innocence. (See also p. 100). The climax of Mrs. Grose's denial comes in the second lake scene with Flora. Mrs. Grose is with the governess at one end of the lake, and the governess directs the housekeeper's eyes to what she believes to be the specter of Miss Jessel. Instead of the triumphant confirmation she expects, she meets only with "a burst of high disapproval," a "deep groan of negation, of repulsion, compassion," and the most explicit denial possible: "What a dreadful turn, to be sure, Miss! Where on earth do you see anything?" (p. 115).

In the same climactic lake scene, the governess relinquishes her vow of discretion and asks Flora directly, "Where, my pet, is Miss Jessel?" (p. 113). Like Mrs. Grose's reactions, Flora's answer is a flat denial. "I don't know what you mean. I see nobody. I see nothing. I never have. I think you're cruel. I don't like you!" (p. 116).[4]

As opposed to the $a+a-$ technique in which Mrs. Grose's and Flora's reactions were limited to a denial or a questioning of the governess's view, in the $a+b+$ category characters do not only negate the governess's view but also offer a different interpretation of the scene in question. In the three prominent examples of this technique, the governess sees the children's behavior as a confirmation of their contact with the ghosts, but the children themselves immediately explain it in a realistic, commonsense way. This sequence of contrasted singly directed clues renders the scene doubly directed, for both the supernatural and the realistic interpretations make coherent sense of the events, and there is no way of choosing between them.

The first instance is Flora's nocturnal escapade. After a bravely self-confident third encounter with Quint, the governess returns to her room only to realize that Flora's bed is empty and the curtains "deceivingly pulled forward" (p. 72). Although she does not explicitly formulate a hypothesis, her catching her breath with terror and later her unutterable relief when Flora emerges from behind the blind strongly imply, especially after the Quint scene, that she suspects Flora of a fiendish communication. Far from waiting for the governess's question, Flora addresses her with a reproach (is this a sign of her innocence or a calculated policy?): "You naughty; where *have* you been?" (p. 72). She then explains her irregularity "with the loveliest, eagerest simplicity" (real or pretended?).[5] "She [Flora] had known suddenly, as she lay there, that I [the governess] was out of the room, and had jumped up to see what had become of me" (p. 72).

The governess is not content with this general explanation and goes on inquiring about the details, but Flora has an answer ready for every question. While her first answer leaves room for the governess's supposition, her second is an emphatic denial. The governess first wants to know whether "You were looking for me out of the window? . . . You thought I might be walking in the grounds?" (p. 73), to which Flora answers with a vague "someone" that does not preclude the possibility of an apparition: "Well, you know, I thought someone was" (p. 73). Then the governess presses on, "And did you see anyone?" (p. 73). Flora's response, "Ah, *no!*" (p. 73), wittingly or unwittingly denies the referent the governess has in mind. This is not enough to convince the governess (or the reader) of Flora's innocence, and she wants to know, "Why did you pull the curtain over the place to make me think you were still there?" (p. 73). Flora again answers luminously, "Because I don't like to frighten you!" (p. 73). And when the governess challenges her further, "But if I had, by your idea, gone out—?" (p. 74), Flora declines to be puzzled, "Oh, but you know, . . . that you might come back, you dear, and that you *have!*" (p. 74). The supernatural and the realistic explanations thus face each other in an insoluble clash. Either Flora was indeed looking out of the window for Miss Jessel, and her explanation to the governess is a lie, a cover-up, or she was really looking for the governess and planned everything so as not to frighten her. Throughout the nouvelle there are signs that the children are aware of the governess's nervousness, insomnia, and strange behavior, and that they try to calm her down (see Cranfill and Clark 1965, p. 161). Flora's behavior on this occasion may (but need not) fall into the same pattern. A similar clash of opposed explanations occurs a little later when the governess finds Miles has gone out. The realistic explanation this time is that Miles simply felt an urge to be naughty (p. 80).[6]

Another cluster of $a+b+$ singly directed clues, the one supporting a supernatural, the other a natural explanation of the same event, occurs in what the governess considers her first breakthrough with Miles. Sitting at the boy's bedside, the governess makes use of his gentle hints about "this queer business of ours" (p. 102) to clarify the school mystery once and for all. For the first time she feels "a small faint quaver of consenting consciousness" (p. 105), and then she pushes her advantage too far. "I just want you to help me to save you!" she says, and the next thing she feels is "an extraordinary blast and chill, a gust of frozen air and a shake of the room as great as if, in the wild wind, the casement had crashed in" (p. 105).

The wind is not from the outside, she makes sure, for the window is closed tight; yet the candle is out and there is total darkness in the room. What is it that blew the candle? Two opposed explanations are given by the governess and by Miles. The governess establishes a cause-and-effect relation between sequential events, and implicitly assuming supernatural intervention, she sees the gust of frozen air and the extraordinary darkness as an "answer to my appeal" (p. 105). What this implies is an intervention on Quint's part, designed either to combat her approaching victory or to punish her for going too

far, for wanting to know too much (an explanation she again
gives in the last scene of the nouvelle). After this Miles's own
realistic explanation is almost an anticlimax.

> "Why, the candle's out!" I [the governess] then cried.
> "It was I who blew it, dear!" said Miles.

Which explanation is truer to reality? Is the simple explanation necessarily also the more correct? And what if it is a lie?
And even if it is not a lie, does it sufficiently account for the
wind? The wind, again, may be simply a natural phenomenon,
but what evidence is there that it is not a devilish omen? The
clash of singly directed clues once more makes the scene
doubly directed and raises an unanswerable question.

Whereas both forms of balance discussed above are created
between conflicting statements of different characters, another
kind of equilibrium is based on opposed singly directed statements of the same character. In "The Figure in the Carpet"
this technique was limited to oscillation in the narrator's own
view. In *The Turn of the Screw* it is further expanded, operating not only on statements of the governess-narrator but also
on those of her confidante and opponent, Mrs. Grose.

The ups and downs characterizing the governess's belief in
the validity of her theory are either scattered over various parts
of the narrative or sequential. A few examples will suffice to
illustrate both methods.

The prevalent tone in the governess's account is one of
growing belief in the objective validity of the realities she
thinks she perceives behind what she considers deceptive appearances. But every now and then she is seized by a spasm
of doubt. Sometimes her doubt takes the form of apprehension
as to what the reader may think of her story, and even when
she defies the supposedly unbelieving reader, her own hesitation still peeps out (pp. 37, 69). More important are the
intrinsic doubts as to whether what she sees is fact or delusion.
This epistemological problem is fraught with moral dilemmas,
for if the governess is wrong, it is she (and not the nonexistent
ghosts) that causes the children's corruption and destruction.
Thus, when she is about to enter Miles's room, assuming that
he is secretly at watch, a horrible uncertainty takes hold of

her: "he might be innocent; the risk was hideous" (p. 76; see
also p. 79). Even in the very last scene, the possibility of a
fatal error arises, "and within a minute there had come to me
out of my very pity the appalling alarm of his being perhaps
innocent. It was for the instant confounding and bottomless, for if he *were* innocent, what then on earth was *I*?"
(p. 136).

Certainty and doubt often follow each other in the narrative
sequence. Thus, at an early stage, when the headmaster's letter
arrives, the governess first draws the conclusion that Miles
must have been an injury to the others, but then, confronted
with Mrs. Grose's good faith, she "jump[s] to the absurdity of
the idea" (p. 29). The sense of absurdity is reinforced when
she sees Miles. "It doesn't live an instant," she declares to
Mrs. Grose, "My dear woman, *look* at him!" (p. 33). She is
now ready to reverse her former verdict, saying that far from
being an injury, Miles was simply "too fine and fair for the
little horrid, unclean school-world" (p. 40), and it is his
goodness that must have made the headmaster vindictive.[7] But
here the sequence attenuates the praise, just as formerly it
attenuated the condemnation. Following the various argu-
ments in Miles's favor, the governess admits a possible lack of
objectivity in her view. "Of course I was under the spell, and
the wonderful part is that, even at the time, I perfectly knew I
was. But I gave myself up to it" (p. 41). The intimation is that
the preceding hymn in praise of Miles's innocence may be a
result of a spell rather than of a real insight into essences.

With regard to Flora, the governess's conviction of the girl's
secret communications with Miss Jessel's ghost is followed by
the contrary assertion of her innocence: "To gaze into the
depths of blue of the child's eyes and pronounce their loveliness
a trick of premature cunning was to be guilty of a cynicism in
preference to which I naturally preferred to abjure my judgement and, so far as might be, my agitation" (p. 62). But this
too is attenuated by the sequel: "It was a pity that, somehow, to
settle this once and for all, I had equally to re-enumerate the
signs of subtlety that, in the afternoon, by the lake, had made a
miracle of my show of self-possession" (p. 62). And then comes
an attenuation of the attenuation, explaining that the purpose of

indulging in these unpleasant details is simply "to prove there was nothing in it" (p. 63).

Sequences like "my certitude that she [Flora] thoroughly saw was never greater than at that instant" (p. 114) and "I felt my own situation horribly crumble" (p. 115) recur throughout, but I feel that the point has already been sufficiently illustrated.

As if to balance the oscillation in the governess's thoughts and statements, Mrs. Grose also changes her attitude toward the central question as well as toward secondary ones. And like the governess's vacillation, Mrs. Grose's wavering can take either the scattered or the sequential form. On the whole, Mrs. Grose's reaction is one of disapproval, but from time to time she confirms the governess's view. To illustrate, after the governess's unusual absence from church, neither the children nor Mrs. Grose allude to this strange violation of her customary behavior. The governess meditates that Mrs. Grose's silence testifies that the children "had in some way bribed her to silence" (p. 98). When she puts this question to the housekeeper, the latter replies, "Oh yes, they asked me to say nothing; and to please them—so long as they were there—of course I promised" (p. 98). So the governess's intuition concerning this minor issue is confirmed. There are also sporadic confirmations of the major issue, culminating in the following conversation which occurs after Flora's delirious night. Mrs. Grose says she must get Flora away.

> "Far from this," she pursued, "far from *them*—"
> "She may be different? She may be free?" I seized her almost with joy. "Then, in spite of yesterday, you *believe*—"
> "In such doings?" Her simple description of them required, in the light of her expression, to be carried no further, and she gave me the whole thing as she had never done. "I believe." [P. 123][8]

On several occasions confirmation and repudiation or confirmation and its attenuation follow each other in the sequence of the same conversation or even of the same sentence. Under the governess's pressure, Mrs. Grose admits that Miles sometimes dishonestly denied having been with Quint (she thus retracts her previous affirmation of Miles's complete goodness, the only exception being the kind of frolics without which a child is not a child [p. 30]). But when the governess presses further, asking, "So that you could see he knew what was between the two wretches?" Mrs. Grose cautiously retreats from her condemnatory position. "I don't know—I don't know!" she replies (p. 65). And presently she engages in a defense of Miles, denying even the implications of her own recent accusation: "And if he was so bad then as that comes to, how is he such an angel now?" (p. 65). Thus, a sequence which started with an accusation ends on a note of defense.

The opposite procedure is employed in chapter 18, when the governess expounds her theory that Flora is outside with Miss Jessel, and Miles, who has finished playing the piano, is intensely communicating with Quint. Mrs. Grose's first reaction, "Lord, Miss!" (p. 108), is one of astonishment and doubt. But a little later, when the governess asks her to look for Flora upstairs, she says, "With *them?*" (p. 109), thus expressing her fear of an encounter with the ghosts. If this is not a complete acceptance of the governess's view and of the condemnation of the children which it implies, at least it shows Mrs. Grose as (half-consciously?) envisaging the possibility of ghosts.

When Mrs. Grose is about to take Flora away, the governess's last injunction is, "There's one thing, of course, . . . they mustn't, before she goes, see each other for three seconds" (p. 120). Mrs. Grose begins by assuring the governess that the children have not met, but she ends her comforting words with a vague unfinished expression which leaves room for the possibility that they have.

> "Ah, Miss, I'm not such a fool as that! If I've been obliged to leave her [Flora] three or four times, it has been each time with one of the maids, and at present, though she's alone, she's locked in safe. And yet—and yet!" There were too many things.
> "And yet what?"
> "Well, are you so sure of the little gentleman?" [p. 121]

In other words, although Flora was locked in safe, there is no guarantee that Miles did not take the initiative in devising a meeting. Mrs. Grose's, "Well, are you so sure of the little gentleman?" can also be taken as an attempt to change the subject. The reader becomes aware of the second possibility because this is how the governess understands Mrs. Grose's question. The governess's answer is therefore not restricted to the problem of whether the children have met, but bears upon the prospects for saving Miles. "I'm not sure of anything but *you*. But I have, since last evening, a new hope. I think he wants to give me an opening" (p. 121). Although both possibilities coexist in the context, it seems to me that they do not have equal weight in it and that Mrs. Grose's question is therefore predominantly a singly directed suggestion (though no more than a suggestion) in spite of the undeniable touch of double-directedness. The governess's answer, I feel (though I find it impossible to prove), is indicative mainly of her own blindness to the suggestion implicit in Mrs. Grose's question, not of the housekeeper's actual intention. The interpretation of Mrs. Grose's words has decisive influence upon the way we take Miles's final surrender of Quint's name and (as I shall show later), since Mrs. Grose's words are suggestive but not definitive, they allow for two readings of the so-called confession.

Doubly Directed Clues

Just as many of the singly directed clues emphasize the doubly directed character of the scene in which they appear, owing to the sequential juxtaposition of opposed statements made by different characters, so many of the doubly directed clues derive their double-directedness from an interaction between the reader's hypothesis and a character's statement, thus resembling (but only resembling) a sequence of singly directed clues.

The doubly directed clues in *The Turn of the Screw* are of four kinds: psychological, cognitive, causative, and linguistic. It is mainly clues of the first category that often seem to border on a combination of conflicting singly directed clues.

A psychological clue is one that indicates a possible explanation of the motives underlying a character's statement or behavior. In *The Turn of the Screw* such clues become doubly directed in three different ways. (1) The governess gives a "twist" to a statement, act, or look that the reader is otherwise likely to take at face value. It should be noted that the governess's undermining interpretation is not made conclusive, and therefore it does not replace the straightforward, commonsense explanation, but rather coexists with it. (2) The reader gives a "twist" to the governess's statement or explanation in a context which again makes both possibilities equally tenable. (3) The reader himself infers from the micro- and macrocontext two opposed explanations of an unexplained statement or act. The first two categories are akin to each other, the difference being mainly in perception-direction, depending on whether a straightforward explanation is implicit in the description itself and is then felt to be "twisted" by the governess, or whether the reader is first aware of a "twisted" explanation and then supplies the commonsense possibility. In many cases, both methods operate in the same scene. All three kinds of psychological double-directedness abound in the text, and I shall therefore have to select only a few examples of each.

The governess's "twist" applies not only to the children's behavior and statements but also to the appearance and disappearance of her own visions. In the two lake scenes Flora betrays no sign of communicating with the ghost of Miss Jessel. This, of course, can be taken to indicate the absence of communication. But the governess interprets it as an act of duplicity on the girl's part, as an unsuccessful attempt to conceal her indulgence in forbidden games.

> The revelation then of the manner in which Flora was affected startled me, in truth, far more than it would have done to find her also merely agitated, for direct dismay was of course not what I had expected. Prepared and on her guard as our pursuit had actually made her, she would repress any betrayal; . . . To see her, without a convulsion of her small pink face, not even feign to glance in the direction of the prodigy I announced, but only, instead of that, turn at *me* an expression absolutely new and unprecedented and that appeared to read and accuse and judge me—this was a stroke that somehow converted the little girl herself into the very presence that could make me quail. [P. 114; see also pp. 55, 73]

Does Flora see nothing or does she only pretend not to see? Does she throw a look of accusation at the governess because she resents her unjustified condemnatory questions, or because she is angry and disappointed that the governess has discovered her secret?

Like Flora, Miles is often described as "gentleness itself" (p. 80), "a little fairy prince" (p. 80), but as in the case of Flora, the governess often feels that this gentleness is no more than a mask. When the boy explains his nocturnal escapade, the governess ruminates, "It was his brightness indeed that gave me a respite. Would it be so great if he were really going to tell me?" (p. 80). And in another late evening conversation, vaguely and ambiguously concerning "this queer business of ours," the governess is touched by what she considers Miles's efforts at deception. "So unutterably touching was it to see his little brain puzzled and his little resources taxed to play, under the spell laid on him, a part of innocence and consistency" (pp. 102–3).

When the two children are described together, their charm is frequently interpreted as "studied" (p. 67), and their silence as a calculated concealment. The governess tells Mrs. Grose, "The more I've watched and waited the more I've felt that if there were nothing else to make it sure [that the four perpetually meet] it would be made so by the systematic silence of each" (p. 81). And when the governess thinks of escaping, she imagines that "my little pupils would play at innocent wonder about my non-appearance in their train" (p. 96).

Even the temporary cessation of her own visions is not taken as an indication of an objective disappearance of the ghosts, but rather as a dangerous symptom of the children's protected communications with the fiends. "What I had then had an ugly glimpse of was that my eyes might be sealed just while theirs were most opened" (p. 87).

Thus the governess's "twist" prevents the reader from taking things at face value. But the opposite process also occurs. The governess's statements concerning Mrs. Grose, Flora, Miles, the uncle, as well as her own role and reliability are often "twisted" by the reader. Having been recurrently confronted with Mrs. Grose's disbelief, the reader tends to treat with suspicion (though not with a flat denial) statements like, "She

[Mrs. Grose] believed me, I was sure, absolutely; if she hadn't I don't know what would have become of me, for I couldn't have borne the business alone" (p. 77). In addition to the straightforward intended relation between the two parts of the statement, the second may also be taken as the unconscious cause of the first, thus turning the whole statement into an expression of wishful thinking. In other words, according to the "twisted" reading, it is because the governess is incapable of bearing the business alone that she convinces herself of Mrs. Grose's belief. The second lake scene contains many openings for an undermining reading side by side with an accepting one. It will be remembered that Mrs. Grose first refuses to follow the governess to the lake and then changes her mind. The governess explains the change in her own way: "and I knew that, whatever, to her apprehension, might befall me, the exposure of my society struck her as her least danger" (p. 110). The real danger of which Mrs. Grose is afraid, the governess intimates, is that of having to encounter the ghosts alone. But the reader may also interpret Mrs. Grose's decision to go to the lake as a result of her fear to leave the half-insane governess alone (Cranfill and Clark 1965, p. 144). Standing together by the lake, the governess triumphantly points to the opposite bank, where she so clearly sees Miss Jessel's specter, and she takes Mrs. Grose's "dazed blink" not as an unavailing effort to see, but as "a sovereign sign" that she does see (p. 114). Furthermore, the housekeeper's failure to see is not taken by the governess as casting a doubt on the reality of what she herself sees, for she feels that "in spite of her blindness" Mrs. Grose is convinced "that something awful had occurred" (p. 117). The implication is that although Mrs. Grose has seen nothing, she senses the reality of the horror perceived by the governess. The reader's "twist" of this implication may substitute the causal *because* for the governess's concessive *in spite*. What if Mrs. Grose is convinced that something awful had occurred not in spite of her exemption but because of it? The "something awful" will then not be the encounter with the ghost, but the governess's liability to hallucinations, of which Mrs. Grose's "blindness" is an immediate evidence.

The question of whether Flora saw Miss Jessel by the lake

is subject to a similar double-directedness. The governess will not let Mrs. Grose press the girl on the topic (retracting her own suggestion earlier), either in a desire not to make her lie (p. 57) or in unconscious rationalization of a fear of contradiction.[9] Later, when Flora is supposed to have rowed the boat across the lake, the governess assumes that she is in search of Miss Jessel (p. 110), but the reader may think that the girl is simply trying to escape from her insistent governess. A similar desire for a respite may be inferred from Miles's behavior toward the end of the narrative. When the child is left alone with the governess, he interrupts their conversation by looking through the window with what the governess describes as an "embarrassed back" (p. 129). For her, this is a sign that he is seeking Quint in vain (pp. 129–30). However, Miles's turning to the window may also be an attempt to evade the conversation which the governess intends to begin.

The governess's explanation of her motives for respecting the uncle's injunction of silence in the face of the worrying situation at Bly may unwittingly suggest the psychological causes of her predicament. She will not write because she cannot face "his derision, his amusement, his contempt for the breakdown of my resignation at being left alone and for the fine machinery I had set in motion to attract his attention to my slighted charms" (p. 84). Perhaps the suspicion she indirectly imputes to the uncle is true in a different way. The reader may infer from her words that unconsciously she has indeed set in motion the whole fine machinery of hallucinations in order to attract the uncle's attention to her slighted charms.

On various occasions the governess's insistence on her absolute reliability provokes the opposite reaction on the part of the reader. The double possibility is often verbally reinforced by the governess's use of a negative expression which brings to mind the opposite affirmative possibility. Thus, in describing the first "encounter" with Miss Jessel, the governess says, "There was no ambiguity in anything; none whatever, at least, in the conviction I from one moment to another found myself forming as to what I should see straight before me and across the lake as a consequence of raising my eyes" (p. 54). "There was no ambiguity in anything" inadvertently encourages the reader to notice precisely the troubling ambiguity of the situation. He may then regard the governess's "none whatever, at least, in the conviction I from one moment to another found myself forming . . ." as a qualification, suggesting behind her back that although there may have been no ambiguity in *her* conviction, this does not mean that there was none in the situation. Indeed, the narrative sequence proves how fallacious the governess's conviction is, her expectations to see Peter Quint being immediately belied by the appearance of Miss Jessel (pp. 56–57). Similarly, when the governess says to Mrs. Grose, "I go on, I know, as if I were crazy; and it's a wonder I'm not. What I have seen would have made *you* so; but it has only made me more lucid, made me get hold of still other things" (pp. 81–82), the reader may either take her words the way she intends them or surreptitiously omit the "as if" and "not," turning the passage into a suggestion of insanity.

As distinct from the two techniques discussed above, namely the governess's "twist" of a character's statement, act, or look, and the reader's "twist" of the governess's statements, the third kind of doubly directed psychological clues is based completely on the reader's own inferences from the micro- and macrocontext. Therefore, these clues are more likely to be perceptible after a full recognition of the ambiguity than in a first tentative reading. In a reading which is not fully governed by a consciousness of the ambiguity, the passages in question are liable to be grasped either as vague or as containing a missing link (like analogous passages in "The Figure in the Carpet"). A reader who is aware of the overall ambiguity will realize that he can fill in the gap in mutually exclusive ways and that both are equally tenable in the context. This points out an interesting circularity in the perception of ambiguity (as of many other governing principles in literature): on the one hand, it is the details that give rise to the ambiguity, and on the other hand, a recognition of the ambiguity is almost a prerequisite for the perception of many more ambiguous details.

In a relatively early conversation between the governess and Mrs. Grose, the housekeeper's motives are left unexplained, calling for conflicting explanations on the part of the reader. The governess expresses surprise that the children never mention Quint, and the following dialogue ensues:

> "Oh, the little lady doesn't remember. She never heard or knew."
> "The circumstances of his death?" I thought with some intensity.
> "Perhaps not. But Miles would remember—Miles would know."
> "Ah, don't try him! broke from Mrs. Grose. [P. 50]

What are Mrs. Grose's motives for asking the governess not to try Miles? Unlike the later episode, where the governess asks the housekeeper not to question Flora (p. 57), here there isn't even a one-sided explanation which the reader can either accept at face value or reverse against the speaker. However, the context gives rise to two explanations, the one consistent with the innocence of the boy, the other with his corruption. The innocent interpretation would say that Mrs. Grose wishes to shield Miles from upsetting memories of the dead. The "twisted" interpretation, on the other hand, would see Mrs. Grose's injunction as an attempt to prevent the forbidden relationship between Miles and Quint from coming to light (remember that this is still an early stage of the narrative, preceding the housekeeper's own hints concerning the relationship).

After the church incident, Mrs. Grose admits that the children "bribed" her into not talking with the governess about her absence from the service, adding, "they said you would like it better. Do you like it better?" (p. 98). The missing link is the reason for which the governess is expected to "like it better." Saying that she actually likes it worse, the governess then tries to clarify the matter. "Did they say why I should like it better?" (p. 98). But Mrs. Grose's answer does not supply the missing link: "No; Master Miles only said 'We must do nothing but what she likes!'" (p. 98). Again the reader can form two hypotheses, the one creditable to the children, the other discreditable. The creditable interpretation takes into account various signs, distributed throughout the narrative, of the children's awareness of the governess's troubled state of mind, suggesting that they do not want to burden her further by insisting on explanations. The discreditable interpretation, on the other hand, argues that Miles has his own interest in mind, not the governess's. From his point of view, the subject is better avoided, because he does not want his desire to go back to school to be pried into.

In the preliminary sparring contest leading up to the crucial final scene, Miles is felt to be on the verge of a confession when he expresses the wish to go out (p. 132). Why does Miles want to go out at this point? We are not told, but we can infer two explanations from the drift of the whole scene. One hypothesis is advanced by Dorothea Krook: "What this signifies, we are meant to see, is that he wants first to confront Peter Quint and finally sever his connexion with the power of evil before he submits himself to the power of good" (1967, p. 120). Equally possible is the opposite, less optimistic hypothesis, that Miles wants to gain time and get away from the governess's relentless inquiry. "It was as if he were suddenly afraid of me," the governess says a little earlier (p. 131).[10]

So far for the psychological clues. The doubly directed cognitive clues could in fact be classified as a subcategory of the psychological, but because they differ significantly from the other clues discussed under that heading and because they become the pivot of two crucial scenes, I have decided to treat them separately. Whereas the doubly directed psychological clues concern the motives underlying a character's statement or behavior, the cognitive clues do not concern motivation, but the process by which a character arrives at what he knows or thinks he knows. Cognitive clues become doubly directed when the process of cognition can be defined in mutually exclusive ways. Such double-directedness is similar to Todorov's definition of propositional ambiguity as the inclusion of one proposition in two or more (mutually exclusive, one should add) sequences at the same time. But whereas the names Todorov gives to the sequences may be mutually exclusive in the abstract, but need not be so in a particular context (this being, in fact, one of the weaknesses in his theory), the names I shall give to the cognitive sequences may perhaps not be mutually exclusive in the abstract, but they are so in *The Turn of the Screw*.

The two crucial scenes which raise the problem of defining or labeling the cognitive process are Mrs. Grose's "identification" of Quint and Miles's final "confession." Both scenes are crucial because were they singly directed, as many critics think they are (Beardsley 1958, pp. 243–44; Reed 1960, p. 198; Waldock 1960, p. 172), they would conclusively tip the scale in favor of one or the other of the mutually exclusive hypotheses, thus rendering the ambiguity of *The Turn of the Screw* temporary rather than permanent. In fact, the process of cognition they dramatize can be defined either as "identification" or as "inference," and there is no way of choosing between the two sequence names. If the scenes dramatize an identification, they support the apparitionist hypothesis. If, on the other hand, they dramatize an inference based on a high degree of suggestibility, they support the hallucinationist hypothesis. The governess, of course, chooses the first possibility, but the reader may describe the process of cognition differently by establishing different links between the details of the dialogue in question.

At first sight, the conversation between Mrs. Grose and the governess about the stranger seems to fulfill all the requirements of an identification scene, for the governess describes someone she does not know in a way that enables Mrs. Grose to identify him as Quint. As Mrs. Grose knows (but the governess does not yet), Quint is dead, and the governess's precise description therefore means that she has seen the ghost of the late valet. To my knowledge, Goddard, in the twenties, was the first critic to question the authenticity of the identification, and I shall reproduce the main points in his argument. Mrs. Grose, the argument goes, "identifies" Peter Quint only because her mind was toying with this idea even before the governess's detailed description, and she would probably have identified as Peter Quint anybody the governess might describe. Two of the governess's statements may have brought Quint to Mrs. Grose's mind. The first is the horrified exclamation, "He's—God help me if I know *what* he is!" (p. 45), where the emphatic "what" suggests that it is something not altogether human, and Quint

(Mrs. Grose knows) is dead, hence no longer human. The second is the governess's hint that this "horror" is a menace to the children, unwittingly reminding Mrs. Grose of the arch-menace to the children, namely Peter Quint. When Mrs. Grose does identify Quint, she picks up the least characteristic points in the governess's description. Why, Goddard acutely asks, "does her identification rest not at all on the red whiskers or the thin mouth, but of all things on the two facts that the stranger wore no hat and that his clothes looked as if they belonged to someone else?" (1970, p. 71). Mrs. Grose probably pays scant attention to the detailed verbal picture the governess is drawing because "an image is already hovering at the background of her mind waiting to rush into the foreground at the faintest summons" (Goddard 1970, p. 71), and the mention of the hat is enough to supply a decisive touch.[11] Owing to the high degree of her suggestibility, Mrs. Grose identifies without really identifying.

Mrs. Grose's initial predisposition is reinforced by a series of shaky inferences which Cranfill and Clark sum up in the following way:

> What finally convinces her that the governess has indeed seen a ghost and that the ghost is Quint? The ghost wears no hat, he is decidedly not a gentleman, he is handsome, he looks like an actor and is therefore not dressed in his own clothes. She offers no comment and asks no questions about the long, pale face, the red hair and whiskers, the dark, arched, mobile eyebrows, the small, sharp, strange eyes, the wide mouth, the thin lips, the tall stature, the erectness of figure. But she knew Quint: he was handsome, but no gentleman. Quint wore—"well, there were waistcoats missed", so Quint must have "borrowed" or stolen them and worn them. The ghost is dressed "In somebody's clothes". That somebody could only be the master. Quint did not, however, wear the master's hat. The ghost wears no hat. Ergo, the ghost is Quint. [1965, pp. 104–5][12]

The second crucial doubly directed scene is Miles's final "confession," in which the mention of Miss Jessel and of Peter Quint is often taken as a conclusive proof of the children's communications with the evil ghosts. But the conclusiveness is again undermined by the possibility that Miles's "supreme surrender of the name," as the governess calls it, is a result of inferences rather than of incriminating knowledge. As the governess herself vaguely suggests, the idea of Miss Jessel may be a "sequel to what we had done to Flora" (p. 138). This assumes a meeting between the two children before the removal of Flora, and Mrs. Grose's earlier incomplete statement, "and yet—and yet!" (p. 121) has left room for such a possibility. In fact, Goddard argues, the very mention of Miss Jessel by Miles does not simply assume a meeting between the two children but proves its existence.

> Bear in mind that, all through, it is Miss Jessel, according
> to the governess, who has been visiting Flora, while it is
> Quint who has been holding communication with Miles. Why,
> if the boy has been in the habit of consorting with the spirit
> of Quint and if he senses now the nearness of a ghostly
> visitant, why, I say, does he not ask if *he* is here? Surely,
> then, his "Is *she* here?" is the best possible proof that the
> idea of a spiritual presence has been suggested not at all by
> past experiences of a similar sort but precisely by something
> he has overheard from Flora, or about her, plus what he
> gets at the moment from the governess. [1970, pp. 79–80]

The governess says that it is not Miss Jessel, but it is at the window, and Miles infers the "he" by a process that can be paraphrased, "If, then, it is not *she,* you mean it must be the other one of the two who were always together?" (Goddard 1970, p. 80). The governess, determined not to be the first to mention the name, asks, "Whom do you mean by 'he'?" and Miles's "Peter Quint" is the self-evident answer after the gradual process of inferences. Thus the confession scene does not definitively prove Miles's intercourse with the ghost of Peter Quint. Nor does it prove the absence of such intercourse. The contradictory hypotheses coexist to the very end.

The third type of doubly directed clues in *The Turn of the Screw* can be called causative, since it is created either by a hesitation concerning the relations between sequence and consequence or by the interchangeability of cause and effect.

The governess's first encounter with Quint is preceded by her thoughts "that it would be as charming as a charming story suddenly to meet someone" (p. 35). This "someone" is, of course, the master, and all she wants is that he should stand before her and mutely express his gratitude by a kind, charming smile. She is then taken aback by "the sense that my imagination had, in a flash, turned real" (p. 35). In the clear twilight she sees a figure on the tower, and only after some time does she realize that this is not the master. What is the relation between the governess's romantic thoughts at dusk and the sudden appearance of the stranger? Is it only a chronological sequence, emphasizing the frustration of expectations caused by seeing the stranger, not the master, on the tower? Or is the stranger on the Freudian tower a result of the governess's romantic daydreams?

The question of whether the thought is an intuitive anticipation of an impending event or a catalyst producing an event of the mind recurs throughout *The Turn of the Screw*. Goddard takes the hallucinationist view of such instances of "perfect synchronization."

But perhaps the most interesting and convincing point in this whole connection is the fact that the appearance of the ghosts is timed to correspond not at all with some appropriate or receptive moment in the children's experience but very nicely with some mental crisis in the governess'. In the end their emergence is a signal, as it were, of a further loss of self-control on her part, an advance in her mania. "Where, my pet, is Miss Jessel?" she asks Flora, committing the tragic indiscretion of mentioning the interdicted name. And presto! Miss Jessel appears. "Tell me", she says, pressing Miles cruelly to the wall in their last interview, "if, yesterday afternoon, from the table in the hall, you took, you know, my letter". And instantly Peter Quint comes into view "like a sentinel before a prison". But the last instance of all is the most revealing. With the ruthlessness of an inquisitor she has extorted from Miles the confession that he "said things" at school. It is not enough that he tells her to whom he said them. She must follow it up to the bitter end. "What *were* these things?" she demands unpardonably. Whereupon, "again, against the glass, as if to blight his confession and stay his answer, was the hideous author of our woe—the white face of damnation." [1970, p. 83]

But in all these instances the ghosts need not be figments of the governess's imagination. They can also be objective realities which she often senses in advance and only too often provokes by an unpardonable behavior. Quint's appearance in the last scene, for example, may be a "punishment" for her stern inquiry, an attempt on the devil's part to stay Miles's confession.

In an earlier scene the governess broods over her role as screen and savior. "The more I saw, the less they would. I began to watch them in a stifled suspense, a disguised excitement that might well, had it continued too long, have turned to something like madness. What saved me, as I now see, was that it turned to something else altogether. It didn't last as suspense—it was superseded by horrible proofs. Proofs, I say, yes—from the moment I really took hold" (p. 53). The proof she so confidently speaks of is the first encounter with Miss Jessel by the lake, and a proof it may indeed be. But it may also be a symptom of precisely the madness she dismisses, for the appearance of the ghost may be a perfect example of the governess's "accepting," indeed "inviting" (p. 50) an occasion for martyrdom.

The governess's initial state of weariness, insomnia, and wavering between the extremes of joy and depression can be taken as one of the reasons for her difficulty in coping with apparitions. Nonapparitionists, on the other hand, would explain the cause-and-effect relation differently: "She is sufficiently sleepless and nervously overwrought to invite hallucinations" (Cranfill and Clark 1965, p. 32).

Cause-and-effect relations become double-edged from the moment the event can be seen both as causing anticipatory intuitions and states of mind and as being the psychological result of such thoughts and mental states. Since the structure of *The Turn of the Screw* is such that events are almost invariably surrounded by foretelling and retrospective interpretations (see Costello 1960, pp. 312–21), doubly directed causative clues are pervasive, and my few examples have by no means exhausted the subject.

The ambiguous network of psychological, cognitive, and causative clues is reinforced by a variety of doubly directed linguistic clues, much richer than in "The Figure in the Carpet." As in the later and most complex ambiguous novel, *The Sacred Fount,* doubly directed verbal elements in *The Turn of the Screw* appear both in the language expressing the narrator's own thoughts and in her/his rendering of dialogues with other characters. But whereas in *The Sacred Fount* the doubly directed linguistic elements function differently according to whether they belong to the first or the second category, in *The Turn of the Screw* the functions overlap, and there is therefore little practical justification for using the above categories as a starting point for a classification of verbal ambiguities. Consequently, I shall content myself with an enumeration of the various kinds of double-directedness in the language of *The Turn of the Screw* without assigning them to more inclusive aspects of discourse.

Pronouns in *The Turn of the Screw* are rendered doubly directed either by having two situational referents or by being assignable, with equal plausibility, to two different pronominal categories. In an early conversation between the governess and Mrs. Grose, the governess asks about "the lady who was here before."

> "The last governess? She was also young and pretty— almost as young and almost as pretty, Miss, even as you."
> "Ah, then, I hope her youth and her beauty helped her!" I recollect throwing off. *"He* seems to like us young and pretty!"
> "Oh, he *did,"* Mrs. Grose assented: "it was the way he liked everyone!" She had no sooner spoken indeed than she caught herself up. "I mean that's *his* way—the master's."
> I was struck. "But of whom did you speak first?"
> She look[ed] blank, but she coloured. "Why, of *him."*
> "Of the master?"
> "Of who else?"
> There was so obviously no one else that the next moment I had lost my impression of her having accidentally said more than she meant. [Pp. 30–31; my emphasis on "he"]

Who is this "he" who seems to like them young and pretty? No referent is explicitly mentioned in the text, and the pronoun is therefore exophoric. However, one would hardly notice a referent problem were it not for Mrs. Grose's answer. Without

it, the context strongly suggests a uniquely recoverable referent
—the master. But Mrs. Grose's use of the past tense hints that
it may be somebody else, for the master is still alive and still
likes them young and pretty. The shadow of the other, the
unspecified possibility becomes more, rather than less, substantial by Mrs. Grose's subsequent denial of it. "I mean that's *his*
way—the master's." This explanation being uncalled for, it
makes the impression of an evasion, and the reader is left with
the feeling that Mrs. Grose may have another referent in mind.
We cannot know in a first reading what the unspecified referent
may be, nor can we definitely establish that Mrs. Grose is
thinking of somebody other than the master. "There was so
obviously no one else," the governess tells us. The exophoric
pronoun thus opens two possibilities: the one specified (the
master), the other—a suggested though unspecified person who
belongs to the past. The importance of this doubly directed
pronoun lies not only in the suspense it arouses and in the
eventuality of ambiguity for which it prepares us, but also
(perhaps mainly) in the retrospective recoverability of the
second, the unspecified referent as Peter Quint. Nor does this
retrospective recoverability resolve the ambiguity. Rather than
supplanting the first possibility, it coexists with it, and Mrs.
Grose's "catching herself up" may indeed convey an apprehension that she has betrayed something she did not wish to
betray, but it may also convey a realization on her part that
her phrasing allowed for more than one person in a situation
in which only one is possible. In addition to suggesting two
possibilities to the reader, the exophoric "he" may have suggested to the governess the presence of someone other than the
master. If so, this hint of an unknown man may (but need not)
be held responsible for providing the romantic, frustrated governess with an undefined love object to be presently material-
ized in her hallucinations (Goddard 1970, pp. 66, 69).

Another doubly directed pronoun appears in the so-called
identification scene. The governess describes the man she saw
as tall, active, erect, but never a gentleman. To this Mrs. Grose
answers, "A gentleman? . . . a gentleman *he?*" (p. 47). The
ambiguity of this question is created by the fact that "he" can
be taken either as anaphoric or as exophoric. Anaphorically it

refers back to the governess's previous description and means roughly, "How can a person like the one you've described be a gentleman?" But the pronoun can also be exophoric, referring to something in the situation, not in the verbal context. The situational referent is someone whom Mrs. Grose knows and who cannot possibly be a gentleman. This, of course, is how the governess understands Mrs. Grose's question, asking her with the joy of expected confirmation: "You know him then?" (p. 47). But this is not the only possibility, and Mrs. Grose offers no direct confirmation. Instead, she asks another question with a similar ambiguous "he", "But he *is* handsome?" either wishing to find out if they are talking about the same person, or simply reacting to the governess's description and remarking that although the unknown "he" is not a gentleman, he makes the impression of a handsome man. Whether the pronoun is taken anaphorically or exophorically influences our view of whether the whole scene dramatizes an identification or only a guided inference. And just as the pronoun is doubly directed, so is the scene as a whole.

The third example yields two different anaphoric referents. It occurs in the conversation between Miles and the governess after the removal of Flora. The boy tells the governess how glad he is that Bly agrees with him and how much he enjoyed his free day. "Oh yes, I've been ever so far; all round about— miles and miles away. I've never been so free." Keeping up with the child's tone, the governess asks, "Well, do you like it?" and Miles answers with a question, "Do *you?*" (p. 130). Both questions are doubly directed. The "it" in the governess's words can refer either to Bly or to the feeling of being free. Similarly, Miles's elliptical question can mean either "Do you like Bly?" or "Do you like my being free?"[13] This linguistic ambiguity is less crucial than the previous one, but it reinforces the double interpretation of Miles's behavior in this as well as in other conversations with the governess. "Do you like Bly?" is innocent, while "Do you like my being free?" may be deliberately provocative, as the governess's preceding question probably is.

The ambiguity of the last scene of the nouvelle is reinforced by a doubly directed pronoun which has been singled out by several critics (for example, West 1964, p. 286). The governess sees Quint at the window, but she has a feeling that Miles sees nothing and that he is finally liberated from the devilish haunting presence. " 'No more, no more, no more!' I shrieked, as I tried to press *him* against me, to my visitant" (p. 137; my italics).

The most obvious way of construing the reference of the pronoun is by relating it anaphorically to the previous sentence, in which the governess speculates about the possibility of Miles's liberation. The sentence then reads, "I shrieked 'no more' to my visitant, as I pressed Miles against me," and may even suggest that she gradually causes the child's death by adding physical pressure to her austere inquiry (West 1964, pp. 284–87).[14] Perhaps less obvious, but equally possible from a syntactic point of view, is a cataphoric link which would read, "I pressed my visitant against me and shrieked 'no more.' " This would mean that she herself now becomes possessed, and by so doing she acts as a screen between Miles and the ghost and frees the child—an act of salvation which she contemplated on several occasions (see, for example, p. 50).

The example with which I would like to conclude the discussion of pronouns differs from the others in that its double-directedness is created not so much by the problem of pronoun reference as by that of determining the syntactic role of each referent. Another difference is that this time the ambiguity is resolved in the sequel, but in spite of the resolution, a residue of the discarded possibility remains and is related to other hints in the same spirit. The governess and Mrs. Grose discuss the nature of the relations between Quint and Miles, the governess starting with the assumption that

> "He was looking for little Miles." A portentous clearness now possessed me. *"That's* whom he was looking for."
> "But how do you know?"
> "I know, I know, I know!" My exaltation grew. "And *you* know, my dear!"
> She didn't deny this, but I required, I felt, not even so much telling as that. She resumed in a moment, at any rate: "What if *he* should see him?"

"Little Miles? That's what he wants!" She looked immensely scared again. "The child?"
"Heaven forbid! The man. He wants to appear to *them*."
[P. 49]

Take Mrs. Grose's question, "What if *he* should see him?" How can we determine which referent is intended to function as the subject and which as the object? In other words, does the question mean, "What if Miles should see Quint?" or "What if Quint should see Miles?" The governess's subsequent question is intended to clarify the issue, but in fact it is as ambiguous as the ambiguity it wishes to dispel. "Little Miles" can be either a specification of the subject, of "he," or a specification of the object, of "him." And therefore her conclusion, "That's what he wants," can again mean either "That's what Quint wants" or "That's what Miles wants." That the second reading is the one the governess has in mind is made clear in the last sentence of the quoted passage. But the possibility of the child's actively seeking Peter Quint remains a hovering presence, joining both anterior and posterior passages in which there are hints at the child's active solicitation of a contact with the ghost of the depraved valet.

Another source of linguistic ambiguity in *The Turn of the Screw* are elliptical, vague, or indeterminate constructions. I shall deal with all these phenomena together because their double-directedness is created in the same way.

It is important to note that the elliptical, vague, or indeterminate constructions are not ambiguous in themselves. They become so because of the cumulative effect of the mutually exclusive systems developing in the macrocontext of the narrative. It is these systems that give rise to conflicting completions of what otherwise would have remained informational lacunae. Therefore, such ambiguous completions are more clearly operative toward the end of the narrative, when the mutually exclusive hypotheses are fully formed, than at its early stages, where such expressions are simply grasped as incomplete or not sufficiently specified (in a first reading, I mean).

When the desperate Mrs. Grose tells the governess that the

only way out of their intolerable predicament is to make the master come down to Bly, the governess asks, "By writing to him that his house is poisoned and his little nephew and niece mad?" (p. 83), and Mrs. Grose replies, "But if they *are,* Miss?" (p. 83). Mrs. Grose's words may be a somewhat oblique way of saying, "But if they are mad, it's your duty to let their uncle know." But these words may also be a colloquial way of casting doubt upon the fact, saying something like, "But who says they are mad?" or "Are they really mad?" In itself, this second interpretation seems less likely than the first, but it is immediately reinforced by the governess's counterquestion, "And if I am myself, you mean?" (p. 83). Mrs. Grose's words can thus be taken both as confirming and as repudiating the governess's view of the state of affairs at Bly.

The conversation between Miles and the governess on the way to church yields several ambiguities arising out of elliptical or incomplete sentences. Miles objects to the governess's implicit comparison between Flora and himself, and the governess asks, "Don't you, then, *love* our sweet Flora?" Miles answers in incomplete sentences, "If I didn't—and you too; if I didn't—" and when the governess repeats his words, hoping for clarification, Miles throws the ball back to her, implying that she already knows the answer. "Well, you know what!" (p. 93). The text does not tell what it is that the governess is supposed to know, and Miles goes on, "Does my uncle think what *you* think?" (p. 93). Wondering with the governess how Miles knows what she thinks, the reader can conjecture two alternative completions. The first is that Miles believes the governess to assume that he can do without school, the second, that he is referring to the governess's interpretation of his expulsion from school. The difference between these two completions is in the degree of innocence they attribute to Miles—innocence of the governess's troubled state of mind in connection with him. The double reading continues when Miles again insists:

> ". . . But I mean does *he* know?"
> "Know what, Miles?"
> "Why, the way I'm going on." [P. 94]

Is Miles merely referring to the lack of formal education, or is he trying to find out whether his uncle knows about the strange supernatural happenings at Bly? Is he or is he not innocent?

In the evening conversation between Miles and the governess after the incident on the way to church, Miles admits that he was thinking of the governess and "of this queer business of ours" (p. 102). The demonstrative "this" leaves its referent unspecified, implying that it is self-evident, and the governesses's attempts to extract from Miles the missing information end in failure.

> "Of what queer business, Miles?"
> "Why, the way you bring me up. And all the rest!"
> I fairly held my breath a minute, and even from my glimmering taper there was light enough to show how he smiled up at me from his pillow. "What do you mean by all the rest?"
> "Oh, you know, you know!" [P. 102]

As in the preceding clash on the way to church, here too Miles can be taken to refer either to the matter of school or to that of the ghosts. If "the way you bring me up" momentarily seems to tip the scale in favor of the first possibility, it is followed by a vague "And all the rest," which again gives rise to the other possibility. And as in the church incident, Miles declines specification, intimating that the governess actually knows the answer. "Oh, you know, you know!" The common focus assumed (or feigned) by Miles is precisely the absent element in the conversation, and it is this absence that increases the reader's share in the "writing" of the story, allowing him to supply either an innocent or a culpable interpretation of that which the dialogue leaves unspecified. A little later Miles goes on with his accusation of the governess. "You'll have to tell him [the uncle]—about the way you've let it all drop; you'll have to tell him a tremendous lot!" (p. 104). "A tremendous lot" is again vague, and its logical relation to the first sentence is doubly directed. It can be either an apposition or an addition. If it is an apposition, it refers back to "the way you've let it all drop," which is probably linked to the matter of schooling, although the "all" renders even this vague and possibly more inclusive. If, on the other hand, it is an addition, it means

something like, "You'll have to tell him not only about the
way you've let it all drop, but about many other things as
well." The "other things" are far from being defined, but at
this stage there is nothing to prevent the reader from tentatively detecting an allusion to the strange business of the ghosts.

Another salient example of the use of this technique occurs
in the conversation between Mrs. Grose and the governess
before the removal of Flora. Mrs. Grose says that she heard
"From that child—horrors!" and adds, "On my honour, Miss,
she says things—!" (p. 122). There is no specification of the
"things" or "horrors" the housekeeper heard from the hysterical girl, the absence of specification being "motivated" by
Mrs. Grose's breakdown at this point. Therefore the reader can
infer from the context of the previous scenes either that Flora
told Mrs. Grose about Miss Jessel, or that the child said terrible
things about her present governess. The first possibility confirms the governess's contention, the second undermines it,
though not conclusively, for Flora's outburst against the governess may express her shock at being discovered, just as it
may convey her resentment of the atrocities she has been
accused of. Thus, the second possibility is itself doubly directed. The governess, it transpires, takes Mrs. Grose's report
as a confirmation of her view, saying triumphantly, "It so
justifies me!" (p. 122). But a link is missing here, the kind of
missing link I have described in my analysis of "The Figure
in the Carpet." It is not clear what it is that justifies her and
why it does so. Assuming that the governess understands Mrs.
Grose to be saying that Flora told her horrors about Miss
Jessel, the report "justifies her" in the sense of confirming her
theory. On the other hand, assuming that the governess understands that she herself was the object of the horrors uttered by
little Flora, the justification can have several meanings: either
the governess is justified in her decision to send the child away
because the things she said in her delirium prove how much
she hates the governess, or because they prove that Flora is lost
and that all efforts of salvation should therefore concentrate on
Miles, or—in a typical inconclusive "twist"—the awful things
said against the governess may confirm the child's depravity
rather than the governess's harmful perversion. Mrs. Grose's

answer, "It does that, Miss!" is again doubly directed, meaning either that Flora's outburst justifies the governess's whole theory or that it justifies her decision to send the child away. It should be noted that a few lines later Mrs. Grose explicitly explains that Flora's shocking language referred to her present governess, but as we have seen above, even this possibility is doubly directed. It is also noteworthy that the implicit conclusion that Flora must have acquired such appalling language from Miss Jessel (pp. 122–23) leaves the issue of the ghost completely open, for it is quite possible that the corrupting instruction took place in Miss Jessel's lifetime.

Similarly dependent on an absence of specification is the ambiguity of tone. But whereas the kind of vagueness, incompleteness, or ellipsis discussed above resides in actual statements of the characters, the ambiguity of tone is created by the omission of "stage directions" concerning the manner in which statements are uttered. Take, for example, the first conversation between the governess and Mrs. Grose about the stranger.

> "How long was he here?"
> "Till I came out. I came to meet him."
> Mrs. Grose at last turned round, and there was still more in her face.
> "*I* couldn't have come out."
> "Neither could I" I laughed again. "But I did come. I have my duty."
> "So have I mine," she replied. [P. 46]

There is no indication of the tone in which Mrs. Grose replies, and the wording of her answers as well as the framework of the situation admit of opposed tonal realizations. "I couldn't have come out" may express either admiration for the governess's courage or disapproval of her rashness. And when the governess explains her behavior by her sense of duty, Mrs. Grose again answers in a doubly directed way. If "So have I mine" is said admiringly, it may be paraphrased as "I also have my duty, and nevertheless I wouldn't have been able to summon up the courage to come out." If, on the other hand, it is deprecating, it means roughly, "I also have my duty and therefore I wouldn't have come out so hastily and irresponsibly." Equally doubly directed is Mrs. Grose's homely exclamation, "Laws!" which occurs in two different scenes. The first is in chapter 12, where the governess gradually unfolds her theory to the dismayed housekeeper. The presentation culminates with an explanation of the ghosts' motives for haunting Bly. "And to ply them [the children] with that evil still, to keep up the work of demons, is what brings the others [the ghosts] back" (p. 82). Mrs. Grose expresses her astonishment in one word, "Laws!" which the governess interprets as a confirmation of her view. "The exclamation was homely, but it revealed a real acceptance of my further proof of what, in the bad time . . . must have occurred" (p. 82). But Mrs. Grose's exclamation is in no way an unambiguous confirmation. Without an indication of the tone in which it was said and with the weight of conflicting hypotheses developed in the micro- and macrocontext, "Laws!" can convey either the housekeeper's shock at the vision of the demons' plan and of the children's depravity—in which case it confirms the governess's theory—or her astonished rejection of such insubstantial figments of an "infernal imagination" (p. 85). Similarly, in chapter 19, when the governess expresses her conviction that Flora took the boat and "went straight over" to the other side of the lake, Mrs. Grose again cries, "Laws!" For the governess, this is an evident sign that "the chain of my logic was ever too much for her" (p. 111), meaning either that Mrs. Grose couldn't follow the argument or that she was appalled by the possibility. But Mrs. Grose's ejaculation may also convey astonishment at the patent *absence* of a chain of logic in what she sees as the governess's strange mental leaps. Is this one of the housekeeper's "plunges of submission" (p. 111), or is it "a burst of high disapproval" (p. 115)?

Close to the ambiguity of tone, but designating not the vocal realization of an attitude but the codified form of speech suited by convention to a given occasion, is the double-directedness of register (Halliday's term, 1964, p. 97 and elsewhere). The most salient example is the headmaster's letter. All the governess says about this crucial but never quoted letter is that "They go into no particulars. They simply express their regret that it should be impossible to keep him" (p. 29). Despite the governess's conclusion that "That can have only one meaning.

. . . That he's an injury to the others" (p. 29), the expression of regret is far from being univocal. It may indeed belong to the register of formal, polite business writing, in which case it is simply a conventional way of sugaring the bitter pill of rejection. But it may also be an expression of real regret, in which case it repudiates the governess's condemnatory interpretation. Perhaps Miles was very good at school, and the headmaster really regrets that it should be impossible to keep him, but nothing can be done either because the boy is too young or because the initial agreement was for one term only and cannot be altered (p. 21; Cranfill and Clark 1965, p. 74). It should be noted that the reasons for discontinuing Miles's schooling are finally disclosed, with a reasonable degree of definiteness, in the "confession" scene, but in the meantime this temporary gap with its considerable duration has played a central part in the ambiguity concerning Miles's innocence or corruption.

As I have pointed out in the theoretical part of this study, the context can have a drastic effect on semantic and syntactic elements included in it. The different meanings of words or sentences which in isolation from a context are grasped as unrelated to each other and sometimes even as opposed to each other may become closely related in the contextual framework. And conversely, related meanings may become distanced and even polarized by the context. In *The Turn of the Screw* the contextual polarization of related meanings is on the one hand made possible by the mutually exclusive narrative hypotheses, and, on the other hand, it reinforces the mutually exclusive character of the same hypotheses. To illustrate, when the governess sits by Miles's bed, trying to make him talk about his past, the boy turns to her with a tortured look, gently asking to be let alone. The governess, however, cannot stop. She feels that "merely, at this, to turn my back on him was to abandon or, to put it more truly, to lose him" (p. 105). In the context "to lose him" may mean either to lose him to the powers of evil or to lose possession of him. Although in isolation the two meanings are related to each other, in *The Turn of the Screw* each of them reinforces a diametrically opposed interpretation of the governess's behavior. The first meaning supports the view of the governess as a self-appointed savior; the second substantiates the interpretation of the motivating force behind her actions as an egoistic need for possession. Both possibilities are reinforced in the succeeding paragraph, where "it made me drop on my knees beside the bed and seize once more the chance of possessing him" and "I just want you to help me to save you!" (p. 105) appear one after the other in the textual continuum.

The last sentence of the nouvelle also becomes doubly directed in a similar way. "We were alone with the quiet day, and his little heart, dispossessed, had stopped" (p. 138). Is the boy's heart cruelly deprived of life, or is it also "dispossessed" in the sense of "rid of an evil spirit," so that at least his soul is saved?

Like semantic nuances, syntactic relations are also polarized in *The Turn of the Screw*. When Mrs. Grose first tells the governess that she herself has seen nothing, the latter is reluctant to accept this as a complete denial of the reality of the ghost she so distinctly perceived. Her understandable reluctance corresponds (or seems to correspond) to something in Mrs. Grose's demeanor: "yet she accepted without directly impugning my sanity the truth as I gave it to her, and ended by showing me, on this ground, an awe-stricken tenderness, an expression of the sense of my more than questionable privilege, of which the very breath has remained with me as that of the sweetest of human charities" (pp. 48–49). There are three foci of verbal double-directedness in this passage: "without directly impugning"; "on this ground"; and "my more than questionable privilege." The first is not based on syntactic relations but on a double possibility of prosodic realization. If the main stress falls on "impugning," the meaning will by and large be that Mrs. Grose did not question the governess's sanity. But the main stress can also be made to fall on "directly," in which case the expression will be read "behind the governess's back" rather than "with her." The adverb "directly" will then be grasped as concealing the ironic possibility that if Mrs. Grose did not *directly* question the governess's sanity, she did so *indirectly*.

It is this double-directedness that renders ambiguous the reference of "this" in "on this ground." On what ground? Is it on the ground of her acceptance, or on the ground of her indirect impugnment of the governess's sanity? Both readings are consistent with what follows, for Mrs. Grose's awe-stricken tenderness may result either from her acceptance of the reality of the ghosts or from compassion aroused by the governess's liability to hallucinations. The governess herself calls her liability a "more than questionable privilege"—an expression which is again doubly directed, depending on whether we take "questionable" to modify that which is described as a privilege or only the adequacy of the term "privilege" when applied to such a predicament.

The same chapter contains another doubly directed sentence. Mrs. Grose describes Peter Quint as a man who was "too free with everyone!" (p. 50), and the governess silently ponders this description. "I forebore, for the moment, to analyse this description further than by the reflection that a part of it applied to several of the members of the household, of the half-dozen maids and men who were still of our small colony" (pp. 50–51). The problem for interpretation is in deciding what part of the description "applied to several of the members of the household." Is the governess saying that, like Quint, other members of the household are too free with everyone, or is she drawing the inference that Quint was too free with other members of the household, not only with Miles? The various semantic nuances of the adjective "free" are also activated in this context. Thus the complaint may concern Quint's disrespect for those in higher ranks—his impudence, familiarity, taking of liberties. But it may also hint at his sexual forwardness, and in retrospect this would make Miss Jessel the hidden referent of Mrs. Grose's vague "everyone" and would reinforce the second syntactic possibility. The nonsexual interpretation, it should be noted, fits both syntactic possibilities equally well.

An interesting doubly directed modifying relation of a comparative clause occurs in the third "encounter" between the governess and Miss Jessel, but its contribution to the central narrative ambiguity is indirect. More directly, it effects a figurative identification between the governess and Miss Jessel —another instance of "the full image of a repetition" (see McMaster 1969, pp. 377–82; Bewley 1952, p. 110). The governess has just returned from church after the perplexing conversation with Miles, and "Tormented, in the hall, with difficulties and obstacles, I remember sinking down at the foot of the staircase—suddenly collapsing there on the lowest step and then, with a revulsion, recalling that it was exactly where, more than a month before, in the darkness of night and just so bowed with evil things, I had seen the spectre of the most horrible of women" (p. 96). To whom does the comparative "and just so bowed with evil things" refer? Was it Miss Jessel who, a month before, was just as bowed with evil things as the governess is now? Or was it the governess herself who, a month before, just as at present, was "bowed with evil things" when she saw Miss Jessel's ghost? Both syntactic relations are cataphoric, referring forward to the succeeding phrase. But the succeeding phrase provides both "I" and "the spectre of the most horrible of women" as plausible referents of "just so bowed with evil things." This purely grammatical interchangeability of the governess and Miss Jessel reflects and reinforces the symbolic identification which crosses the governess's mind.[15] And the identification itself contributes to the central ambiguity by adding to the prevalent juxtaposition of the good governess with the evil Miss Jessel the gruesome possibility of an identification between two evil governesses. A qualification is needed here perhaps. The grammatical ambiguity I have just pointed out is predominantly local, for if we turn back to the previous "encounter" we realize that it was Miss Jessel and not the governess who was bowed on one of the lower steps (p. 74). Nevertheless, the local ambiguity leaves some hovering impression of evil attached to the governess, for at present she *is* bowed with evil things, and the reader may choose to project onto the previous scene a figurative, if not a factual, state of being bowed down.

To conclude the analysis of ambiguous syntactic relations, I propose to examine the end of the story, where the ambiguity is intensified by the double-directedness of the addressee. The passage has been often quoted and often discussed.

> I was so determined to have all my proof that I flashed into ice to challenge him. "Whom do you mean by 'he'?"
> "Peter Quint—you devil!" His face gave again, round the room, its convulsed supplication. "*Where?*"

They are in my ears still, his supreme surrender of the
name and his tribute to my devotion. "What does he matter
now, my own?—What will he *ever* matter? *I* have you,"
I launched at the beast, "but he has lost you for ever!"
[P. 138]

As has so often been remarked, Miles's "you devil!" may refer
either to Peter Quint or to the governess. The governess, of
course, chooses the first possibility, taking it as an expression
of the boy's complete rejection of evil. But the cry can also be
directed against the governess, accusing her of infernally in-
stilling a consciousness of evil into an innocent soul.

Similarly, the governess's "*I* have you, . . . but he has lost
you for ever!" may be addressed either to Miles or to Quint. If
it is addressed to Miles, it expresses the governess's feeling of
victory: it is she who now possesses the child, and the devil has
lost him forever. On the other hand, if the words are addressed
to Quint, they mean that the governess has now become
possessed by the devil ("*I* have you"), thus freeing Miles, who
has consequently lost Quint forever. This double possibility is
sustained by the two meanings of "I launched at the beast." If
launch means "throw oneself," then "I have you" is addressed
to Miles. If, on the other hand, *launch* signifies "say vigor-
ously," the whole speech is addressed to Quint, the "beast"
(West 1964, pp. 286–87).

The last category of ambiguous linguistic clues to be discussed here is doubly directed images. In *The Turn of the
Screw* these are all found in the governess's language, and their
double-directedness results from the fact that they can be
understood both "with" the governess and "behind her back."
The governess's first description of the stranger includes the
following note of certainty, "the man who looked at me over
the battlements was as definite as a picture in a frame" (p. 37).
The common quality mentioned in the closed simile is definiteness, but the reader may wish not to ignore other connotations
of "picture," connotations which link it with the world of
illusion and may, boomerang-like, undermine the governess's
certainty. On the same page she again asserts her conviction:
"So I saw him as I see the letters I form on this page" (p. 37).

And again the straightforward intended meaning may be under-mined by the possibility that the governess forms, creates, the figure of the stranger just as she forms the letters on the page. In a later chapter, the governess describes Mrs. Grose's receptivity with the help of an image that can easily turn against her own intention. "She [Mrs. Grose] offered her mind to my disclosures as, had I wished to mix a witch's broth and propose it with assurance, she would have held out her large clean saucepan" (p. 78). Instead of emphasizing Mrs. Grose's receptivity, as the governess does, the reader may wish to focus on the other half of the image and stress the governess's role as a witch, poisoning the minds of both housekeeper and children. Similarly, when the governess expresses her intention to save Miles by appealing to his intelligence, her own description may point to a danger of which she is unaware. "Wasn't there light in the fact which, as we shared our solitude, broke out with a *specious glitter* it had never yet quite worn?—the fact that (opportunity aiding, precious opportunity which had now come,) it would be preposterous, with a child so endowed, to forego the help one might wrest from absolute intelligence?" (p. 127; my italics). It is the speciousness of the glitter that implies not only its fair appearance but also its potentially deceptive nature and hence the potential mistake in the governess's assault on the child's intelligence. Quint's reappearance in chapter 24 may indeed be symptomatic of her mistake. And his reappearance is again described in a doubly directed image, "like a sentinel before a prison" (p. 133). While the governess probably sees Quint as the jailer, the reader may reverse the picture, seeing her as imprisoning Miles and thereby causing Quint's return.

With *The Turn of the Screw* there is a marked increase in the complexity of the system of clues used to create and maintain the ambiguity. A further development in this direction can be found in James's next ambiguous work, *The Sacred Fount*.

6 *The Sacred Fount*

Like *The Turn of the Screw, The Sacred Fount* is a first-person narrative, its ambiguity arising from the equal plausibility of the narrator's hypothesis about the Newmarch guests (a) and its negation ($\bar{a}$) or its counterpart (b). Very early in the novel, the narrator forms the theory that Mrs. Brissenden's second bloom and beauty are a result of her unconscious draining of her husband's vitality in their intimate relationship of sublime passion. Applying this hypothesis to Long's intellectual improvement, he believes it to be the work of an intelligent woman who therefore "must logically have been idiotised" (pp. 102–3). In his search for the "right" woman he becomes gradually convinced that Mrs. Server is "the missing word" in the puzzle (p. 56), but he also becomes aware of his own tenderness for her and of his wish to protect her from Mrs. Brissenden's acute perception. To complete the symmetrical theory, the narrator discovers, or thinks he discovers, that Mrs. Server and Guy Brissenden are drawn together by their common plight as the "sacrificed" and analogously that Mrs. Brissenden and Gilbert Long become conscious of their own bond as sacrificers. Is this a penetrating insight into what is happening beneath the smooth surface of the weekend party or is it a figment of the narrator's own "private madness" (p. 118)? Both possibilities can be fully supported by evidence from the text, and we are faced with mutually exclusive "finalized hypotheses," the one asserting the relations perceived by the narrator, the other firmly denying them.

THE CREATION OF THE AMBIGUITY

As in "The Lesson of the Master" and "The Figure in the Carpet," the first step toward narrative ambiguity in *The*

Sacred Fount is the omission of a central 'bead' from the 'string' of events—to use James's own metaphor in "Glasses" (in *The Complete Tales,* 9:317). The detective story structure thus underlies the composition of *The Sacred Fount* as much as it does that of "The Figure in the Carpet," and the gap in both works is perceptible in advance. The propelling factor in *The Sacred Fount* is the attempt to find out whether "vampirish" relations do indeed exist between the two analogous couples. But it is precisely on this subject that we are confronted with a central informational gap. There is no independent dramatization of the relationships between the different characters which would enable us to solve the enigma for ourselves. Independent, I mean, of the narrator's rendering of the facts—a rendering which, we soon discover, may (but need not) be strongly colored by his own imagination. Not only are the objective facts replaced by their effects, but even as effects their reverberations in the consciousnesses of the other characters are subject to the narrator's rendering. The other characters are never allowed to speak for themselves; they are always quoted by the narrator. *Quoted* is perhaps not the appropriate word, for although some remarks of the other characters *are* quoted, others are the narrator's own phrasing of what he considers the import of his interlocutor's words. Thus, for example, after "quoting" Mrs. Server, the narrator says, "These remarks—of which I give rather the sense than the form, for they were a little scattered and troubled, and I helped them out and pieced them together—these remarks had for me, I was to find, unexpected suggestions—not all of which was I prepared on the spot to take up" (p. 47).

Other instances are even further removed from quotation, being not the narrator's formulation of the general meaning of what his interlocutor *said,* but his interpretation of what his interlocutor did *not* say. Again in connection with Mrs. Server, the narrator "quotes" what he believes to be her thoughts, adding, "I finally felt, in a word, so qualified to attribute to my companion some such mute address as that" (p. 105). Similarly, people's looks seem to the narrator to say things which he takes upon himself to translate into words (pp. 24, 80). Whether they do mutely "say" these things or whether they only seem to him to say them is what the absence of objective dramatization prevents us from knowing.

But making this central gap technically possible is not enough. It is also necessary to make it thematically plausible. The permanent gap in *The Sacred Fount* is "motivated" in different ways, all mediated through the characters' incapacity or deliberate refusal to obtain or divulge information. Concern for the aesthetic, or quasi-aesthetic, causes the narrator to omit many details, for, "The links, in fact, should I count them all, would make too long a chain. They formed, nevertheless, the happiest little chapter of accidents, though a series of which I can scarce give more than the general effect" (p. 24).

Discretion and consideration prevent some of the characters from obtaining knowledge of the facts. Thus, Ford Obert says that as long as the search is confined to "psychologic evidence," there is nothing ignoble about it. "What's ignoble is the detective and the keyhole," and the narrator concurs: "If I had a material clue I should feel ashamed: the fact would be deterrent" (p. 57). Similarly, Mrs. Briss scorns to pick up "a little loose collateral evidence" as to Mrs. Server's predicament because of a discretion which the narrator sincerely appreciates (p. 64). Lady John later says that people's civility, including her own, prevents them from discussing Mrs. Server's strange behavior (p. 124). The narrator's own tenderness and consideration for Mrs. Server prevent him from comparing notes with the other characters (p. 75), and thus the hypothesis is never put to test. The fun of the game, the "high application of intelligence," would also be spoiled by a "material clue" (p. 57). Toward the end of chapter 4, Obert remarks that he has his own idea, but, "He didn't say what it was, and I [the narrator] didn't ask, intimating thereby that I held it to be in this fine manner we were playing the game" (p. 58). Or, earlier on the same page, "I hadn't really made out at all what he was impressed *with*, and I should only have spoiled everything by inviting him to be definite."

Firm trust is another excuse for not asking for objective evidence. When, in the final encounter, Mrs. Briss emits the shattering (or seemingly shattering) information that Lady John is the woman involved with Long, the narrator pleads for proof. The only proof Mrs. Brissenden is prepared to offer is that she had this information from her husband, but she cannot tell the eager narrator how her husband had learnt the crucial fact: "I take his word" (p. 211). Similarly, the insignificance of the evidence in hand is used as a pretext for evasiveness. When the narrator urges Mrs. Briss to repeat the words which convinced her of Long's irremediable stupidity, she replies, "Not a word to repeat—you wouldn't believe! He does say nothing at all. One can't remember. It's what I mean" (p. 202). And again we are left without the evidence which could decide for us the question of Long's stupidity.

The technical role of the omission of information is thus fully "dissimulated." But the creation of the gap and its motivation in the Formalist sense are still not enough. There must also be motivation in the psychological sense, that is the creation of desire on the part of the reader to fill in the gap. Without this motivation, the reader would never join in the game of fitting clues together and would never discover their mutually exclusive nature. Motivation in this sense is provided by the very centrality of the gap, by its being the object of the quest and the subject of the talk of all the characters in the novel. The gap and its filling in are what the novel is about, and to read the novel at all is to engage in the search for this all-important missing presence.

The mutually exclusive sets of clues are balanced in the two ways I have discussed elsewhere, namely, the equilibrium of singly directed clues and the presence of doubly directed clues. But whereas in "The Lesson of the Master" this balance is grasped only in retrospect, and in "The Figure in the Carpet" and (somewhat differently) in *The Turn of the Screw*, it runs parallel to the narrative sequence, in *The Sacred Fount* the opposing clues do not always appear in linear succession. They are often scattered over various parts of the narrative, so that there can be, for example, a "suspended" $a+$ "waiting for" its negation $(a-)$ or for its counterpart $(b+)$ which will appear at a later stage of the story. This, of course, makes for a greater disparity between the linear and the supralinear than there is in "The Figure in the Carpet" and *The Turn of the Screw*.

Singly Directed Clues

The equilibrium of singly directed clues in *The Sacred Fount* takes two forms: the balance of confirmations and repudiations of the same interpretation, here the view advanced by the narrator $(a+a-)$; and the balance of evidence for one interpretation by counterevidence for other interpretations $(a+b+)$.

As in *The Turn of the Screw*, the narrator's theory is examined both by the other characters and by the narrator himself. The discussions between the narrator and his fellow characters are intended to test either the narrator's view of the other participants in the drama or his theories about his interlocutors, and I shall start with the first type.

Even before the substance of the conversation is analyzed, it is important to note who initiates the conversation or, in the narrator's language, who gives the cue. The balance between cues given by the narrator and those given by the other characters is complete. The narrator gives Long the cue as to the change in Mrs. Brissenden. "I had then given him his cue by alluding to my original failure to place her. What in the world, in the year or two, had happened to her? She had changed so extraordinarily for the better. How could a woman who had been plain so long become pretty so late?" (p. 19). It is again the narrator who asks Long whether he had noticed a change in Guy Brissenden.

> After dinner, but while the men were still in the room, I had some talk again with Long, of whom I inquired if he had been so placed as to see "poor Briss." [P. 30]

With Ford Obert the narrator starts discussing the Brissendens, drawing his yet unconscious attention to "the air of disparity in the couple I have just named" (p. 33). And to Mrs. Brissenden he suggests that Lady John is not Long's fount but only his screen for the real woman (pp. 37–39).

Four cues, then, are given by the narrator. Four other cues are suggested by other characters. Mrs. Brissenden is the one who first comments on the change in Long (although the narrator had noticed it before). "She put it to me frankly that she had never seen a man so improved: a confidence that I met with alacrity, as it showed me that, under the same impression, I had not been astray" (p. 21). It is again Mrs. Briss who suggests that her husband is Lady John's screen for Long (p. 22), and it is she who has the sudden inspiration that May Server is Long's real "fount." "We have her," she says upon seeing May Server, and it is only "by her insistence in fact that my [the narrator's] thought was quickened" (p. 44). The change in Mrs. Server was even earlier suggested by that acute observer, Ford Obert. She is not the same woman whom he had once painted. "Her imagination had, for the time, rested its wing. At present it's ready for flight—it seeks a fresh perch." And a little later, "She's too beastly unhappy" (p. 28).

Once the cues (four and four) are given, the discussions go on, and the narrator's views are either confirmed or repudiated by his interlocutors. Long confirms the narrator's impression of the change in Mrs. Briss, recalling that he had not placed her at first himself (p. 19). Briss confirms his view of May Server (pp. 88–91), while Mrs. Briss confirms his perception of her own improvement, assuring him that it had been noticed by other people (p. 21). It is she again who corroborates his naming of Lady John (p. 21), while Ford Obert strengthens his point about the disparity between Mrs. and Mr. Briss. He does so by mistaking the relations between their ages. "Why had so fine a young creature married a man three times her age?" (p. 33). These are all direct confirmations (that is, the interlocutor agrees with the narrator). Additional confirmation is derived indirectly by unwitting repetition on the part of two characters of the same judgment. Ford Obert describes the change in May Server by saying, "Well, a part of it is that she can't keep still. She was as still then [when he painted her] as if she had been paid for it. Now she's all over the place" (p. 55). These words are almost literally repeated by Mrs. Briss in the ensuing chapter: "She was all over the place . . . She couldn't keep still. She was different from the woman one had last seen. She used to be so calm—as if she were always sitting for her portrait" (p. 63).

These confirmations, five direct and one indirect, are balanced by the same number of direct and indirect repudiations of the narrator's view. Long noticed nothing about Guy Bris-

senden, and he answers the narrator's hint at a striking change
with a hard look and an ironic, " 'Strikes' me—in that boy?
Nothing in him, that I know of, ever struck me in my life. He's
not an object of the smallest interest to me!" (p. 31). He
definitely sees nothing in poor Briss, "No, confound you!" (p.
32). Mrs. Brissenden disagrees with the narrator's dismissal of
Lady John as Long's sacred fount, saying, "It proves nothing,
you know, that *you* don't like her" (p. 37). Mrs. Server associates Lady John with Obert, not with Long (p. 47), thus top-
pling (or seeming to topple) a hypothesis that the narrator is
still playing with. Obert, on his part, is sure that Long cannot
be Mrs. Server's lover, for "she collared him much too markedly. The real man must be one she doesn't markedly collar"
(p. 56). Another of the connections "discerned" by the narrator, the secret bond of sympathy between Mrs. Server and Guy
Brissenden, is unwittingly rejected by Lady John's belief that
poor Briss is "in terror" of May Server. "Most of the men here
are, you know, and I've really assured myself that he doesn't find
her any less awful than the rest. He finds her the more so by
just the very marked extra attention that you may have
noticed she has given him" (p. 123). To these five direct repudiations is added one instance of indirect repudiation by
unwitting repetition. When Ford Obert changes his view of
May Server's condition, the narrator's wonder "came from the
fact that Lady John had also found Mrs. Server all right," and
the rejection of such a crucial point in his theory thus seems
doubly strengthened (p. 160).

Both confirmations and repudiations are subject to retraction
in the course of the novel. Both Ford Obert and Mrs. Brissenden withdraw from their initial positions and deny the truth of
observations they were the first to make. A crucial blow comes
from Ford Obert in chapter 11. May Server, he affirms, is no
longer beastly unhappy, and even when he said she was, he
knew "that beastly unhappiness wasn't quite all of it" (p. 160).
Everything that Obert had ever said about Mrs. Server was
only a result of "the torch of your [the narrator's] analogy"
(p. 152), and therefore "I assure you I decline all responsibility. I see the responsibility as quite beautifully yours" (p.
·149). The second blow comes from Mrs. Brissenden in the

grand *volte face* which, in spite of its relative brevity in terms of *fabula* time, occupies a quarter of the novel's length. About the relations between May Server and Gilbert Long she now says, "It's nonsense. I've nothing to tell you. I feel there's nothing in it and I've given it up" (p. 173). May Server "isn't in it" (p. 174), and Gilbert Long is the same "prize fool" he always was (p. 201). It was Mrs. Brissenden, we remember, who first commented on Long's improvement, and it was her choice which originally alighted on Mrs. Server. Like Ford Obert, she now retracts not merely a confirmation, but an originally independent impression, and like him, she now attributes the initial impression to the narrator's infernal powers of persuasion (p. 198).

As if to match these retroactive repudiations, the same scenes contain rectifications of an equal number of former repudiations. Thus, if early in the novel Mrs. Briss discarded the idea of Lady John's involvement with Gilbert Long, she now reaffirms it by an emphatic triple repetition (p. 209). Similarly, when at an early stage of the quest, the narrator tactlessly suggested to Mrs. Briss a bond of sympathy between her husband and Mrs. Server, she treated it as a broad joke: "Is it your idea to make out . . . that she has suddenly had the happy thought of a passion for my husband?" (p. 64). It is this broad joke which she affirms as literal truth in the final scene. May Server, she now says, didn't dash, "she settled. She stuck . . . She made love to him [Briss]" (p. 217). Ford Obert's new affirmation that Mrs. Server's lover "isn't there" (p. 155) is a retraction of his repudiation of the same idea when insincerely and testingly suggested by the narrator (on p. 57 Obert says about the same lover, "I'm sure he is [here]. She tells me he's near").

Perfect balance, we have seen, is maintained between confirmations and repudiations by the different characters of the narrator's views of the other principals. Nor is the balance limited to an analysis of "the others." On some occasions the subject of discussion is the narrator's interpretation of a character's own "mute addresses" and "eloquent silences." Again, half of his intuitions are confirmed, the other half denied.

Upon seeing May Server and Ford Obert, the narrator interprets the latter's look as hinting to him, "Don't—there's a good fellow—leave me any longer alone with her!" (p. 24). Obert later admits that his look was indeed intended to call the narrator to his rescue, as he was frightened "at a sort of sense that she wanted to make love to me" (p. 27). Another plea for rescue is discerned by the narrator in the "look or two of dim suggestiveness" that Guy Brissenden seems to give him while "thinking secludedly together" with Lady John (pp. 79, 81). Again his intuition is confirmed. When left alone with the narrator, Briss immediately confesses, "I'm glad you turned up. I wasn't especially amusing myself" (p. 84).

Two other interpretations are, however, blandly repudiated by the characters concerned. The narrator interprets Obert's avoidance of his eyes as a sign that "something or other had happened as a consequence of which Obert had lost the impulse to repeat to me his odd invitation to intervene" (p. 139). When he puts this idea to Obert, he is rewarded with an ironic, commonsensical answer: "A man engaged in talk with a charming woman scarcely selects that occasion for winking at somebody else" (p. 149).[1] When Mrs. Brissenden informs the narrator of her desire to talk to him, he infers from the way she faces him a defiant intimation that she would do everything not to travel back with him, as well as "a world of invidious reference to the little journey we had already made together" (p. 136). Later it transpires that all Mrs. Brissenden's look was intended to convey was that she preferred to see him privately and quietly, after all the others had retired. "I wanted to see you quietly," she explains two chapters later, "which was what I tried—not altogether successfully, it rather struck me at the moment—to make you understand when I let you know about it" (p. 170).

The narrator's intellectual adventure is not limited to the erection of the magnificent "palace of thought" which is his complex and symmetrical theory. What he knows (or thinks he knows) about the other characters is not enough for his intellectual appetite. He also craves knowledge about himself, about *how* he knows what he knows. The searchlight, now turned upon himself, reveals two contradictory answers to the question of *how* he knows, and these, in turn, provide—this time from his own point of view—the same mutually exclusive solutions to the original problem of *whether* he knows. When the answer to the question of how he knows seems to the narrator to be either "by logical induction" or "by artistic inspiration," he rejoices in the triumph of his theory. "It appeared then that the more things I fitted together the larger sense, every way, they made—a remark in which I found an extraordinary elation. It justified my indiscreet curiosity; it crowned my underhand process with beauty. The beauty perhaps was only for *me*—the beauty of having been right" (p. 96). Emphasizing the artistic aspect of this "underhand process," he says, "I was positively—so had the wheel revolved—proud of my work. I had thought it all out, and to have thought it was, wonderfully, to have brought it" (p. 97).

His self-approval often verges on hubris and makes his ecstatic reveling in his "supernatural acuteness" (p. 94) or "the sweetness of [his] wisdom" (p. 106) unpleasant to many readers and critics. But these hubristic certainties often give way to more somber moods in which "creating results" seems synonymous with "fabricating" them, and in which the whole theory seems to him a palace of cards with no foundation in reality. The following passage records one of these moments of gnawing doubt: "I remember feeling seriously warned, while dinner lasted, not to yield further to my idle habit of reading into mere human things an interest so much deeper than mere human things were in general prepared to supply" (p. 114). His perceptions now seem to him "extravagant" (p. 114) and the grounds of his theory "fantastically constructive" (p. 69).

The clash between the possibilities of truth and delusion is underscored by the frequent contiguity of the narrator's exultation and his misgivings. Thus, an outburst of elation ends with a recognition of the absence of proof: "I had puzzled out everything and put everything together: I was as morally confident and as intellectually triumphant as I have frankly here described myself; but there was no objective test to which I had yet exposed my theory" (p. 105). Even before the elaborate theory is formed, the narrator records his impressions of the change in Guy Brissenden and his own sense of being on the track of a law, and then adds, "A part of the amusement they [the phenomena] yielded came, I daresay, from my exaggerating them—grouping them into a larger mystery (and thereby a larger "law") than the facts, as observed, yet warranted" (p. 30). Later, when every new piece of evidence seems to fit into the theory, the narrator describes the aesthetic beauty of the symmetry as well as its danger: "These opposed couples balanced like bronze groups at the two ends of a chimney-piece, and the most I could say to myself in lucid deprecation of my thought was that I mustn't take them equally for granted merely *because* they balanced. Things in the real had a way of not balancing: it was all an affair, this fine symmetry, of artificial proportion" (p. 130). The opposite sequence can also be found. After seeing Mrs. and Mr. Briss together, the narrator decides to get rid of his obsession, but he soon finds it "perched" again on his shoulders when the vision of Long in "the warm darkness" seems so perfectly to fit his theory (pp. 142–43).

In addition to direct self-criticism, the sequence may also express indirect judgment by analogy. Thus, after the narrator's analysis of Long's former stupidity and present improvement, the narrator himself fails to recognize Mrs. Briss, "after which I reflected that she might easily have thought me the same sort of ass as I had thought Long" (p. 18). The point of the sequence is to throw the shadow of a doubt upon the narrator's preceding affirmation of Long's stupidity; just as Mrs. Briss might have thought the narrator an ass for what seems a justified failure to recognize her, so the narrator himself may be pronouncing Long a fool on the basis of slight evidence. Similarly, when the narrator sees Gilbert Long sitting next to Lady John and poor Briss next to Mrs. Server, he starts brooding on the juxtaposition, and then, characteristically, starts looking at his own brooding from the outside: "My cogitations —for I must have bristled with them—would have made me as stiff a puzzle to interpretative minds as I had suffered other phenomena to become my own" (p. 74). And just as they may misinterpret his cogitations, so he himself may be misreading the "evidence" in front of him.[2]

The narrator's ambivalent attitude toward his theory is not confined to matters of factual validity. He is also spasmodically tormented by moral compunctions. His curiosity sometimes seems to him as "wanting in taste" (p. 44) and beneath his conception of moral behavior: "To nose about for a relation that a lady has her reasons for keeping secret—" (p. 57). It is not only on the count of discretion that the "immersion, intellectually speaking, in the affairs of other people" is reprehensible (p. 72). A much more serious result of the narrator's prying (if a result it is) is the communication of a consciousness to the "victimizers"—an act which, the narrator believes, is responsible for their dissimulation in the last scenes (see, for example, pp. 189–90).

These moral scruples, however, are balanced both by the narrator's sporadic assertions that the beauty of his system "justified my indiscreet curiosity" (pp. 96, 203), and by Obert's reassuring statement that an enquiry confined to "psychological evidence" is "not only quite inoffensive . . . but positively honourable" (p. 57).

The examples of singly directed clues discussed so far are all members of the category $a+$, $a-$, that is, the creation of equilibrium between confirmation and repudiation of the same hypothesis. It is a natural consequence of the definition of ambiguity that $a-$ automatically becomes $b+$, and I shall now proceed to examine how the b, the alternative interpretation (or interpretations), is suggested, and how it is prevented from becoming more plausible than a.

Whereas throughout the novel Mrs. Brissenden either confirmed or repudiated the narrator's theory, at the end she does not only reject every detail of it, but also counters it with a theory of her own. Gilbert Long, she says, is the same "prize fool" he always was. No wonder, then, that he *is* Lady John's lover, for, as described in the dialogue between the narrator and Mrs. Brissenden, "He would have no need then of her having transformed and inspired him"; "Or of her having *de*formed and idiotized herself" (p. 210). May Server is not intellectually depleted but merely "horrid": She made love to poor Briss. Thus the different "pieces" in the narrator's theory are fitted into a new "structure" which, interestingly enough, leaves out one of the central "bricks" in the narrator's "palace of thought," Mrs. Brissenden herself. It is precisely this brick that the narrator picks up in his silent criticism of the newly erected structure. Mrs. Briss, he is convinced, has a reason to

keep herself out of the symmetrical relations and has hypo-
critically constructed her theory in order to protect herself.
There is no independent evidence which would enable us to
judge whether Mrs. Briss does indeed lie, or whether the
narrator imputes this to her for fear of having to admit his
defeat.

Moreover, the narrator himself oscillates between belief and
disbelief, and a zigzag movement is maintained throughout the
last chapters. At the beginning of the interview, the narrator
has premonitions of her triumph (pp. 167–68). Then he speaks
about a "flaw in her confidence" (p. 169) and about the "fine
dishonesty of her eyes," "the light of a part to play" (p. 170).
All these thoughts precede the conversation between them, and
intimate either that she is going to lie or that the narrator
believes she is. When Mrs. Brissenden advances her first
counterargument, the narrator immediately interprets it as a
fib invented in collaboration with Long, and thus he is para-
doxically able to take this seeming blow as another proof of
"the kingdom of thought I had won" (p. 176). This certainty
is, however, shaken when she pronounces him crazy. Rather
like the governess in *The Turn of the Screw*, he then risks "the
long laugh which might have seemed that of madness" and
wonders "if perhaps I mightn't be" (p. 192). A little later he is
again sure that she lies (pp. 202, 208), but then another spasm
of doubt seizes him: "What if she *should* be right?" (p. 210).

Thus just as the narrator's theory was tested against the
other characters' confirmation or repudiation, so Mrs. Brissenden's "now finished system" (p. 218) is assessed by the narrator's acceptance or rejection of it.[3] And the same balance that
was maintained between the characters' views of the narrator's
theory is also preserved in his alternating attitudes towards
Mrs. Brissenden's dazzling structure. Perfect ambiguity as to
the truth value of Mrs. Brissenden's theory is ensured by the
omission of all independent evidence and the oscillation between the narrator's confident dismissal of it and his sporadic
reluctant allowance of its possible validity.

Whereas Mrs. Brissenden's theory is fully stated in the last
chapters, another counterhypothesis is only gently hinted at in
the novel and more than fully developed by Blackall in

Jamesian Ambiguity and The Sacred Fount (1965). Unlike the two other theories, each of which is propounded by one character, the third suggestion is constructed by the reader on the basis of hints dropped by various characters. This is why the third possibility can become an implicit corrective to the exclusion of the self which characterizes both Mrs. Brissenden's and the narrator's suppositions.

The first hint is dropped by Ford Obert so early in the novel that in a first reading one is likely to overlook its potential significance. Talking about May Server's unfortunate tendency to "make love" to every man in the company, Obert adds, "It seems to me . . . that she began on it to you [narrator] as soon as she got hold of you. Weren't you aware?" (p. 27). Later, in a discussion between the narrator and Mrs. Brissenden about May Server, Mrs. Brissenden senses that the narrator's denial of the change in May Server is an attempt to shield the disintegrating lady. This she immediately points out to him: "Does it inconveniently happen that you find you're in love with her yourself?" (p. 61), and, "Perhaps what you don't like is that my observation may be turned on *you*. I confess it is" (p. 63). A possible connection is thus established between the narrator and Mrs. Server. Evidence from a different quarter is provided soon enough in the form of two statements of the narrator's which become the two premises in a syllogism concluded by the reader. In chapter 6 the narrator considers Mrs. Server's avoidance of Long's company as indicative of a relation between them. Immediately following this, he recalls that he himself consistently escapes being pounced upon by her (p. 74), a statement which he repeats at the beginning of the next chapter (p. 87). If avoidance is a sign of a particular interest, and if May Server consistently avoids the narrator, is not the narrator the man who accounts for her being "all gone"? Some such question forms itself in the reader's mind and is immediately supported by the narrator's idea that "there was something quite other I possibly might do with Mrs. Server than endeavour ineffectually to forget her" (pp. 74–75; see also p. 54).

The other side of the coin, May Server's possible tenderness for the narrator, is also presently reinforced by the narrator's impression of a difference between her behavior with him and with all the others. "What made the difference with *me*—if any difference had remained to be made—was the sense of this sharp cessation of her public extravagance" (p. 98). Ford Obert, having watched May Server with the narrator, explains, "She darts from flower to flower, but she clings, for the time, to each. You've been feeling, I judge, the force of my remark" (p. 54). It is also Obert who says that Mrs. Server's affection is likely to be fixed on the last man who could be believed of her (p. 59), on the one man "she doesn't markedly collar" (p. 56)— an idea which is brought to mind when the narrator mentions her consistent avoidance of himself. To the narrator's declaration that he has watched everyone except Obert, the latter answers that he, on his part, has watched everyone *including* the narrator (p. 154). What he has watched, Blackall suggests, is this possibility of a relation between the narrator and Mrs. Server. "Presumably the analogy that holds Ford Obert's attention all day, the analogy which has brought him to believe that May is in love with the narrator and the narrator, possibly, in love with May—Obert is still making up his mind in Chapter XI—is this one: Briss obviously adores his wife: Mrs. Briss is off talking to the narrator. May Server constantly flits to Briss for company; in whom else may she have an interest? Perhaps in the narrator" (1965, pp. 66–67). The whole novel, according to Blackall, is a joke at the expense of the narrator, who "himself is the man for whom he seeks, the person whose presence accounts for May Server's strange behaviour" (p. 62).

But this "collectively implied" possibility is far from being conclusive. For, to begin with the narrator's role in it, there is complete balance between his tenderness for Mrs. Server and his cold, clinical study of her predicament. "The question of her happiness [the narrator says] was essentially subordinate; what I stood or fell by was that of her faculty" (p. 161). The question of Mrs. Server's happiness is "essentially subordinate" because what is at stake for the narrator is not May Server as a human being, but the validity of his own theory. This is why he can reflect on her condition in a detached calculating manner: "and peace therefore might rule the scene on every hypothesis but that of her getting, to put it crudely, worse. How I remember saying to myself that if she didn't get better she surely *must* get worse!" (p. 78).

As for Mrs. Server's hypothetical love for the narrator, the basic opening of gaps is again in operation. Her emotions are never directly exhibited, and we depend for our conclusions on hints dropped by the other characters. While these hints are substantial enough, they are also balanced by attenuating factors which either precede or follow them in the narrative sequence. Thus Ford Obert's revealing hint that he had watched the narrator is followed by, "I admit that I made you out for myself to be back on the scent" (p. 154). Is this all his watching revealed? Even more surprising, perhaps, is the sequence of the insinuating, "Oh, I've watched *you*" (p. 154) and the resigned, "For I've been looking too [for May Server's lover]. He isn't here" (p. 155). If the narrator is the man, how can Obert assert that he is not there? Is this delicacy on his part, or is it a blow to the hypothesis he himself helped to promote?

The narrator's own impression that with him Mrs. Server "folded up her manner in her flounced parasol" (p. 98) is followed by his intuition that she is actually waiting for poor Briss (p. 99). Although he still maintains that the change in her behavior is produced by himself, the sequence—Guy Brissenden's appearance—may suggest otherwise.[4] The only hint which is not attenuated by the sequence is Mrs. Brissenden's, but it turns only on the narrator's feeling for Mrs. Server, not on her feeling for him, which is the more crucial aspect for the theory. This crucial possibility is, in fact, indirectly denied by Mrs. Brissenden's statement that her husband is the man to whom May Server made love.

Reinforcing the network of singly directed hermeneutic clues discussed so far is a similar balance at the verbal level. Contrasted lexical collocations and opposed image clusters support sometimes one, sometimes the other, of the two sets of singly directed clues, intermittently treating the narrator's activity either as a dignified quest or as a ridiculous or even sinister pursuit. On the dignified side are terms and images deriving from logic, art, and drama. The narrator initially describes himself as "just conscious, vaguely, of being on the track of a law, a law that would fit, that would strike me as governing the delicate phenomena" (p. 30). He later speaks of "induction" (p. 35), "postulate" (p. 61), "collateral evidence" (p. 64), "working hypothesis" (p. 75), "demonstration" (p. 99), and "verification" (p. 125).[5] Side by side with the language of logical reasoning is that of the intuitive, imaginative pursuit of truth through creativity. We have already encountered the narrator "overtaken by a mild artistic glow" (p. 81) and reveling in "the joy of determining, almost of creating results" (p. 151). His theory, it seems, is a work of art, and as such may have reasons that reason itself does not know. To introduce this variation of Pascal's dictum is to suggest an opposition between logical thinking and the creative imagination as two ways of searching for the truth. An opposition indeed there is, but in *The Sacred Fount* neither method fares better than the other. The exercise of each is shown to be either a source of great light or a self-contained activity, having no point of contact with the existential and fostering truths which are alien to it.

Images from the theater also operate in this double way. On the one hand, the narrator sees himself as an author or a director of a play and finds "a rare intellectual joy, the oddest secret exultation, in feeling her [Lady John] begin instantly to play the part I had attributed to her in the irreducible drama" (p. 80). On the other hand, the characters may not be playing the parts he attributes to them, but simply playing a part, pretending in a way independent of and even opposed to his preordained plan. "Just this fine dishonesty of her eyes, moreover—the light of a part to play, the excitement (heaven knows what it struck me as being!) of a happy duplicity—may well have been what contributed most to her present grand air" (p. 170). Blackall justly comments, "Judging by these images, one might tentatively conclude that the narrator is both dignified and detached despite his excessive self-confidence; that his inquiry is essentially serious despite the fact that, pursued in a given social context, it may have comic or pedestrian implications" (1965, p. 77). Even if he is wrong, his intentions are of a high order.

However, opposed to the elevating clusters there are words and images which degrade the search and relegate it to the level of playing a game, snuffing, prying, and hunting. The narrator and Obert are "playing [a] game" (p. 58); Long comes to him for "the high sport" (p. 119); with Mrs. Briss he feels that "we shall 'burn', as they say in hide-and-seek" (p. 39); and in his "own inner precincts" he tosses and catches a ball (p. 125). Seen as a game, his quest is trivialized. Seen as the activity of a prying newspaperman, it becomes positively unpleasant; there are scenes, he thinks, in which "any preposterous acuteness" might suffer "such a loss of dignity as overtakes the newspaperman kicked out" (p. 114).[6] The unpleasant aspect is maintained in images like "I was on the scent of something ultimate" (p. 30), "I seem to snuff up . . . the sense of a discovery to be made" (p. 35), and becomes more menacing in images of hunt and prey. "Discretion," the narrator meditates, "played an odd part when it simply left one more attached, morally, to one's prey" (p. 74). The prey is May Server, who is again described in similar terms when the narrator approaches her in the wood and feels "as if I were trapping a bird or stalking a fawn" (p. 98).

Doubly Directed Clues

Three kinds of doubly directed clues can be found in *The Sacred Fount*: psychological, causative, and linguistic.

What is open to two interpretations in the psychological clues are the real or imputed hidden motives behind what is or seems a straightforward statement. The "psychologist" is invariably the narrator; the stimulus, a character's repudiation of the narrator's views. Whenever a character agrees with him, the narrator takes his words at face value and rejoices in the confirmation. But when a character repudiates his hypothesis, the narrator immediately turns the searchlight from the statement itself to the speaker, and indulges in an analysis of the possible psychological reasons for the repudiation. Thus, in addition to the balance between characters' confirmations and repudiations of the narrator's view, the repudiations themselves become doubly directed as a result of the (never conclusive) psychological interpretation given to them by the narrator. To justify the "psychological twist," the narrator usually draws our attention to a strangeness in his interlocutor's behavior which aroused his suspicion. Long denies the change in Briss "with some sharpness," with "impatience," and seems "uneasy" throughout the discussion (pp. 30, 31, 32). May Server summons to her defense "the heart-breaking facial contortion . . . by which she imagined herself to represent the pleasant give-and-take of society" (p. 109). Ford Obert denies his responsibility in a manner which the narrator again characterizes as "uneasy" (p. 149), and Mrs. Brissenden is "nervous" in the last interview (p. 168).

Why the sharpness? Why the impatience? Why the nervousness and uneasiness? Clutching at these external signs, the narrator inwardly imputes insincerity to his interlocutor. If Long feels uneasy, "this was exactly a proof of his being what Mrs. Briss, at the station, had called cleverer" (p. 31). In other words, Long does see the change in Briss, but chooses to pretend to have noticed nothing. "To be so tortuous, he must have had a reason" (p. 32). The reason, apparently, is his realization that just as poor Briss pays for Grace Brissenden's bloom, someone must be sacrificed to his own amazing improvement. It is in self-protection that Long denies the change in Guy Brissenden, and his denial is thus made to confirm not only the narrator's view of Briss but also his impression of Long's new-found cleverness. But is Long tortuous? Does he necessarily pretend to see nothing, or does he see no change because there is no change to be seen? His conversation with the narrator offers equal evidence for both possibilities, and again in the form of a zigzag sequence. The narrator tries to test Long's frankness by dropping a hint and then pausing "long enough to let his curiosity operate if his denial had been sincere." "But," he concludes, "it hadn't. His curiosity never operated" (p. 31). A little later the narrator drops another hint, this time in connection with Mrs. Brissenden's transformation, and Long "showed as relieved to be able to see what I meant" (p. 32). So perhaps he really saw no change in Guy Brissenden? The pendulum swings again in the other direction when the narrator comments that Long had no reason to "show as relieved," for "that wasn't at all what I meant" (p. 32). Is Long then in the dark about Mrs. Brissenden as well? No sooner is the possibility suggested than it is dispelled by the narrator's formulation of what he did mean which, it now transpires, is not substantially different from what Long thought he meant (p. 32). When he perceives, he perceives correctly and expresses his perceptions. Perhaps, then, he really perceived nothing wrong with poor Briss? If so, what is the cause of his uneasiness and impatience? There are two possible answers to this question. The first is the one explicitly offered by the narrator, namely the strain of lying and playing a part. The second possibility is also suggested by the narrator, but with no conscious awareness on his part. "I recognized after a little that if I had made him, without intention, uncomfortable, this was exactly a proof of his being what Mrs. Briss, at the station, had called cleverer" (p. 31). Rather than being a proof of his cleverness, Long's uneasiness may simply be a result of the narrator's relentless insistence, thus bringing to mind one interpretation of Flora's boat escapade in *The Turn of the Screw*. Long's failure to see the change in Briss (assuming for the moment that such change does exist) may also be ascribed to his stupidity, and would thus support Mrs. Brissenden's final contention that Long is the same prize fool he always was. For the narrator this is a nonexistent possibility, as it contradicts his basic assumption concerning the miracle of his interlocutor's intellectual improvement (see Krook 1967, p. 175).

Mrs. Server, Long's supposed fount, is also subject to the narrator's psychological speculations, and there is no knowing whether her mention of Obert (p. 47) is or is not a "legend," and, more complicatedly, whether her alleged dismissal of poor Briss (pp. 105–7) is sincere or insincere or even whether it occurs at all (these two scenes will be analyzed in detail under doubly directed *linguistic* clues).

It is again by imputation of insincerity that the narrator can turn Ford Obert's crucial withdrawal of confirmation into an exhilarating proof of the profundity of his own "plunges of insight" (p. 151). And again the conversation contains evidence for and against his interpretation. Obert's uneasiness (p. 149), like Long's, is double edged: it may argue either his anxious attempt to conceal his hypocrisy, or his exasperation with the narrator's endeavor to shift the responsibility to him and involve him again in "a chase of which I washed my hands" (p. 149). And as in the case of Long, the sequence offers evidence for both possibilities. At one moment Obert explains his avoidance of the narrator's eyes in a witty, commonsense way: "A man engaged in talk with a charming woman scarcely selects that occasion for winking at somebody else" (p. 149). Later he interprets the same evasion as intended "to mark for you the difference" (p. 162)—the difference between the disintegrating, pouncing May Server and the May Server who is now "all there." Following this statement Obert adds, "I was a little ashamed of myself. I had given her away to you, you know, rather, before" (p. 162). Should this suggest to us the possibility of his present views being an expiation of his shameful exposure of Mrs. Server rather than a rendering of literal truth?

"The meaning" of the grand meeting with Mrs. Briss is "so different from its form" (p. 188) not only because the narrator is not "properly honest" but also (the narrator believes) because, "She had come down to square me; she was hanging on to square me; she was suffering and stammering and lying; she was both carrying it grandly off and letting it desperately go: all, all to square me" (pp. 188–89). Is the tone of triumphant assurance a proof of the validity of his view, or is he protesting too much—too vehemently, even a trifle frenziedly ("all, all to square me")—to conceal from himself a want of confidence in his view?

The double-directedness of the final encounter with Mrs. Brissenden is maintained to the last sentence of the novel, thus making the end an evasion of an ending—an ingenious avoidance of tipping the scale for one or the other of the mutually exclusive interpretations by the sheer act of putting it in the winning position of the finale.

She had so had the last word that, to get out of its planted presence, I shook myself, as I had done before, from my thought. When once I had started to my room indeed—and to preparation for a livelier start as soon as the house should stir again—I almost breathlessly hurried. Such a last word—the word that put me altogether nowhere—was too unacceptable not to prescribe afresh that prompt test of escape to other air for which I had earlier in the evening seen so much reason. I *should* certainly never again, on the spot, quite hang together, even though it wasn't really that I hadn't three times her method. What I too fatally lacked was her tone. [P. 219]

This is a classical example of a "conclusion in which nothing is concluded": the narrator's cogitations can be read either as a sincere admission that his "palace of thought" had indeed come "tinkling to the ground" (Levy 1962b, p. 383), or "as an ironic comment on his midnight conversation with Grace" (Andreach 1962, pp. 197–216). If it is an admission of defeat, then the theory is "dead," and the narrator will be the butt of our retrospective reading of the novel. If, on the other hand, this is an ironic comment, the end is still open to two interpretations. Either the narrator is even now ignorant of his mistake, but the reader is not (Andreach 1962, p. 211), or both the narrator and the reader know his theory to be true and see Mrs. Brissenden's seeming victory as a cheap use of underhand techniques (Segal 1969, p. 166).

The juxtaposition between the narrator's method and Mrs. Brissenden's tone operates both "with" him and "behind his back." If we take the juxtaposition in accordance with the narrator's intention, we shall conclude that, far from being an admission of real defeat, the attribution of Mrs. Brissenden's victory to her tone simply means that the narrator is not half as insolent and brash as she is and would clearly scorn to use her own weapons. But we need not take the juxtaposition in this way alone. On the basis of the frequent "psychological twists" administered by the narrator to his interlocutors' statements, we should not put aside the possibility that Mrs. Brissenden's tone, however brash and insolent, may nevertheless express the objective truth of what she articulates, and that the narrator finds it easier to attribute her victory to tone, an external and often deceptive element, than to veracity. "Method," the term juxtaposed with "tone," is also open to two interpretations. While it may indeed be what the narrator takes it to be, namely the way of attaining the truth, it can also be, and especially in *The Sacred Fount,* a self-contained procedure, a symmetrical and beautifully balanced superstructure which (alas) may be subject to "the wretched accident of its weak foundation" (p. 214). The narrator's having "three times her method" may actually be his main weakness, and the reader may wish to draw this adverse conclusion from his self-congratulatory penultimate sentence. Tone and method juxtaposed still "put us altogether nowhere," and the ambiguity is maintained to the last sentence of the novel.

The imputation of insincerity is one way of putting in doubt the validity of a conflicting view. Another way is the postulation of inferior intelligence on the part of the dissenter. This is the treatment given to Lady John's "clumsier curiosity" (p. 125), whose potentially upsetting ideas the narrator treats as "too commonplace for me to judge it useful to gather them in" (p. 132). That her "commonplace ideas" about May Server coincide with those of the perceptive observer, Ford Obert, is taken not as proof of her perceptiveness but rather of the imperceptiveness of Obert's revised view: "My wonder came from the fact that Lady John had also found Mrs. Server all right, and Lady John had a vision as closed as Obert's was open. It didn't suit my book for both these observers to have been affected in the same way" (p. 160). Thus, not only the direct repudiations but also the indirect ones are twisted against themselves by the narrator. And as in the direct repudiations, the narrator's twist here is not conclusive, for the same argument can also suggest that Lady John's vision is as open as Obert's.

As in *The Turn of the Screw,* the doubly directed causative clues call into question the relationship between sequence and consequence. In *The Sacred Fount* the sequence is that of the narrator's thoughts and their "materialization," and the double-edgedness is created by the age-old problem of whether *post hoc ergo propter hoc.* The narrator suggests it is. The reader may have some reservations.

Seeing Lady John with poor Briss, the narrator speculates that, "She had held out on the possibility that Mr. Long—whom one *could* without absurdity sit in an arbour with—might have had some happy divination of her plight" (p. 82). His "intuition" immediately proves true. "Well, the 'proof' I just alluded to was that I had not sat with my friends five minutes before Gilbert Long turned up" (p. 82). While this may indeed be a proof, it may also be mere coincidence.

A similar situation recurs when the narrator divines (or thinks he divines) that "it was to alight on poor Briss that May Server had come out" (p. 99), and not long afterwards poor Briss comes to join them (p. 111).

The sight of Gilbert Long and Grace Brissenden "in familiar colloquy" is so startling, because "I had a few minutes before, in the interest of the full roundness of my theory, actually been missing it" (p. 129). But this time the argument from coincidence is not left to the reader. It is the narrator himself who says, "Yet—now that I did have it there—why should it be vivid, why stirring, why a picture at all? Was *any* temporary collocation, in a house so encouraging to sociability, out of the range of nature?" (p. 129).

As if to complicate matters even further, the use of sequence to *dis*prove a relationship is also made double edged. Watching Mrs. Server, who "confessed with every turn of her head to a part in a relation" (p. 69), the narrator and Mrs. Briss are convinced that the man behind the tree is Gilbert Long. But a minute later the object of their curiosity "offered himself to our united, to our confounded, anxiety once more as poor Briss" (p. 69). Does this mean that Mrs. Server's demeanor did not really confess to a part in a relation, or does it imply the reality of her relation with Guy Brissenden? Both possibilities are suggested in the sequence of one sentence: on the one hand the narrator feels inclined to say with Mrs. Briss, "Whoever he is, they're in deep!" but on the other hand, and in the same sentence, he recognizes that his grounds for such a statement would be "quite as recklessly, as fantastically constructive as hers" (p. 69).

As in the other works, double-directedness is reinforced by linguistic clues of different kinds, and in *The Sacred Fount* these are richer and more complex. Ambiguous verbal elements can appear either in the language expressing the narrator's own thoughts or in his rendering of dialogues between himself and the other characters. I have already pointed out that all the dialogues in the novel, even those which appear between quotation marks, are rendered by the narrator, often in his own language. And yet, there are differences between the use of doubly directed linguistic clues in reported dialogues and the employment of the same device in the language expressing the narrator's own descriptions, speculations, and analyses.

In the language expressing the narrator's thoughts, doubly directed clues usually operate to counter the meaning intended by the narrator with a contrasted alternative meaning hinted at "behind the narrator's back," though, ironically, through his own words. Particularly suitable for this purpose are verbs of perception, as they have subjective as well as objective connotations. To illustrate, when the narrator affirms that Obert's "eyes indeed most seemed to throw over to me" an expression of surprise at Long's intelligent interpretation of the picture (p. 49), are we to understand that the professional painter is indeed surprised and that his eyes unmistakably express his amazement; or are we to take "seem" as registering a figment of the narrator's imagination and believe that Obert's eyes expressed nothing of the sort? Stronger in the suggestion of delusion are expressions like "might have seemed to ask" (p. 19), in which the subjective sense of "seem" is intensified— made doubly subjective, as it were—by the grammatical mood. That "seeming" may be a function of the distorting vision of the beholder is again intimated by Mrs. Brissenden in the following snatch of conversation with the narrator:

"Long *isn't* what he seems?"
"Seems to whom?" she asked sturdily. [P. 181]

Similarly, when the narrator interprets what he believes to be Mrs. Server's reaction to his mention of Guy Brissenden, the verb *to appear* arouses in us a double attitude toward his impressions:

"Poor Briss?" her face and manner *appeared* suddenly to repeat . . . Wherein did poor Briss so intimately concern her? [P. 106; my italics]

Does the appearance correspond to a reality, is it pretense, or is it present only to the narrator's imagination?

To read into also has the potential of double-directedness: "I read into Lady John's wonderful manner—which quite clamoured, moreover, for an interpretation—all that was implied in the lesson I had extracted from other portions of the business" (p. 80). Is he "reading into" in the sense of interpreting the data, or is he "reading into" in the sense of imposing conclusions derived "from other portions of the business" on Lady John's "wonderful manner"?[7]

In describing May Server's behavior in the scene cited above, the narrator says, "I quickly saw in it, from the moment I had got my point of view, more fine things than ever" (p. 107). "From the moment I had got my point of view" may simply mean "from the moment I began to see my way," "from the moment I found out how to look at things," and the narrator's words will then express an intuitive perception of truth. But the same expression may also suggest—behind the narrator's back—a dangerous flaw in his approach, for he starts with a point of view and not with the facts in front of him. Interestingly enough, a similar twist occurs in Mrs. Brissenden's argument concerning May Server's role as the hidden source of Long's intellectual improvement. Having explained her view, she adds, "When one knows it, it's all there. But what's that vulgar song?—'You've got to know it first' " (p. 60). Later she adds, "but when one has had the 'tip' one looks back and sees things in a new light" (p. 63). What she says in order to reinforce her theory can also undermine it from within by pointing to the circularity involved in its formation; first you have to know it, and then you will certainly find it so.

The use of oxymora is another way of inviting two contrasted readings, making one component suggest the existence of the phenomenon reported by the narrator, while the other component operates to put it in doubt. This is the case of expressions like "the gentleman *mutely named* between us" (p. 82); "what, in the way of *suppressed communication,* passed between us" (p. 102); and "some such *mute address*" (p. 105; my italics). Are we to put the emphasis on "named," "communication," and "address," as the narrator would like us to do, and see the situation as some kind of supraverbal exchange of comments, or are we, on the other hand, to stress "mutely," "suppressed," and "mute" and conclude that there was no "real" communication at all?

An oxymoron can express not only the possible lack of correspondence between the actual and the imaginary, but also the discrepancy between the real and the feigned. Thus the narrator speaks of the "special shade of innocence" (p. 178) which is, as he believes, Mrs. Brissenden's lie. And he himself uses expressions like "candidly" (p. 172) and "sincerely" (p. 173) while cold-bloodedly lying to Mrs. Brissenden.[8]

Literary allusions and idiomatic expressions in the narrator's language also tend to take effect both "with" him and "behind his back." These doubly directed literary and cultural clues in *The Sacred Fount* appear as casual or seemingly casual allusions in their immediate context, and they are all concentrated in the crucial last conversations with Ford Obert and Mrs. Brissenden. The problem of how much can legitimately be made of casual allusions lies beyond the scope of this study. However, I do wish to make the point that the concentration of the doubly directed allusions in the last part of the novel suggests the legitimacy of making as much of them as the context allows. For by the time the reader has reached this part of the novel, his attention has been so engaged by every detail, in case it should prove a definitive clue, that he is hardly permitted to treat anything as merely casual. Thus, allusions that would perhaps carry less weight at earlier stages of the novel are now endowed with particular significance. At this stage, I believe, the reader is encouraged to ponder over the implications of each echo or allusion, and it is by so doing that he discovers their doubly directed character.

Challenging Ford Obert to destroy his now completed theory, the narrator says, "*Mon siège est fait*—a great glittering crystal palace. How many panes will you reward me for amiably sitting up with you by smashing?" (p. 145). All the French idiom means on the surface is that the narrator is here presenting a theory about which he has made up his mind to his entire satisfaction. But, as Littré's dictionary tells us, the expression originated in an "allusion à l'abbé Verlot, qui, ayant longtemps attendu en vain des notes exactes sur le siège de Rhodes, en avait terminé l'histoire avant qu'elles arrivassent et se contenta de dire: J'en suis fâché, mon siège est fait" (1963). What this anecdote dramatizes is an opinion formed before the facts; hence the expression "mon siège est fait" can have the connotation of an ill-formed opinion. The narrator has only the first meaning in mind (that is, "my opinion is formed"), but by making him use the French expression Henry James intimates that his opinion may be ill-formed and baseless. Or is the narrator self-ironic, forestalling Obert's objections by a note of self-deprecation? In any case, his opinion imprisons the other characters as well as himself, enchaining his thoughts to its own self-contained logic, as the independent connotations of the word *siège* suggest.

On the same page the narrator describes his theory as "Sorry stuff, perhaps—a poor thing but mine own!" The second part of this sentence is a quotation from Shakespeare's *As You Like It* (5. 4. 55–56). The expression has since passed into the language, and may perhaps not be recognized as a quotation from the play. Nevertheless, a reader who does remember that these are Touchstone's words to the Duke Senior, introducing Audrey, his future wife, will be able to activate various aspects of the Shakespearean line in the new context. The personality of the original speaker is brought to bear upon the quoter, and Touchstone, we know, is a somewhat uncertain personality. Sometimes he seems a choric wise fool, a possessor of real insight, a touchstone. In other scenes he becomes a different kind of touchstone; not being precious in himself, he serves as a contrastive measure of the preciousness of others. It is mainly in the repartees with Rosalind that Touchstone's wit dwindles and his insights are shown as highly pedestrian. The implications of this for the two possible attitudes toward the narrator of *The Sacred Fount* are too clear to need explication. As for the quotation itself, unlike "mon siège est fait," Touchstone's description of Audrey is not ambiguous in the original context but becomes so in *The Sacred Fount*. When the narrator describes his theory as perhaps a "poor thing but mine own," are we to take his words as a conscious or partly conscious admission of the dubious validity of his theory, and link this deprecation to the "sorry stuff" which precedes the Shakespearean line? Or are we intended to take the expression as it is often taken in colloquial use and detect a note of pride, of false modesty, in the narrator's belittling declaration?

In measuring his possible guilt for having communicated a consciousness to Mrs. Brissenden and thereby having made her lie to protect herself, the narrator reflects, "And I could only say to myself that this was the price—the price of the secret success, the lonely liberty and the intellectual joy. There were things that for so private and splendid a revel—that of the exclusive king with his Wagner opera—I could only let go, and the special torment of my case was that the condition of light, of the satisfaction of curiosity and of the attestation of triumph, was in this direct way the sacrifice of feeling" (p. 203). "The exclusive king with his Wagner opera" refers to Ludwig II of Bavaria, who was Wagner's patron and used to have "private theatricals" of Wagner's operas with himself as sole spectator. Ludwig II is also known for his mania for building, and in this, as well as in his "splendid isolation," he resembles the narrator of *The Sacred Fount*, who attempts to build "a perfect palace of thought." In June 1886 Ludwig was declared insane.

While the narrator's comparison focuses on the "private and splendid revel" as the common quality between him and the Bavarian king, the reader may want to extend the comparison further and transfer Ludwig's madness to the narrator. Thus, behind the narrator's back (or is there again a note of self-irony?), his private revel can be seen as a symptom of insanity, and his palace of thought as a product of mad fancy. But the double-directedness of this reference is even more complex. "Yet, this inference about the quality of the narrator's argument need not rule out the possibility that his palace of thought is to be understood as having a viable life of its own. Ludwig's palaces still stand despite their wild origins. And might not the narrator's palace of thought exist as a work of art exists, irrespective of whether it corresponds to literal fact?" (Blackall 1965, p. 94).

Popular descriptions of Ludwig in England at the end of the nineteenth century vary between sentimental defense of a misunderstood artistic genius and ironic exposure of a megalomaniac crackpot. It is strange that Blackall, who quotes many of these descriptions, finally draws an unequivocal conclusion: "Hence it is unlikely that James would have made this allusion if he had wished the narrator to be taken seriously as a type of the artist, or his theory to stand as a work of art, because at best Ludwig is an ambiguous figure and at worst he is a ridiculous one" (p. 113). But, to follow her own argument, it is also unlikely that James would have made this allusion had he wished the narrator to be taken only as a ridiculous madman, for "at best Ludwig is an ambiguous figure." It is the coexistence of conflicting attitudes toward Ludwig that made James introduce the allusion, thereby raising again the unanswerable questions: Is the narrator an artist, or is he rather an *artiste manqué?* Is his activity allied to madness, or does it yield the kind of insight that so-called normal people are incapable of?

The "mania for building" which the narrator of *The Sacred Fount* shares with King Ludwig of Bavaria provides him with two palace metaphors which recall a well-known literary text. "Remember . . . that you're costing me a perfect palace of thought!" the narrator pleads with Mrs. Brissenden in their last interview (p. 214). The description of his theory as "a palace of thought" is significantly contrasted with Mrs. Brissenden's previous admonition that all he builds are "houses of cards" (p. 181). It is also significantly reminiscent of the title of one of Tennyson's most famous poems, "The Palace of Art" (1832). Like the poet-speaker in Tennyson's poem who builds his soul a beautiful and artificial palace where she "would live alone unto herself," the narrator of James's novel erects a "frail but quite sublime" structure of the beauty which "*I* alone was magnificently and absurdly aware—everyone else was benightedly out of it." (p. 127).[9] I have already remarked that the narrator often speaks of his theory as a work of art, but doing so with the help of the Tennysonian echo suggests a possible limitation of a self-contained theory which will not stand up to a confrontation with reality (see, for example, the ball image on page 125). For the soul in "The Palace of Art" was very happy in her artistic ivory tower for three years only. "On the fourth she fell." She could no longer stand her seclusion.

> When she would think where'er she turned her
> sight
> The airy hand confusion wrought,
> Wrote "Mene, mene" and divided quite
> The kingdom of her thought.

Incidentally, "the kingdom of her thought" is another expression adopted by James's narrator in congratulating himself for "the kingdom of thought I had won" (p. 176). Tennyson's poem suggests that a kingdom of thought may be insubstantial, and that art divorced from life may lead to despair. Rather than offering a clear-cut solution to the dilemma of art and life, the poem dramatizes its complexities. Its end is characteristically open: the soul abandons her palace, but commands that it should not be pulled down, for

> Perchance I may return with others there
> When I have purged my guilt.

The echo from Tennyson thus helps to make the narrator's expression doubly directed.[10]

All the echoes and allusions discussed above appear in the narrator's descriptions of his own theory. There is, however, one allusion that modifies not only the narrator's theory but also Mrs. Brissenden's anticipated showdown. The allusion occurs in a conversation between the narrator and Ford Obert just before the grand nocturnal encounter with Mrs. Brissenden. To the narrator's question whether the place is "wholly cleared" of the ladies, Obert answers, "Save, it struck me, so far as they may have left some 'black plume as a token'." And the narrator completes the quotation, saying, "Not, I trust, . . . of any 'lie' their 'soul hath spoken!' But not one of them lingers?" (p. 144). That the sentences about the black plume and the lie are a direct quotation from a literary text, not simply an evocation or an echo, and that both Obert and the narrator are conscious of quoting such a text is indicated by the inverted commas surrounding the borrowed expressions. The quotation is from the seventeenth stanza of E.A. Poe's "The Raven."

> "Be that word our sign of parting,
>   bird or fiend!" I shrieked, upstarting—
> "Get thee back into the tempest and the
>   Night's Plutonian shore!
> Leave no black plume as a token of that
>   lie thy soul hath spoken!
> Leave my loneliness unbroken!—quit the
>   bust above my door!
> Take thy beak from out my heart, and
>   take thy form from off my door!"
>   Quoth the Raven, "Nevermore."[11]

Occurring just before the narrator's attempt to find out whether Mrs. Brissenden has lingered, the quotation may first be taken as an anticipatory hint that she is going to lie. But the context of "The Raven" may also encourage us to relate the quotation to the narrator's subjective view of things, and conclude that the narrator expects Mrs. Brissenden to lie— which, of course, is different from asserting that Mrs. Brissenden is in effect going to lie. The lines quoted above appear after one of the raven's ominous "Nevermore's," this time in reply to the speaker's poignant question about the possibility of meeting his deceased beloved in another world. From a realistic point of view, the raven's answer is, unfortunately, no lie, and the speaker's accusation can be seen as rationalization on his part, as an attempt to talk himself into believing that he can reasonably hope to see Lenore once more. Similarly, the narrator of *The Sacred Fount* can be viewed as imputing deception to Mrs. Brissenden in order to shield himself from a recognition of his own mistake. But there is a sense in which the raven's words in the poem are close to a lie, and another turn of the screw is thus given to the quotation in its Jamesian context. After all, the raven does not really answer the speaker's question. It does not mean anything by its reiterated "nevermore", for it is the only word the bird can say, the only answer it can give to any question. This can also be related to Mrs. Brissenden, suggesting that her final declaration is a studied speech and not a real answer to the narrator's theory. As with the other allusions, the conflicting possibilities again face each other in an insoluble deadlock.

Whereas the doubly directed linguistic clues in the narrator's own language always refer to something outside themselves (for example, the narrator's theory), in the dialogues the ambiguous element is itself the subject of discussion. An interesting example of this kind of ambiguity is the use of exophoric pronouns with a double situational referent. Three exophoric pronouns enact the ambiguity of three central scenes in *The Sacred Fount*. Knocking away the assumption of the existence of a common focus between speaker and addressee—an assumption which usually underlies the use of exophoric pronouns—James makes it possible for each interlocutor to take the pronoun to refer to someone else. This does not only lead to a misunderstanding between the characters, but also simultaneously reinforces the two contradictory interpretations of the novel. If we take the pronoun to refer to one character, it offers evidence in support of one interpretation; if, on the other hand, we take it to refer to the other situational possibility, the opposite interpretation seems confirmed. Exophoric pronouns thus reenact at the verbal level the main structural technique of the novel, namely the omission of a central piece of information and the supplying of mutually exclusive clues for filling in the gap. The first of these scenes appears at the beginning of chapter 4. The narrator and Mrs. Server are discussing Guy Brissenden and Lady John. Mrs. Server confidentially opines that Guy Brissenden is interested only in Lady John (p. 47) and that Lady John, on her part, does not even give him a thought because "there's only one person she's interested in." Who this undefined "one" is she does not say, probably because she assumes a common focus between herself and the narrator ("Isn't it rather marked that there's only one person she's interested in?" she says [p. 47]). The narrator is "thoroughly at sea," and is convinced that the referent of the undefined "one" is Gilbert Long. At this point they reach "the great pictured saloon," and Mrs. Server replaces the undefined "one" by the seemingly defined exophoric "he": "Why, here he is!" If the narrator or the reader expected this exclamation to provide a solution he was completely mistaken, for the situation is a perfect dramatization of ambiguity. "Here he is!" says Mrs. Server, directing the narrator's attention to *two* men, Gilbert Long and Ford Obert. Which of the two is the referent of the pronoun? In order to test his hypothesis that Long is the man, the narrator mentions Obert, to which May Server answers yes with a beautiful look and a laugh. There are two possibilities, then, and how are we to choose between them? Choice, although impossible, is important for the whole theory, as both Lady John and May Server have been associated with Long. If the narrator is right in supposing that Long is the hidden referent of the exophoric pronoun, this would support Mrs. Brissenden's initial (and later also final) view of the affair between him and Lady John. If, however, Obert is the man in whom Lady John is interested, it would discredit the Lady John-Gilbert Long relationship, but on the other hand it would reinforce the idea recently proposed by Grace Brissenden that there is something between May Server and Gilbert Long. This impression is reinforced by the narrator's mental qualification of her mention of Obert as a "legend"—a polite way of saying a "lie"—which enables her to keep Gilbert Long for herself. As we have seen, the imputation of insincerity to an interlocutor is one of the devices used to make motivation doubly directed. It is also a way of preventing a potential resolution of linguistic ambiguities from becoming conclusive.

The second example of an ambiguous exophoric pronoun occurs in another conversation between the narrator and Mrs. Server four chapters later. Sitting with Mrs. Server in a secluded spot, the narrator inwardly speculates about "the sense of common fate" (p. 104) which she must share with Guy Brissenden and the greater solace she could derive from Briss's company than from his own. In direct continuation of his thoughts he then turns to her, saying, "I parted with him some way from here, some time ago. I had found him in one of the gardens with Lady John; after which we came away together" (p. 105). Although it is clear that the narrator has only Briss in mind, the pronoun is open to two interpretations, both of which could accommodate the company of Lady John. This is why May Server "had had an uncertainty . . . as to whom I meant" (p. 105). *Him* could mean either Briss or Long, and in either case Mrs. Server would have a reason to worry about Lady John's company ("You found him with Lady John?"). If it is Long she is thinking of, the narrator's former interpretation of her expression, as indicative of the solace that only Briss can give, may prove wrong. But, on the other hand, her thinking of Long will confirm that part of the narrator's theory concerned with the relations between the two. If it is not Long but Briss she is thinking of, this may confirm his previous speculations, but the attempt on her part to conceal the referent may also suggest a different kind of relationship between her and Guy Brissenden. All this "happens" only in the narrator's mind. Mrs. Server says nothing apart from enigmatic short ejaculations: "Do you mean—a—do you mean—? . . . There are so *many* gentlemen!" (p. 106). The narrator finally specifies, "Poor Briss, you know, . . . is always in her clutches" (p. 106) —a specification which might have resolved the ambiguity. But it does not, for (in an analysis which actually belongs to doubly directed *psychological* clues), the narrator interprets her expression as saying, "Wherein did poor Briss so intimately concern her?" If this is a correct interpretation of her expression (which, of course, is left open), does she simply feel the mention of Briss, with whom she has no relationship, to be a disappointing anticlimax? And does this in turn confirm her relationship with Long? Or is she trying to conceal her bond with Briss, as the narrator supposes? ". . . the relation that had established itself between them *was,* for its function, a real relation, the relation of a fellowship in resistance to doom" (p. 107). If the narrator is right about the embarrassed concealment, this would be consistent also with a relationship that is "real" in a different sense, the sense later confirmed (though again not conclusively) by Mrs. Brissenden's affirmation that May Server made love to her husband. Bearing in mind the possible tenderness on Mrs. Server's part for the narrator himself, still another interpretation suggests itself: she does not mention any name in order to prevent the narrator, in whom she is really interested, from taking for granted her affection for any other man.

The third example of ambiguous pronouns is less complex, as in this instance the alternative interpretations are a result of a misunderstanding which is clear to both narrator and reader. The narrator informs Ford Obert that in a message sent with Guy Brissenden "she" expressed her wish to see him immediately. We know that "she" is Mrs. Brissenden, but Ford Obert does not know this and takes the pronoun to refer to May Server. The narrator recognizes his interlocutor's mistake quite late in the conversation, and even then does nothing to correct it: "I left him under this simple and secure impression that my appointment was with Mrs. Server" (p. 164). The interest of the misunderstanding is that it is because the message is delivered by poor Briss that Obert automatically associates it with Mrs. Server. Obert's reaction thus confirms (or seems to confirm) the bond between May Server and Guy Brissenden, though not, of course, the *nature* of the bond—whether they are bound by their common position as victims of their vampire spouses (the narrator's hypothesis), or whether they are lovers (Mrs. Briss's final explanation, or pseudo-explanation). The anticipated duplicity which the narrator imputes to the unnamed "she" coheres with his previous imputations of insincerity to both May Server and Grace Brissenden and need not be true of either.[12]

Closely related to ambiguous pronouns are doubly directed substitutions, of which there is only one example in *The Sacred Fount*. Having separated poor Briss from Lady John, the narrator perfunctorily apologizes to Guy, who answers frankly, "I'm glad you turned up. I wasn't especially amusing myself" (p. 84). This confirms the narrator's own view, and he therefore says self-confidently, "Oh, I think I know how little!" (p. 84). Briss now meets him half way, the narrator feels, with an incomplete "You 'know'?" (p. 84), to which he receives an even more self-confident answer, "Ah, . . . I know everything!" (p. 85). It is the interposition of the indefinite and all-embracing *everything* which makes the ambiguity of Brissenden's reply technically possible. "You know I decidedly have too much of that dreadful old woman?" asks Briss (p. 85). Without the interposition of *everything*, "that dreadful woman" would have unequivocally referred to Lady John, the subject of the previous discussion. But the word *everything* opens new possibilities, and the narrator takes "his disgusted allusion as to Mrs. Brissenden" (p. 85). Only later does he realize that Briss had only Lady John in mind. The substitution is not ambiguous to Guy Brissenden. It is only ambiguous to the narrator, and only for a short time. But for the reader the resolution of the ambiguity does not completely dispel the portentous possibility of Brissenden's having too much of his wife.

Another type of linguistic ambiguity is that arising out of an elliptical construction. In the first chapter of the novel, when Mrs. Brissenden tells the narrator that she had hardly recognized Gilbert Long, the narrator answers, "He hinted to me that he had not known you more easily" (p. 21). The second part of the comparison (than . . .) is omitted, and Mrs. Brissenden's ensuing question, "More easily than you did?" (p. 21), gives rise to two possible completions. Without her question we would have assumed the meaning to be "more easily than you [Mrs. Briss] had known him [Long]," but when the question is asked, the narrator's own failure to recognize Mrs. Brissenden is introduced into the picture. This occurs too early in the novel to contribute to the yet undeveloped central issue, and its effect is mainly one of compression, of bringing together three of the failures of recognition with which the novel begins.

The conversation between the narrator and poor Briss in chapter 7 provides a more significant example of ellipsis in the service of ambiguity. The subject of this delicate discussion is the special bond between Guy Brissenden and May Server. The narrator, as usual taking the lead, cautiously asks, "And isn't the matter also, after all, that you simply feel she desires you to be kind?" Brissenden's reply is short and enigmatic: "She does that. . . . It *is* that she desires me. She likes it." (p. 92). The ambiguity arises not from the existence of two possible completions of the ellipsis, but from the impossibility of deciding whether there is an ellipsis at all. "It *is* that she desires me" can read as a shortening of "It *is* that she desires me to be kind," and Brissenden's words will then confirm the narrator's view of the sympathy between the two victims. But the sentence may not be an ellipsis at all. With the strange emphasis on *is*, which requires a second stress on *desires*, Briss may be affirming that May Server simply desires him, an affirmation which will support his wife's final contention. The *it* in "She likes it" can replace both "my being kind to her" and "desiring me." The ambiguity in this conversation, not being commented on by either of the interlocutors, is consequently all for the reader.

Similar in this respect is the use of polysemies. The discussion between the narrator and Mrs. Server quoted above for its ambiguous pronouns starts with Mrs. Server's question, "Isn't he [Briss] curiously interesting?" (p. 46). The narrator is "too struck with her question for an immediate answer" because it seems so flatly to contradict his own view of Briss as dull and depleted, and if she is right, he must be wrong. On the other hand, if the narrator is right about Brissenden, Mrs. Server's failure to realize the complete absence of interest in him may prove either how deeply she is in love with him or how far her own disintegration has already gone, and may thus confirm another part of the narrator's theory. The adverb *curiously* suggests yet another possibility, for it does not only mean "in a way which deserves or excites curiosity" and "exquisitely," but also "strangely," "singularly," "queerly." Mrs. Server may be thinking of Briss as really interesting, and then either she is right and the narrator wrong about him; or she is wrong and the narrator right about both Brissenden and Mrs. Server herself. But she may also be thinking of Briss as interesting in a strange way, interesting as a phenomenon, and this would confirm the narrator's view of the depleted gentleman, but would simultaneously attenuate somewhat his conviction of Mrs. Server's tenderness for her fellow victim.

In the last interview with Mrs. Briss, the narrator compliments her on being an exciting adversary: ". . . pulling against you," he says, "also had its thrill. You defended your cause" (p. 178). While her "cause" may simply be her theory, it may also conceal a sly hint at her self-interest.

Like the doubly directed ellipses, not all polysemies are ambiguous only for the reader. Sometimes they are the focus of a misunderstanding between two characters, as in the following passage:

> "Good-night, Brissenden. I shall be gone tomorrow before you show."
> I shall never forget the way that, struck by my word, he let his white face fix me in the dusk. " 'Show'? *What* do I show?"
> I had taken his hand for farewell, and, inevitably laughing, but as the falsest of notes, I gave it a shake. "You show nothing! You're magnificent." [P. 159]

The narrator uses *show* in the sense of "appear," but poor Briss, whose main concern (according to the narrator's hypothesis) is not to let his sacrifice show, symptomatically takes the verb in its other sense. He would also, of course, take it in the other sense if what he was anxious not to "show" was (according to Mrs. Briss's account in the last scene) that he was being pursued by May Server.

The foregoing analysis of the ambiguity of *The Sacred Fount* and the techniques employed in its creation has concentrated on an examination of the application of the narrator's theory of the sacred fount to the four principals involved. But what about the substance of the theory, the idea which was the germ of the novel and which gave it its metaphoric title? (see James's *Notebooks*, 1961, pp. 150–51). The sacred fount theme, though overshadowed by the quasi-epistemological enquiry, successfully fuses some insights which, as Krook has indicated, are to be taken up again in James's later works.

> The insistence equally on the destructive power of passion, symbolized in the 'eating up' of the adoring by the adored, and on its creative power, expressed in the miraculous transformation of the adored by the selfless passion of the adoring; the view that a love which is grounded in passion is essentially sacrificial, and as such rich in the most 'sublime' beauty and pathos; the suggestion that the spring of all human energy is ultimately in the passions, and that passion therefore (and in particular sexual passion) is the sacred fount of all significant moral life; these are some of the themes subsumed, directly or indirectly, by the image of the sacred fount. [1967, p. 189]

The fount is a source of vitality and efflorescence for some characters, but at the same time, and as a necessary consequence, a source of depletion for others. It is a double-faced phenomenon of the kind poignantly described by James in the preface to *What Maisie Knew:* "No themes are so human as those that reflect for us, out of the confusion of life, the close connexion of bliss and bale, of the things that help with the things that hurt, so dangling before us for ever that bright hard medal, of so strange an alloy, one face of which is somebody's right and ease and the other somebody's pain and wrong" (in Blackmur, ed., 1962, p. 143).

Vocabulary, imagery, allusions, and tone all collaborate to create the double-edgedness of the sacred fount process. The terms chosen to describe it are taken from a world of noble, almost religious sacrifice on the one hand, and from a ruthless universe of vampires and blood-draining on the other: "They [Guy Brissenden and May Server] had truly been arrayed and anointed, they had truly been isolated, for their sacrifice" (p. 122), and, "Mrs. Briss had to get her new blood, her extra allowance of time and bloom, somewhere; and from whom could she so conveniently extract them as from Guy himself? She *has*, by an extraordinary feat of legerdemain, extracted them; and he, on his side, to supply her, has had to tap the sacred fount" (p. 34).

Images of blood-draining are not restricted to Mrs. Brissenden and Gilbert Long, the unconscious vampires according to the narrator's theory. The effect on the narrator himself of Brissenden's appearing, sacrificially, with his wife's message is also described as a filling-up process. It "renewed my sources and replenished my current" (p. 157). Does the narrator, then, drink from a spiritual sacred fount to the depletion of his victims, as Folsom and other critics suggest? (Folsom 1961, p. 140).

The victim's sacrifice often acquires tragic overtones, as in the description of May Server's disintegrating consciousness (p. 102). But it is also occasionally treated in a lighthearted tone, as in the image of the turkey and the greedy man (p. 34). or that of "administering" intellect "by the spoonful" (p. 23).[14]

A possible interchangeability of victim and victimizer is suggested by the allusion to the lips and the cheeks. Reflecting upon the Long-Server relationship, Mrs. Brissenden says, "It's only an excessive case, a case that in him happens to show as what the doctors call 'fine', of what goes on whenever two persons are so much mixed up. One of them always gets more out of it than the other. One of them—you know the saying—gives the lips, the other gives the cheek" (p. 66).

The saying is as old as Aristophanes's *The Frogs*—"There is always one who kisses and one who only allows the kiss" (1. 755); and its meaning is straightforward enough to make the narrator's "Yet the cheek profits too" surprising. For, as Mrs. Brissenden immediately points out, it's the cheek that profits most, it's the cheek that allows the kiss, that receives. The narrator's paradoxical interpretation is, I suggest, partly based on the biblical "He gives his cheek to him that smiteth him" (Lam. 3: 30) and "Whoever shall smite thee on the right cheek, turn to him the other too" (Matt. 5: 39). In these verses what the cheek receives is not a kiss but a blow, and therefore if it profits at all, it does so as a result of suffering (hence "yet"). The interesting suggestion behind this reversal is that although on the surface the "vampires" are obviously the benefiting party and the kiss may also be a vampire kiss, they may lose by gaining—lose in human and moral stature— and, in just the same proportion, the victims may become humanly and morally sublime by their very act of sacrifice and thus, in a profound sense, profit most. Victim and victimizer may both either prosper or decline. Physically, intellectually, and morally the transference of vitality is a double-edged process, associated on the one hand with "the innumerable legendary and poetic fountains of youth and love" (Melchiori 1965, p. 304) and on the other with the well of Archimago, Spenser's hypocritical villain (*Faerie Queene,* bk. 1. And see Folsom 1961, p. 144). The fount, then, is not only a source of plenitude for one character and of depletion for another; it also spells a paradoxical coexistence of growth and diminution for each party and is itself both a sacred stream of living water and a well "of somewhat dubious sanctity" (Folsom 1961, p. 144). Could there be an ambiguity in the adjective itself, an indissoluble coexistence of *sacred* in the sense of "holy" and *sacred* in the rarer sense of "accursed"?[15] Could that be the ambiguity not only of *The Sacred Fount* but also of the sacred fount?

Beyond Ambiguity?

A hunt after clues does not tell us whether the narrator's theory and its application to the Newmarch guests are profound truths or mere moonshine. It only shows how perfect the ambiguity is. And yet while constantly frustrating our detectivelike search for an unequivocal solution, it also creates an urge to stop the perpetual oscillation and break out of the labyrinth. Where is the way out? May we not be on the wrong track when confined to clues dispersed in the story itself? Should we not stop grouping evidence for and against the narrator's theory and start examining its foundations from a point of view external to itself though actually underlying it and suggested by it? This is what Blackall does—though undeclaredly and again one-sidedly—when she enumerates the flaws in the narrator's theory:

> Finally, then, the reader may distrust the narrator not only because he leans heavily on analogy as a basis for conviction; advances a theory that is not supported by other characters, themselves clever persons . . . and forms his new estimate of Long on slight evidence, namely an instance of his being well-mannered; but also because the narrator maintains a position that is logically suspect. He commits the fallacy of unnecessary complexity in an inductive inquiry, and it is legitimate to challenge him on this ground because he prides himself on his logic. [1965, p. 53. See also pp. 47, 50, 51, 52]

While support (or lack of support) from the other characters and evidence (or its absence) for Long's improvement refer us back to the text and consequently to the ambiguity we have demonstrated,[16] the points about complexity and analogy summon judgments from the outside, from the discipline of logic. No sooner is *outside* mentioned than we are bound to realize that in *The Sacred Fount* the *outside* is made *inside*. James has ingeniously introduced criteria for logical judgment into the novel and has even more ingeniously rendered their validity ambiguous. Thus, the attempt to examine the foundations of the narrator's theory from a point of view external to itself finds itself again enclosed within the text.

As Blackall suggests, the narrator does indeed complicate matters, and we often want to check his cogitations by plain common sense. This is particularly so when his logical reasoning is taken to an extreme. The naturalness of Mrs. Server and Long, he says, is "the only precaution worth speaking of" (p. 48); Long's stupidity is only "a represented, a fictive ineptitude" (p. 202), which actually makes him doubly acute; the unusual separation of Lord Lutley and Mrs. Froome "offered somehow the relief of a suggestive analogy," in the light of which the exceptional "juxtaposition" of May Server and Gilbert Long can be explained. However, the reader may feel that the naturalness of Mrs. Server and Gilbert Long need not be a precaution at all but rather a proof of the absence of a relationship; Long's stupidity may be nothing more than downright stupidity and the Lutley-Froome inverse analogy is plainly ridiculous as proof. Such criticism is valid and is actually built into the narrative itself by James. Having once argued that naturalness is "the only precaution worth speaking of," the narrator later brings it as proof of the *absence* of relations (p. 63). Another of the narrator's complex explanations is commonsensically criticized by Ford Obert in the passage already quoted about winking in the company of a charming lady (p. 149). But the argument from commonsense is not only incorporated into the novel. It is also made inconclusive within it. Obert's commonsensical answer, we have already seen, is later discarded in favor of a more complex interpretation of his behavior, and Mrs. Briss, who becomes at the end the representative of commonsense, earlier sees the complex as truer to reality than the commonsense. She interprets the quick parting of Long and Mrs. Server as a proof "that they're afraid to be seen" (p. 62), rather than as a straightforward indication that they simply have nothing more to say to each other. And a little later, when the narrator commonsensically points out that the man beside May Server in the tree was not Long, Mrs. Briss turns this possible blow into a subtle proof of her point. "We shouldn't have been treated to the scene if it *had* been. What could she possibly have put poor Briss there for but just to show it wasn't?" (p. 71). The narrator's opponents, we have seen, also "commit the fallacy of unnecessary complexity in an inductive inquiry," and if his view is to be discredited on this count, so are theirs, leaving us again without a view to endorse. Moreover, commonsense may not yield the most satisfactory or true results; it is not an infallible touchstone in complex situations.

So much for commonsense. What about analogy? The all-embracing analogy in the narrator's theory is composed of balancing opposites and parallels. The two members of each couple are opposed to each other: Mrs. Brissenden's second bloom and beauty are contrasted with her husband's physical depletion and results from it. Likewise, Long's intellectual improvement is contrasted with the unknown lady's reduction to idiocy and dependent on it. The two couples parallel each other; in both one of the parties draws his (or her) vitality from the other, although—another contrast within the parallel —in one couple the benefiting party is a woman (Mrs. Briss) and in the other it is a man (Gilbert Long). The sympathy between the supposed victims (May Server and Guy Brissenden) is also paralleled by the affinity of the victimizers (Mrs. Briss and Gilbert Long). A "change back" of any of the participants would necessitate a parallel reversion of the others:

> If *he* [Long] "changed back," wouldn't Grace Brissenden change by the same law? And if Grace Brissenden did, wouldn't her husband? Wouldn't the miracle take the form of the rejuvenation of that husband? Would it, still by the same token, take the form of *her* becoming very old, becoming if not as old as her husband, at least as old, as one might say, as herself? Would it take the form of her becoming dreadfully plain—plain with the plainness of mere stout maturity and artificial preservation? And if it took this form for the others, which would it take for May Server? Would she, at a bound as marked as theirs, recover her presence of mind and her lost equipment? [P. 136]

Exceptional behavior on the part of one couple can be explained by the opposite yet equally unusual conduct on the part of another. The unexpected copresence of May Server and Gilbert Long is explained away by the surprising separation of Lord Lutley and Mrs. Froome: "What I could directly clutch at was that if the exception did prove the rule in the one case it might equally prove it in the other" (p. 117).

It is by "the torch of [his] analogy" that the narrator groups the facts "into a larger mystery (and thereby a larger "law")" (p. 30), and analogy, says Blackall, "to begin with, is not proof" (1965, p. 51). Analogy, the narrator himself also says, may not be proof, and another of the external criteria thus finds itself "internalized." The crucial passage has already been quoted, but because of its centrality it is worth repeating here. "These opposed couples balanced like bronze groups at the two ends of a chimney-piece, and the most I could say to myself in lucid deprecation of my thought was that I mustn't take them equally for granted merely *because* they balanced. Things in the real had a way of not balancing; it was all an affair, this fine symmetry, of artificial proportion" (p. 130).

However, if we conclude from this that James unequivocally agrees with the French adage "comparaison n'est pas raison" we shall find ourselves neglecting a great deal of evidence to the contrary. As in the case of commonsense, analogy is used not only by the narrator but also by the other characters. Mrs. Brissenden's final theory also groups the characters into analogous couples (Long-Lady John; Briss-May Server), and it does so on the basis of the very theory which it rejects. "On the very system you yourself [the narrator] laid down. When we took him for brilliant, she couldn't be. But now that we see him as he is—." The narrator appropriately completes her statement of analogy by a symmetrical sentence, "We can only see her also as *she* is?" (p. 209). The interpretation hinted at by Ford Obert and developed by Blackall is also based on analogy, and it is Obert, in fact, who at one stage finds the narrator's analogy "dazzling." "It's a jolly idea—a torch in the darkness; and do you know what I've done with it? I've held it up, I don't mind telling you, to just the question of the change, since it interests you, in Mrs. Server. If you've got your mystery I'll be hanged if I won't have mine. If you've got your Brissendens I shall see what I can do with *her*. You've given me an analogy, and I declare I find it dazzling. I don't see the end of what may be done with it" (p. 56. See also pp. 152–53, 156). It is true that like Mrs. Brissenden Obert later repudiates the narrator's view, but their repudiations are a necessary balance to their initial enthusiastic acceptance (necessary, I mean, for the ambiguity), and they are further complicated by the contestants' own use of analogy and, of course, by the "psychological twist" given by the narrator.

Opposites and parallels go far beyond the formation of the narrator's theory. They become a prominent quality of his style, the staple of his thought and expression. Perhaps an examination of the stylistic symmetries will give us a clue as to the attitude we are meant to adopt toward the use of analogy. As the narrator's style abounds in symmetries of various kinds, I shall have to confine myself to a few examples of each.

Let us start with the pairs of opposites. First, there are those which convey the opposites in the theory and which, being a necessity of the subject matter, may not be strictly stylistic. For example, the change in Mrs. Brissenden is originally described in the following way: "What I had mainly remembered was that she had been *rather ugly*. At present she was *rather handsome*" (p. 19).[17] Her husband's depletion is a necessary result of her surprising rejuvenation: "Given his wife's *bloated* state, his own *shrunken* one was what was to have been predicated" (p. 58). May Server's condition is such "that if she didn't *get better* she surely *must get worse*" (p. 78). And the difference between the splendor of the one lady and the disintegration of the other is described in another series of contrasts: "What was actually before me was the positive pride of life and expansion, the amplitude of conscious action and design; not the *arid channel forsaken* by the *stream*, but the *full-fed river sweeping* to the sea, the volume of water, the stately current, the flooded banks into which the source had swelled" (p. 171). If at the end May Server is "all right," then Long would logically have to be "all wrong" (p. 161); and if the narrator is "an intelligent man gone wrong," as Mrs. Briss says, then Long is "a stupid man gone right" (p. 201).

More significant from a stylistic point of view is the use of opposites to describe phenomena not directly related to the theory. "It was an occasion, I felt—the prospect of a large party—to look out at the station for others, *possible friends* and even *possible enemies*, who might be going. Such premonitions, it was true, *bred fears* when they *failed to breed hopes*" (p. 17). The contrast between "friends" and "enemies" is reinforced by the repetition of the adjective *possible* in connection with both. Similarly, the "negated repetition" of "bred" versus "failed to breed" emphasizes the contrast between "fears" and "hopes." All this is said before the narrator has even the vaguest glimmer of his theory and may therefore be indicative of something inherent in his thought habits. A little later, when he is struck by the various changes, he wants to compare notes with Ford Obert, about whom he says, "Nothing, naturally, was easier than to turn him on the question of *the fair* and *the foul, type* and *character, weal* and *woe* among our fellow-visitors" (p. 33). People's sitting silently together "proves in general either *some coldness* or *some warmth*" (p. 124). The ladies were at once *so little* and *so much* clothed, *so beflounced* yet *so denuded*" (p. 141). And "there were cases in which fancy, sounding the *depths* or the *shallows* could at least drop the lead" (p. 26).

Having noticed the narrator's tendency to think and speak in opposites, I was glad to find it confirmed in an excellent article by Andreach, although I cannot wholeheartedly accept his conclusions. "An examination of the mental processes of the narrator reveals a mind addicted to thinking in terms of opposites; that is, he points for each particular experience its logical possibilities in terms of contradictory predicates: If an object, logical or existential, is not dark, it is light; if it is fat, it is not thin; if it is not old, it is young; and so on" (1962, p. 202). So far so good. As long as Andreach remains at the level of description, his generalization is accurate and sound. But when he passes "external" judgment upon this stylistic peculiarity, he ignores the extent to which the "external" has been "internalized" in *The Sacred Fount* and consequently arrives at one-sided conclusions which fail to do full justice to all the elements in the text. Andreach's main criticism is that the narrator errs by applying logical rules to the existential:

> Since he perceives human behaviour as conforming to a law of opposites—that is, since he posits for each particular experience its logical possibilities in terms of contradictory predicates—and, closely related to this, since he fails to recognize the existential particularity of human beings beyond mere extensions of his logical analyses, he will inevitably alienate those with whom he comes in contact. Human beings, unlike light rays, cannot be polarized. They are not categorized at either one pole or the other. In normal human relations one perceives fine gradations, shades, and nuances; and human beings are most deeply insulted when they are not recognized in these terms . . . In logical, conceptual analysis one can conclude—so long as one observes the rules of the science of logic—anything one likes. According to the law of the excluded middle (the law of contradictions), A is either A or Not-A. But logical inquiry is not existential experience . . . Logic—like art for Henry James—

imposes order and organization onto the chaos of experience. The predicament of the narrator is that of a man who compulsively orders existential experience to conform to *a priori* conceptual analysis. [Pp. 205–6]

While this may be a profound insight into the relations between the logical and the existential, it is not necessarily the insight provided by *The Sacred Fount*. What we are out to discover is the attitude toward dichotomous thinking implicit in the novel itself. We can then either accept it or reject it, but this would already be a judgment of the inferred attitude, not a description of it. The first problem, therefore, is not what we think of the opposites in the narrator's style but what the implied author of *The Sacred Fount* thinks of them. Does James make his narrator employ opposites so frequently in order to intimate a limitation in his thought processes or because he believes this to be the way in which both logic and art arrive at the truth? This is the central question, and although Andreach has probably answered it to his satisfaction, the evidence offered by the text is not as clear-cut as his presentation suggests. Before tackling the perplexing evidence, I would like to point out several other characteristics of the narrator's style which, although not analyzed by Andreach (or, for that matter, by any other critic I have read), are closely related to the prominence of opposites.

The balance in the narrator's style, like the symmetry in his theory, consists of opposites on the one hand and parallels on the other. The parallel constructions are of the types recognized by traditional rhetoric, and for convenience I shall use the terms accepted in it, and shall confine myself to a few examples of each type. Most of the parallels have expressive functions in the local context in which they appear, but their accumulation singles them out as a group and suggests that they may have a "collective function" in addition to and beyond their separate, local roles.

Anaphora, that is, the repetition of a word or group of words in the beginning of several consecutive sentences or phrases. In describing his recurrent meetings with Mrs. Server, the narrator appropriately repeats the verb *to come upon,* giving the recurrence the force of proof for himself and of quasi-claustro-phobic irritation for the observed: *"I came upon her* in great dim chambers, and *I came upon her* before sweeps of view. *I came upon her* once more with the Comte de Dreuil . . . Only at no moment, whatever the favouring frame, did *I come upon her* with Gilbert Long"* (p. 74). The expression of his desire not to see poor Briss again is intensified by the use of repetition. *"I felt it* with sharpness as I leaned on the sill; *I felt it* with sadness as I looked at the stars; *I felt* once more what *I had felt* on turning a final back five minutes before, so designedly on Mrs. Server" (p. 142). And his sense of the final formidable change in Mrs. Brissenden is emphasized and enhanced in the same way: *"It had been* in her way of turning from me after that brief passage; *it had been* in her going up to bed without seeing me again; *it had been* once more in her thinking, for reasons of her own, better of that; and *it had been* most of all in her sending her husband down to me" (p. 166).

Epistrophe, that is, the repetition of the same word or group of words at the end of several consecutive sentences or phrases. In the only instance of this figure to be found in *The Sacred Fount,* the narrator repeats the expression in order to inculcate the truth-value of his observation: "Mrs. Server confessed with every turn of her head to *a part in a relation;* it stuck out of her, *her part in a relation;* it hung before us, *her part in a relation"* (p. 69).[18]

Epanadiplosis, that is, the repetition of the same word or group of words at the end of one sentence or phrase and at the beginning of the next. The effect is one of elegant patterning and of gradual logical analysis, positing a term and then taking it up for definition or elaboration. This is how the narrator renders his perception of the mute game of intelligence between Gilbert Long and himself: "I had moreover the comfort—for it amounted to that—of perceiving after a little that we *understood* each other too well for our *understanding* really to have tolerated the interference of *passion,* such *passion* as would have been represented on his side by resentment of my *intelligence* and on my side by resentment of his. The high sport of *such intelligence* . . . demanded and implied in its own intimate interest a certain amenity" (p. 119). The more resonant "game" played with Mrs. Brissenden is also symmetrically patterned, first by a chiasmus, then by epanadiplosis: "I don't think, you know, . . . it was *my person*, really, that gave its charm to *my theory;* I think it was much more *my theory* that gave its charm to *my person. My person*, I flatter myself, has remained through these few *hours—hours* of *tension*, but of a *tension*, you see, purely intellectual—as good as ever" (p. 198).

Chiasmus, that is, "a balanced passage whereof the second part reverses the order of the first; especially an instance in which forms of the same word are used" (Shipley 1966). In an attempt to reawaken Obert's curiosity, the narrator reminds him of the identity of their interests in the past. This he does by changing the order of the repeated pronouns: *"Yours was mine*, wasn't it? for a little, this morning. Or was it *mine* that was *yours?"* (p. 147. James's emphasis on *was*). A similar emphasis on mutuality heightens the narrator's scorn of what he considers Lady John's incapacity to perceive connections in a deeper sense. *"Gilbert Long* had for her no connection, in my deeper sense, with *Mrs. Server,* nor *Mrs. Server* with *Gilbert Long,* nor *the husband* with *the wife,* nor *the wife* with *the husband,* nor I with either member of either pair, nor *anyone* with *anything,* nor *anything* with *anyone"* (p. 132).

When used in an unnatural grammatical construction, chiasmus can intimate the fallacy of taking symmetry for granted. *"Poor Briss* was in love with *his wife*—that, when driven to the wall, she [Lady John] had had to recognise; but she had not had to recognise that *his wife* was in love with *poor Briss"* (p. 133). It is the unnatural position of the pronoun *his* in relation to its antecedent ("his wife" . . . "poor Briss") that emphasizes the unnaturalness, the artificiality, of assuming a symmetry, a reciprocity, of feelings. Thus, like almost everything else in the novel, chiasmus is used both to pose (first two examples) and to undermine (third example) that which it describes. It is also used to convey the feeling of inevitability, of something closing in on you from all sides. The possibility of a love relationship with Mrs. Server imposes itself on the narrator's thoughts in the form of an encircling chiasmus. "In *resisted observation* that was *vivid thought,* in *inevitable thought* that

was *vivid observation,* . . . I found myself cherishing the fruit
of the seed dropped equally by Ford Obert and Mrs. Briss"
(p. 75). The change of the adjective modifying *thought* is
heightened by the sameness of the other elements and marks
the diminution of his capacity to resist the disquieting realization.

"Artificial proportion," we have seen, is one of the characteristics of the narrator's style. The difficulty in determining
the implicit attitude toward it derives mainly from the fact that
the narrator's style is the only stylistic norm of *The Sacred
Fount.* It is also the style of Henry James as we know it from
his critical prefaces and letters. Even if we waive for a moment
the problem of the legitimacy of using extratextual evidence in
settling textual issues, the similarity between James's style and
that of his narrator in *The Sacred Fount* can be used to support
two opposed conclusions. It is possible to argue with Ora Segal
that this resemblance rules out the idea of a parody and proves
that the narrator is not meant as an object of ridicule (1969,
p. 160). But it is equally possible that James is here for once
"turning a searchlight on Henry James" (Follett 1936, quoted
by Krook 1967, p. 183).

While the external evidence can be reasoned thus or thus,
decisive internal evidence is not forthcoming. There is no
authorial voice in *The Sacred Fount* which could help us to
assess the narrator's style either by direct comment or by
comparison. Perhaps, then, we should compare the narrator's
style with that of the other characters? We can try this, of
course, but while so doing we must remember that the other
characters never really speak for themselves. Even when they
are quoted, it is the narrator who quotes them after a distance
of time and often in his own style. This said, we turn to an
examination of the language of the other characters and discover that they too speak in opposites and parallels. It is
important to distinguish here between two types of symmetries in the style of the other characters: those which form a
balance with the narrator's preceding words and those which
are symmetrical in themselves. The last contest with Mrs.
Brissenden abounds in examples of the first type:

"You owed it to me to let me know what you thought of me even should it prove very disagreeable?"

That perhaps was more than she could adopt. "I owed it to myself," she replied with a touch of austerity.

"To let me know I'm demented?"

"To let you know I'm *not*." [P. 193]

Or in the analysis of the Long-Lady John relationship, starting with the narrator's observation:

"He [Long] would have no need then of her having transformed and inspired him."

"Or of her having *de*formed and idiotised herself." [P. 210; James's italics]

Or again:

"If Briss came down with Lady John yesterday to oblige Mr. Long—"

"He didn't come", she interrupted, "to oblige Mr. Long!"

"Well, then, to oblige Lady John herself—"

"He didn't come to oblige Lady John herself!"

"Well, then, to oblige his clever wife—"

"He didn't come to oblige his clever wife!" [P. 212]

Ford Obert also parallels the narrator with a symmetrically constructed opposite:

"If she isn't now beastly unhappy—?" [the narrator asks]

"She's beastly happy?" [P. 153]

Even more significant than the reply itself is the narrator's comment on it: "he broke in, getting firmer hold, if not of the real impression he had just been gathering under my eyes, then at least of something he had begun to make out that my argument required." The significance of this statement lies in the indication that the symmetry in the interlocutors' language (granted that it is their language and not the narrator's phrasing of their thoughts) may not be an inherent quality of their style but a reaction conditioned by his own. This is part of what both Obert and Mrs. Brissenden mean when they speak of the narrator's infernal powers of persuasion. It also reenacts at the level of language the central technique of subjecting everything in the novel to the narrator's vision and rendering of his vision.

Had the symmetries in the language of the narrator's inter-locutors been limited to echoing and countering him, we might have dismissed their value as a foil against which to determine the implicit attitude toward the peculiarities of his own style. But the statements of the other characters are sometimes sym-metrical in themselves, although less frequently than the nar-rator's—in proportion, perhaps, to the relative sparsity of their speeches compared with his. Using a pair of opposites, Long describes the matrimonial predicament: "That's the awfulness, don't you see? of the married state. People have to get used to each other's *charms* as well as to their *faults*" (p. 20). And a little later he says, "Youth is—comparatively speaking—beauty," an observation which he himself balances by, "Well, if you like better, beauty is youth" (p. 32). Mrs. Brissen-den similarly contrasts *mind* and *talk* on the one hand with *delicacy* and *consideration* on the other (p. 66). Later she tells the narrator that in order to recover from mistakes such as his theory, "One thinks a little," but realizing that it was in fact thought that had led the narrator astray, she immediately makes the opposite statement: "Well, then . . . I must have stopped thinking" (p. 187). In speaking about Mrs. Server's condition, Ford Obert uses chiasmus to intimate that the two possible ways of looking at it are in fact one. " 'She's all *in* it,' he insisted. 'Or it's all in *her*. It comes to the same thing' " (p. 59; James's italics). And Mrs. Brissenden uses the same de-vice to reinforce her declaration of complete discretion: "I've not spoken to a creature" and then "Not a creature has spoken to me" (pp. 184–85).

If the other characters also use symmetrical constructions, perhaps the balance in the narrator's style is not an indication of a limitation on his part? As if to suggest that this inference is too easily drawn, there are two instances in which Mrs. Brissenden uses symmetry in order to point out its artificiality. In one case the symmetry is only in the argument, in the other it is also in the language. When the narrator asks her whether she put the question of the identity of the beneficent lady to Long himself, Mrs. Brissenden answers, "I wasn't imputing to you the same direct appeal. I didn't suppose . . . that—to match your own supposition of *me*—you had resorted to May herself" (p. 185; James's italics). That symmetry may be misleading is linguistically suggested by her in the symmetrical form of a chiasmus: "They say there's no smoke without fire, but it appears there may be fire without smoke" (p. 65). The use of chiasmus to convey the inexistence of chiastic relations in actual experience is intended by Mrs. Brissenden as a kind of parody, employing a conventional rhetorical figure and a traditional proverb only to expose them as fallacious.

Lest this should seem devastating criticism of the narrator's symmetrical thinking, we must remember not only that she herself often thinks on similar lines but also that humorous treatment of parallels is not alien to the narrator. When Mrs. Brissenden says that she initially agreed with the narrator only "because you talked me over," he wittily answers, "And who is it then that . . . has, as I may call it, talked you under?" (p. 185). The wit consists in deviating from an idiom and including within the parallel construction a newly coined antonym ("to talk under"), thus expressing a detached and humorous awareness of the ease with which nonexistent opposites can be formed. He reacts in a similar way to Obert's use of his own theory about changes and changes back:

> "I should have thought," my friend continued, "that he too [Briss] might have *changed back*."
> I took in, for myself, so much more of it than I could say!
> "Certainly. You wouldn't have thought he would have *changed forward*." [P. 160]

Both the narrator and the other characters use opposites and parallels, at the same time being aware of the dangers and limitations involved. Hence, a comparison of styles does not provide an unequivocal clue as to the attitude we are meant to adopt toward the use of analogy. The only element which may be said to transcend the participants and give us a glimpse of some authorial presence is the structure of the novel, although those critics who see the narrator as an author will tend to attribute even that to him.[19] The structure of the novel exhibits several symmetries.

Chapter 1 is symmetrical in itself, consisting of the following episodes: (1) the narrator meets Gilbert Long, (2) the narrator meets Mrs. Brissenden, (3) the narrator and Long discuss the change in Mrs. Briss, (4) the narrator and Mrs. Briss discuss the change in Long. Other symmetries reside not in the sequence of events within one chapter, but in the recurrence of analogous events in different chapters. Chapter 4 (up to the discussion of the picture) and chapter 8 are analogous. In both, the speakers are the narrator and Mrs. Server. In chapter 4 they discuss Briss, Lady John, and X (the man in whom she is interested), the X standing either for Long (the narrator's version) or for Obert (Mrs. Server's version). In chapter 8 the subject of conversation is again an X in relation to Lady John, and again the X can be filled by two different referents: either Long (as in chapter 4) or poor Briss (who in chapter 4 was also connected with Lady John). In both chapters a misunderstanding arises out of the use of an exophoric pronoun: *one* and *he* in chapter 4, *him* in chapter 8, and in both one referent is actually supplied, while the other keeps lingering in the narrator's mind. It is in the light of the other possibility that the narrator imputes insincerity to Mrs. Server's behavior in both chapters. Her affirmation in chapter 4 that Ford Obert is the man in whom Lady John is interested shows the narrator "to what legend she was committed" (p. 47), and her defiant (or seemingly defiant) facial expression upon his mention of poor Briss in chapter 8 is also seen as an attempt to conceal the relationship (p. 107).

These two chapters are to some extent paralleled by chapter 6, in which the narrator, having no interlocutor, discusses with himself the characters and relations figuring in the other two chapters—first Mrs. Server and Long, then poor Briss, Lady John, and Long. In all three chapters Mrs. Server is described in terms of a painting. In chapter 4: "She might have been herself—all Greuze tints, all pale pinks and blues and pearly whites and candid eyes—an old dead pastel under glass" (p. 48). She is later compared to the grinning mask in the ambiguous picture. In chapter 6, "She kept repeating her picture in settings separated by such intervals that I wondered at the celerity with which she proceeded from spot to spot" (p. 73). Again the image of the mask follows that of the picture. The difficulty of Mrs. Server's predicament is that it forces her to uphold a mask, "to shroud" "her whole compromised machinery of thought and speech" and create "the illusion of an unimpaired estate" (p. 77). In chapter 8, "her lovely grimace," which was what she had in common with the mask in the picture, "was as blurred as a bit of brushwork in water-colour spoiled by the upsetting of the artist's glass" (p. 99). If the beginning of chapter 4 was parallel to chapter 8, its end is analogous to the colloquies with Ford Obert in chapter 2. There are two such colloquies in chapter 2, and the subject discussed is Mrs. Server in the first and the Brissendens in the second. The same subjects in the same order constitute the closing conversation of chapter 4.

Chapter 2 and chapter 4; chapters 4, 6, and 8 all exhibit symmetries and parallels. Two of the odd chapters, 3 and 7, also balance each other. All that happens in chapter 3 is a conversation between the narrator and Mrs. Brissenden, first about Lady John in relation to Long, then about May Server in relation to the same gentleman. Chapter 7 similarly consists of one conversation, this time between the narrator and Mrs. Brissenden, and the subjects of discussion are again first Lady John, then Mrs. Server.

An examination of the narrator–Mrs. Server axis in chapters 2 to 5 yields the following results:

Chapter 2   Narrator's conversation *with* Mrs. Server
             Narrator's conversation *about* Mrs. Server
Chapter 3   Narrator's conversation *about* Mrs. Server
Chapter 4   Narrator's conversation *with* Mrs. Server
             Narrator's conversation *about* Mrs. Server
Chapter 5   Narrator's conversation *about* Mrs. Server

Chapters 2 and 4 contain both a conversation with Mrs. Server and one about her, while chapters 3 and 5 include only a conversation about her. "With," "about," "about"; "with," "about," "about"—is the overall symmetrical pattern emerging, and its balance is reinforced by the alternation of the interlocutor in the conversations about Mrs. Server. In chapter 2 it is Obert, in chapter 3 Mrs. Briss; in chapter 4, again Obert; and in chapter 5, once more Mrs. Briss.

The same chapters yield another symmetrical pattern:

Chapter 2   Narrator's conversation *about* Mrs. Briss
Chapter 3   Narrator's conversation *with* Mrs. Briss
Chapter 4   Narrator's conversation *about* Mrs. Briss
Chapter 5   Narrator's conversation *with* Mrs. Briss

Chapter 1, as we have seen, started the reverse pattern of first talking with a character (Mrs. Briss, Long) and then about him.

But, the reader may want to object, is it not mainly because of the division into chapters that these repetitions are grasped as analogies? Precisely. "It is all an affair, this fine symmetry, of artificial proportion." And artificial proportion is precisely the point it makes, inviting us to see both the proportion and the artificiality, the beauty and the terror, the truth and the untruth of parallels and symmetries.

Another kind of symmetry is that imposed on our reading (or our metareading) by the ambiguity of the novel. Like the narrator's style, the ambiguity posits opposites, two mutually exclusive interpretations according to which the various pieces of evidence balance each other in the scales of contradiction. But whereas the narrator chooses with the help of contradictory predicates, the ambiguity makes such choice impossible, balancing the structure he erects by another, eternally coexistent yet symmetrically opposed possibility. The ambiguity encompasses two limited structures within the larger framework of *The Sacred Fount,* and a reading which recognizes the ambiguity necessarily manifests the symmetry arising from a constant oscillation between the two opposed structures, the symmetry of a seesaw movement. Is symmetry then a "torch in the darkness" or a misleading *ignis fatuus?* The symmetry of *The Sacred Fount* is in its ambiguity, and ambiguity, we already know, will not give us the answer. Looking back now on the novel, can we not discover a hint of this unresolved resolution in the very first sentences? They start with opposites— "friends," "enemies"; "fears," "hopes"—but how do they end? ". . . it was to be added that there were sometimes, in the case, rather happy *ambiguities*" (p. 17; my italics).

One such happy ambiguity is dramatized in the-man-and-the-mask episode which reflects in miniature the "little law of composition" (James, quoted by Edel 1953, p. xxx) governing the novel as a whole. It is not an ambiguous scene, but a scene about ambiguity. Its focus is a work of art, "the picture, of all pictures, that most needs an interpreter" (p. 50).

The figure represented is a young man in black—a quaint, tight black dress, fashioned in years long past; with a pale, lean, livid face and a stare, from eyes without eyebrows, like that of some whitened old-world clown. In his hand he holds an object that strikes the spectator at first simply as some obscure, some ambiguous work of art, but that on a second view becomes a representation of a human face, modelled and coloured, in wax, in enamelled metal, in some substance not human. The object thus appears a complete mask, such as might have been fantastically fitted and worn. [Pp. 50–51]

That the picture consists of opposites—the man and the mask, life and death, appearance and reality—is pretty obvious. It is also obvious that Mrs. Server and the narrator interpret it in opposite ways, Mrs. Server taking the commonsense view that the man is life and the mask death, while the narrator characteristically sees the mask, the artifice, as life and the man as death. It is perhaps less obvious that the picture itself offers evidence for both interpretations, that it is "some obscure, some ambiguous work of art." While the man is a living creature, a "reality," the mask is a "representation . . . in some substance not human." It is inanimate, with its fixed "awful grimace" (p. 51); it is artificial and dead—"the Mask of Death." But if we are inclined for a moment to take the man as life and the mask as death, we have only to reread the description of Life to see how deadly it is. For the man wears a black garment, a color traditionally associated with death, and has a "pale, lean, livid face." His dress was "fashioned in years long past," and his face is "like that of some whitened old-world clown." In addition to the death associations aroused by "black," "white," "long past" and "old world," the image of the whitened face is taken from the realm of masks, and the clown is traditionally a figure of someone who has to play a part, who has to laugh even when he wants to cry (*Ridi, pagliaccio* . . .). We thus witness a metaphoric interpenetration of the two figures and this intertwinement is the "objective correlative" of the two mutually exclusive interpretations offered by Mrs. Server and the narrator (for critics' interpretations of the picture, see Gale 1962, pp. 21–33; Isle 1968, p. 260; Krook 1967, p. 177; Folsom 1961, pp. 139–40; Levy 1962b, p. 382; Reaney 1962, p. 144).

To speak of the man as a living creature is already to speak in some sense metaphorically. On a literal level the man is not a bit more living than the mask—they are both inanimate objects in a picture hanging on the wall. It is the picture that gives them "life," and it is in a picture, in art alone, that incompatibles can coexist.

From aesthetic observations the conversation half-playfully glides to identification of the figures in the picture with members of the Newmarch party. The mask is reminiscent of Mrs. Server, while the face recalls poor Briss's. We have already seen that on several occasions Mrs. Server is described in terms of a picture. What links her to the mask in particular is the grimace by which, according to the narrator's interpretation, she tries to conceal her tragic disintegration (see, for example, pp. 99, 109, 110, 139). The implications of this identification are double-edged, for Mrs. Server's likeness to the mask may associate her either with death, by her own interpretation of the mask, or with life, according to the narrator's paradoxical view.

The similarity between poor Briss and the man in the pastel is anticipated by a description in chapter 3:

"The gentleman close to her [to Mrs. Server], with the same support, offered us the face of Guy Brissenden, as recognisable at a distance as the numbered card of a "turn"—the black figure upon white—at a music-hall" (p. 43). The black figure foreshadows the man with the quaint, black dress, and the music-hall is to be recalled by the image of the clown. Toward the end of the novel, Brissenden is again described in terms of a somber picture. "He reminded me at this hour more than ever of some fine old Velasquez or other portrait—a presentation of ugliness and melancholy that might have been royal" (p. 115). In his last interview with the narrator, "he let his white face fix me in the dusk" (p. 159)—a white face like that of the pale, lean, livid portrait. As in the case of Mrs. Server, Brissenden's resemblance to the man in the obscure picture may be interpreted in two mutually exclusive ways, depending on whether we take the narrator's view of the man as a death figure or Mrs. Server's life interpretation.

The picture itself is ambiguous. The interpretations are mutually incompatible and no choice is possible. The position of the characters in front of the picture is analogous to our position in front of *The Sacred Fount*. Beyond the ambiguity, we once more discover, there is nothing. Or rather, beyond the ambiguity there is further ambiguity.

Conclusion: Ambiguity, a Modern Perspective

There are two main ways of accounting for the functions and significance of a given literary phenomenon: mimetic and nonmimetic. The mimetic (or iconic) approach considers the phenomenon as a device used to reflect, express, represent a parallel phenomenon beyond itself—out there, in the world of "reality." The nonmimetic approach, on the other hand, concentrates on the role of the given phenomenon in relation to the process of reading and on the manner in which it draws the reader's attention to itself, becoming a self-reflexive meditation on the medium of art, rather than a mirroring of a reality outside art.

Most studies of the Jamesian ambiguity have been iconic in approach. Dorothea Krook, for example, sees the device as dramatizing a moral and an epistemological theme: the moral theme of "the co-existence or co-presence of good and evil in the human soul" (1967, p. 130) and the epistemological theme of the "incapacity of the enquiring mind to know with certainty whether what it 'sees' is fact or delusion" (p. 167). The ambiguity can be said not only to dramatize "the irremediable uncertainty of our human knowledge" in relation to reality, but also "to call into radical question the validity of the relations between appearances and the reality they profess to represent" (Bewley 1952, p. 82). Is there an objective reality outside the human consciousness, and if so, is it more real than the internal reality of the appearances perceived by our consciousness?

A la question "que s'est il réellement passé à la propriété de Bly?" James répond d'une manière oblique: il met en doute le mot 'réellement.' " [Todorov 1971, p. 167]

The interpretation of evidence, the reading of signs, rather than the problem of reality is made the center of Wiesenfarth's semiotic explanation of the ambiguity of *The Sacred Fount:*

> The novel is not a problem in metaphysics; it is, rather, a
> study in logic and semiosis. *The Fount* is not concerned with
> truth, but with the correct reasoning about signs. That the
> meaning ascribed to the signs conforms with the objective
> reality is impossible to determine because of the ambiguity
> of the novel. The focus of the novel is not the true relations
> persisting among the Brissendens, Long, May Server and
> Lady John. The centre of composition in the novel is formed
> by the logical constructions which the narrator and Grace
> Brissenden fit together from signs that are identical but that
> mean something different to each of them. [1963, pp. 96–97]

Because the characters interpret the same signs in different
ways, real communication among them is inhibited. Thus
Melchiori gives a social slant to the epistemological and social
themes: *"The Sacred Fount* is meant to be a puzzle, a variation
on the theme of the impossibility of knowing man, on the
theme, in short, of incommunicability" (1965, p. 304).

The moral, epistemological, metaphysical, semiotic, and social interpretations are all mimetic, showing James as firmly
rooted in the great humanist tradition to which he belongs. In
contrast, the nonmimetic approach reveals qualities of the
ambiguity which seem to anticipate certain antitraditional
tendencies in twentieth-century literature, art, and aesthetics.
It is this aspect that I would like to emphasize here, claiming
for it neither exclusiveness nor predominance, only relative
neglect on the part of most analysts.

By leaving a central gap open and encouraging the reader to
search for clues, group evidences, and weigh them against each
other, the ambiguity makes the reading process dynamic or,
in modern Structuralist-Marxist parlance, prevents the reader
from being merely a passive consumer and turns him into an
active producer of the text (see, for example, Barthes 1970).
As theorist of his own fiction, James is well aware of the
reader's contribution to the work of art, and decides to exploit
it in solving the problem of how to present evil without de-
tracting from its horror. In the Preface to "The Aspern Papers"
he says about *The Turn of the Screw,* "Only make the reader's
general vision of evil intense enough, I said to myself—and that

already is a charming job—and his own experience, his own imagination, his own sympathy (with the children) and horror (of their false friends) will supply him quite sufficiently with all the particulars. Make him *think* the evil, make him think it for himself, and you are released from weak specifications" (in Blackmur, ed., 1962, p. 176). James's values, according to him, "are positively all blanks" (p. 177), and the reader has to fill them in on the basis of implicit directives in the text. But because in ambiguous works these implicit directives are mutually exclusive, the process of filling in the blanks is one of perpetual oscillation, of endless switches from one alternative to the other. Our interpretation, says Gombrich about visual ambiguities, "can never come to rest and our 'imitative faculty' will be kept busy as long as we join in the game" (1968, p. 240). In thus becoming aware of the movements and fluctuations of his own mind, the reader actively lives James's conception of consciousness as a constant flux, forever receptive, forever modified. Such a conception of reading requires a reader who is willing to collaborate in the enterprise, and James knows what this means for the author. The author, he says, "makes his reader very much as he makes his character" (quoted by Chatman 1972, p. 58, n. 1).

A corollary of the augmentation of the reader's share in "creation" is the breaking of the automatism involved in passive "consumption."

Habit devours everything; objects, clothes, furniture, your wife and the fear of war. "If the complex lives of many people are led without consciousness, it is as if these lives were not led at all." That which we call "art" exists in order to remedy our perception of life, to make things felt, to make the stone stony. The purpose of art is to evoke in man a sensation of things, to make him perceive things rather than merely recognize them. In order to do so art uses two devices: making things strange and complicating the form, so as to increase the duration and the difficulty of perception. For in art the process of perception is an aim in itself and it should be prolonged as much as possible; Art is a means of experiencing a process of 'becoming'; that which has already 'become' is unimportant for art. [Shklovsky, in Todorov, ed., 1965, p. 83; my translation]

Narrative ambiguity frustrates two habitual expectations of the relatively passive reader: the belief that the central enigma will finally be solved is counteracted by the permanent gap, while the hope to be able, at least at the end, to construct a univocal and coherent *fabula* is thwarted by the coexistence of conflicting clues which give rise to mutually exclusive *fabulas*.

The "deautomatization" created by the permanent gap does not only enhance a new perception of the reality represented; it also directs the reader's attention to the medium itself, urging him to scan it with greater attention and in new ways in order to capture the elusive solution. Thus the undisclosed secret in Sebastian Knight's novel prevents the reader-narrator from looking through the text as if it were transparent glass, and instead directs his attention to its own mode of being.

> "I sometimes feel when I turn the pages of Sebastian's masterpiece that the 'absolute solution' is there, somewhere, concealed in some passage I have read too hastily, or that it is intertwined with other words whose familiar guise deceived me. I don't know any other book that gives one this special sensation, and perhaps this was the author's special intention." [Nabokov 1960, pp. 168–69]

The author's "special intention," it is implied, may have been to draw the reader's attention to the words, to force him to divest the words of that "familiar guise" which facilitates automatic recognition, and to make him confront them in their own right. The aesthetic, says Jan Mukařovský of the Prague Structuralist School, "consists in the fact that the listener's attention, which has so far been turned to the message for which language is a means, is directed to the linguistic sign itself, to its properties and composition, in one word, to its internal structure" (1964, p. 36).

Akin in spirit to the Formalist and Structuralist views of literature are Gombrich's observations about the visual arts. Automatic reconstruction, known as "losing the surface," is an experience welcomed not by painters but by the masters of camouflage, who use the familiar to promote routine reactions and prevent the enemy's attention from being arrested by what is to be concealed (1969a, pp. 59, 61). It is at the opposite effect that art aims. Far from being content with making the perceiver recognize the already known, it wishes to make him experience the new and the unexpected.

Thus the visual arts have taken on the role of exercises in the variability of vision. The artist, at least the modern artist, is engaged in a constant fight against the automatisms of perception. He certainly does not want us to look through his representation at what is represented: he does not want his picture to trigger responses that belong to reality . . . I have more or less refrained from discussing works of art [while discussing automatic reconstruction] because the artist wants us to attend to his art. Neither does the poet want his words to become transparent for us so that we disregard their sound for the sake of the message. All art needs an awareness of form. [P. 67]

This focus on the form, or Jakobson's famous "poetic function" (1967, p. 302) is effected not only by the permanent gap but also by the other component of the ambiguity, namely, the mutually exclusive systems of clues. To use an analogy from the visual arts again, here is Gombrich's comment on Thiery's puzzling figure: "It is practically impossible to keep this figure fixed because it presents contradictory clues. The result is that the frequent reversals force our attention to the plane" (1968, p. 241). The result is also a complication and a prolongation of the reading process (see Kooij 1971, p. 60, on verbal ambiguity), culminating in the experience of perpetual "becoming" so dear to Shklovsky.

Taking this endless process of "becoming" one step further, Todorov shows how James's ambiguous narratives tend to locate the solution within the quest itself, rather than in the truth it is expected to yield. "Le récit de James s'appuie toujours sur la quête d'une cause absolue et absente . . . tout, dans le récit, doit finalement sa présence à cette cause. Mais la cause est absente et l'on part à sa quête: l'histoire consiste en la recherche, la poursuite de cette cause initiale, de cette essence première. Le récit s'arrête si l'on parvient à l'atteindre . . . L'absence de la cause ou de la vérité est présente dans le texte, plus même, elle en est l'origine logique et la raison d'être; la cause est ce qui, par son absence, fait surgir le texte.

L'essentiel est absent, l'absence est essentielle" (1971, p. 153). Isn't this also, Todorov consistently suggests, the mysterious secret which is ever present yet never disclosed in "The Figure in the Carpet?" ". . . s'il [le secret] avait été nommé il n'aurait plus existé, or c'est précisement son existence qui forme le secret. Ce secret est par définition inviolable car il consiste en son propre existence. La quête ne doit jamais se terminer car elle constitue le secret lui-même" (p. 183).

From a search which becomes its own end to a text which turns largely upon itself, simultaneously unfolding a story and evolving its own poetics, the distance is small. And, indeed, many ambiguous narratives reinforce their self-reflexive character by self-duplication, often taking the form of a reproduction of the fictional situation in the work's relation with its readers, sometimes adding the technique known as *mise en abyme*. In *The Sacred Fount*, for example, the narrator and his interlocutors ask about the Newmarch party the same questions that we ask about *The Sacred Fount*, and their failure to arrive at a unanimous resolution equals our failure to break out of the labyrinth of ambiguities. Within this self-mirroring novel there is further duplication in the man-and-the-mask scene. Its center is an ambiguous work of art of which the characters offer mutually exclusive interpretations and of which James offers none. The characters' interpretations of the picture reflect their analyses of their fellow guests, but they also enact our own position vis-à-vis *The Sacred Fount*: two opposed possibilities and no choice. A structure of Chinese boxes, constantly revealing the same principle, drawing our attention to different but analogous levels of itself. Similarly, in Pynchon's overplotted *The Crying of Lot Forty-Nine*, there is an equally overplotted Elizabethan play which, like the novel itself, poses the problems of chaos and order, of the madness involved in the search for coherent patterns, of "real" worlds versus "projected" worlds. The *mise en abyme* in Robbe-Grillet's *L'année dernière à Marienbad* is also derived from the realm of art, this time from the art of sculpture. In the middle of the symmetrically patterned garden stands a statue which, like the ambiguous painting in *The Sacred Fount*, elicits conflicting interpretations from the spectators: "c'est vous, c'est moi, ce sont des dieux antiques, Hélène, Agamemnon," and so on. Another image from the visual arts reflects the compositional principle of Nathalie Sarraute's *Portrait d'un inconnu.* Here the image exists only at the verbal level, and it is consciously compared by the narrator to his habits of observation:

> Il y a un truc à attraper pour le saisir quand on n'a pas la chance de le voir spontanément, d'une manière habituelle. Une sorte de tour d'adresse à exécuter, assez semblable à ces exercises auxquels invitent certains dessins-devinettes, ou ces images composées de losanges noirs et blancs, habilement combinés, qui forment deux dessins géométriques superposés; le jeu consiste à faire une sorte de gymnastique visuelle: on repousse très légèrement l'une des deux images, on la déplace un peu, on la fait reculer et on ramène l'autre en avant. On peut parvenir, en s'exerçant un peu, à une certaine dextérité, à opérer très vite le déplacement d'une image à l'autre, à voir à volonté tantôt l'un, tantôt l'autre dessin. [1956, pp. 27–28]

The "dessins-devinettes" referred to are of the Escher type, and it is interesting to note at this point that Escher's own paintings direct attention to their mode of operation not only by the constant switches which they impose on the observer but sometimes also by incorporating miniature images of themselves. In *Belvedere,* a lithograph depicting an impossible building, a lad is seen sitting in front of the building, holding an impossible cube in his hand, apparently oblivious to the similarity between the cube in his hands and the belvedere behind his back (1972, no. 14 and p. 16).

That ambiguous works draw attention to their own compositional principle and become, to a large extent, self-reflexive meditations should by now be clear. What is not yet clear is what this ambiguous focusing on ambiguity reveals. We can start again with the visual arts, where modern experiments like Escher's and Vasarely's make us discover that "pictures are infinitely ambiguous because they present a flat two-dimensional geometrical projection of a three-dimensional reality. To say of such a projection that it 'looks like reality' begs the question" (Gombrich 1963, p. 157).

Or in Escher's own words:

Our three-dimensional space is the only true reality that we know. The two-dimensional is every bit as fictitious as the four-dimensional, for nothing is flat, not even the most finely polished mirror. And yet, we stick to the convention that a wall or a piece of paper is flat, and curiously enough, we still go on, as we have done since time immemorial, producing illusions of space on just such plane surfaces as those. Surely it is a bit absurd to draw a few lines and then claim: "This is a house". This odd situation is the theme of the next five pictures. [1972, p. 15]

A similar ideology underlies the use of ambiguity in the modern antinovel, where the device becomes a credo of doubt, a manifesto of the impossibility of representing a "three-dimensional" reality in a "two-dimensional" medium. Such novels can be read only in literality, and the reader must renounce the illusion of a "third dimension," the illusion of a reflection of reality (and see Barthes's comments on Robbe-Grillet, 1964). Sergio Perosa, who points out the striking similarities between James's *The Sacred Fount* and Nathalie Sarraute's *Portrait d'un inconnu*, concludes that the former, like the latter, is a parable of the pathetic incapacity of art to express—let alone rival— the complexities of life (1963, p. xxxvii).

With due respect to Perosa, it is here, I think, that the differences within the similarities begin to be felt. Ambiguity, whether visual or narrative, can enact not only the limitations of art but also its strength. For it is only in art that the same figure can be either a rabbit or a duck, either white birds flying in one direction or black birds flying in the other, and it is only in art that the existence of ghosts or of vampire relations can be simultaneously asserted and denied. In life we cannot allow equal tenability to contradictories, and although we sometimes realize that the information we have is insufficient for choice, choice itself always seems imperative. Art, on the other hand, makes the coexistence of contradictories possible. Indeed, the creation of ambiguous works is one of art's ways of solving the problem of contradictories—solving it not by choice but by an artistic dramatization of their coexistence. "I have always known life is impossible," says Mosley's narrator. "Stories are symbols in which impossibilities are held" (1968, p. 140).[1] The triumph of art, rather than its bankruptcy, is celebrated by the Jamesian ambiguity, showing not simply how the possible is rendered impossible by art, but mainly how the impossible becomes possible in it. This difference in outlook is perhaps responsible for the difference in technique. In the modern anti-novels the ambiguity is created mainly by the $a+a-$ principle, thus making clues neutralize each other and reducing the sum to zero. In Henry James, on the other hand, the balance of clues is based not only on $a+a-$ but also on $a+b+$, resulting not in zero, but in the "impossible" coexistence of mutually exclusive structures.

Thus, although in many respects the ambiguity of Henry James is an antecedent of the modern impossible objects, it significantly stops halfway, refraining from a denunciation of the very art which created it. In the Jamesian vision, as the famous letter to H.G. Wells amply testifies, "It is art that *makes* life, makes interest, makes importance" (1970, 2:490; his italics).

Notes

CHAPTER 1

1. Tarski calls the first kind of disjunction 'non-exclusive'. One should note that Tarski's examples are not strictly limited to 'truth' versus 'falsity'.

2. When the negation line covers only one sign, it negates this sign alone (for example $\bar{a}$ = not a). When it covers the whole expression, it negates it as a whole, that is, it negates the relation established between its members (for example, $\overline{a.b}$ = not (a and b); a and b cannot be conjoined).

3. Reichenbach also retains this sign for the sake of convenience. He only wishes to make clear that it does not designate something entirely separate and new.

4. 'Empty' should be distinguished from 'meaningless'. An empty formula is one that leaves us entirely uninformed as to the truth-values of the elementary propositions. Both tautologies ('T' for all instances) and contradictions ('F' for all instances) are empty; "tautologies as well as contradictions possess determinate truth-values and are meaningful, although empty" (Reichenbach 1951, p. 37).

5. Ibid., pp. 142–43. The examples are also his. I omit the 'subcontraries' and the 'superalterns' and 'subalterns' because they are not directly relevant to my purpose. The complete square of opposition (scholastic and Boolean) can be found in Copi 1961, p. 161; Reichenbach 1951, p. 93. Blanché's revision of the traditional square can be found in 1966, pp. 23–26.

6. The Principle of the Excluded Middle says that every statement must be either a or *not* a. The formula is $a \lor \bar{a}$.

7. Most readers do this unconsciously or half-consciously, and it is only in an explicit description of this one aspect of reading that the impression of a systematic, almost scientific process is created.

8. "Simplicity" is a relative criterion (relative to the work in question). Sometimes a complex solution is the "simplest," least circuitous, for the narrative under discussion.

9. Eco recognizes the problem that such works raise for the theory of art. "Or, il faut se demander tout d'abord si cette *poétique de l'oeuvre ouverte* . . . est une poétique de *l'oeuvre* ou bien une poétique de la *non-oeuvre*" (p. 120; Eco's italics), but this interesting problem lies beyond the scope of my study. His conception of an open work is less "revolutionary" than Barthes's because it locates the exploration of possibilities within "les limites d'un champ" which is the "physionomie propre" of the work (pp. 318–19); whereas Barthes seems to imply infinite plurality and uncontrolled reversibility.

10. Sometimes an ambiguity results from the uncertainty as to whether we

should take the narrative literally or allegorically, as, for example, in Edgar A. Poe's "William Wilson" or in Gogol's "The Nose." See Tzvetan Todorov 1970, pp. 69–79.

11. Empson also says, "Ambiguity itself can mean an indecision as to what you mean, an intention to mean several things, a probability that one or other or both of two things has been meant and the fact that a statement has several meanings" (pp. 5–6).

12. Monroe C. Beardsley has confined 'ambiguity' to "linguistic expressions that are doubtful in meaning because they could have either, but not both of two possible meanings and provide no ground for a decision between them" (1958, p. 126). This definition is similar to the one I propose. See also Beardsley 1954, p. 38.

13. This is not the only way in which Stanford uses the term 'ambiguity'. He wavers between this highly extended sense and a strict sense, which he defines in the following way: "words or phrases in which two or more distinct meanings are possible, these meanings being mutually exclusive as well as distinct" (p. 132). He often uses 'ambiguity' to designate "puns" (p. 17), "toying with homonyms" (p. 31. The example is Othello's "Put out the light, and then put out the light"), playing on the contemporary and etymological senses of a word (p. 40), exploiting the adjectival meaning of proper names (pp. 35–36), and so on.

14. It can be seen from this passage that Copi's definition of 'ambiguity' is broader than mine.

15. Other weaknesses of the Empsonian scheme, like the coexistence of verbal and psychological criteria, the overlap among the seven types (Empson himself admits this weakness on p. 133 of Seven Types), and the failure to distinguish between associations that belong to the meaning of a given text and those that do not, have been fully commented on by many critics and need not detain us here. See, for example, Schaar 1965, pp. 157–65; Hirsch 1967, p. 62, and footnote no. 24 on the same page; King 1941–42, pp. 161–83; 161 (King's own use of the term is very close to 'multiple meaning').

16. By the way, it may be worth mentioning that the coexistence of the literal and the figurative meanings of a given expression does not always verge on symbolism. Such coexistence is often utilized in advertisements, as, for example, the caption "more than lip service" in an advertisement for lipsalve. The pun here is based on the coexistence of the physical (literal) and the idiomatic (figurative) meanings of "lip service," and yet it has nothing to do with symbolism.

17. Sometimes the context can make the literal and the figurative meanings mutually exclusive. Ambiguity (in the strict sense) then arises as to which is meant.

18. Examples of a union which represents a residue, not an achieved harmony, are "counting one's beads," and "as hard as nails," with which I have dealt above.

19. 'Conjunctive ambiguity' seems to correspond to Empson's first type, while 'integrative ambiguity' corresponds to his second, and 'disjunctive ambiguity' to his seventh, but the parallels are not clear-cut, Empson's types being rather fuzzy.

20. Kaplan and Kris admit that their 'additive ambiguity' is often described as 'vagueness' and their 'integrative ambiguity' as 'complexity', but they prefer to treat all these phenomena together because, from the point of

view of the multiplicity of language, they are "generically identical," and this—they say—is the crucial point of view for the study of poetry (pp. 416–17).

CHAPTER 2

1. Unfortunately, I cannot read the Formalists in Russian and have to rely on English and French translations. Lemon and Reis render *fabula* and *sjužet* as "story" and "plot," respectively. This is a misleading translation because it suggests an identity between the Russian terms and E. M. Forster's terms, and no such identity exists. This is not the place to expound the differences between the two pairs of terms, and a mere statement of their dissimilarity will have to suffice. My own use of "story" is nontechnical and refers simply to the narrative work as a whole. Tomashevsky usually speaks of "motifs" rather than "events," but because the term *motif* will be defined later, I avoid it at this stage.

2. It should be noted, however, that even the *fabula* is not completely raw: it already contains a selection from the completely raw material offered by reality.

3. In complaining that the Russian Formalists saw temporal "deformation" as the only distinguishing feature between the *fabula* and the *sjužet,* Todorov treats their views as more uniform than they actually are and overlooks the differences among the various definitions of *sjužet.*

4. This aspect is distinguished from two other aspects: the semantic (that is, "what the story represents and evokes") and the verbal ("the concrete sentences by which the story is communicated to us").

5. Tomashevsky's examples are not uniform: while all the above examples include an agent or object and an action, another example of a motif includes only an object, "the motif of the revolver" (p. 70).

6. Seymour Chatman (1969, pp. 3–36) mistakenly groups detective and spy novels together as narratives "which approach the condition of pure plot" (p. 5). In fact, detective stories are not so much concerned with what will happen next as with a solution of an enigma that refers back to the past.

7. It is, of course, perfectly legitimate to choose an object of analysis which does not correspond to the governing structural principle of the work, and the units will then be different. I am also aware of the fact that not every work has a single governing structural principle. Some works can have more than one, some can have none, and the units will then be determined by what we want to examine and need not be forced into one governing principle.

8. I cannot here go into the whole notion of the codes, nor is it necessary for the point I am trying to make.

9. The works referred to are, of course, James's "The Figure in the Carpet," *The Turn of the Screw, The Sacred Fount,* and Robbe-Grillet's *Le Voyeur, L'année dernière à Marienbad.*

10. I am grateful to Professor J. F. Kermode for having pointed out this passage to me as well as for his stimulating ideas on the subject of hermeneutic gaps, presented to his postgraduate seminar at University College in 1971–72.

11. Some of the gaps opened by Perry and Sternberg (1968, pp. 263–92; English abstract, pp. 452–449) are of the kind which, because of the con-

ventions of the genre, require no filling in. And see the debate on the article in *Ha-Sifrut* 1969, pp. 580–663 (English abstract, pp. 686–679).

12. Examples of this kind of permanent gaps: Frank Stockton's "The Lady, or the Tiger"; Henry James's "The Figure in the Carpet," *The Turn of the Screw*, and *The Sacred Fount;* Robbe-Grillet's *Le Voyeur, La Jalousie, L'année dernière à Marienbad;* Nathalie Sarraute's *Portrait d'un inconnu;* Thomas Pynchon's *The Crying of Lot Forty-Nine;* and Nicholas Mosley's *Impossible Object.*

13. In Robbe-Grillet's *Le Voyeur* this "trou dans le récit" takes the literal form of blank pages. See Roland Barthes 1964, p. 64.

14. The term is taken from Perry and Sternberg 1968. They speak of "multiple systems of gap-filling clues," not of mutually exclusive ones. The term "gap-filling clues," I admit, is clumsy and not the most felicitous, but I could not find a better one. Whenever used in this study, it should be taken to mean something like "indications relative to the disposal of gaps and to the inference of the missing information."

15. In every narrative there are also logical relations among the units themselves, notably the relation of causality (implication), but they are less central to the present discussion.

16. Even here there is a difference between ambiguous narratives and detective stories, for the latter usually start by stating the presence of an informational gap.

17. It is, of course, possible to reject the view that the context of a narrative is contained within itself, whereas that of a sentence lies beyond itself. One may claim that, just like a sentence, a narrative must be examined against a context wider than itself, and that an ambiguous narrative can be disambiguated by our knowledge of the whole corpus of a writer's works. This, I believe, is a different use of the term *context*, for one does not claim that a verbal ambiguity can be created or resolved by the sum total of sentences pronounced by the same speaker on other occasions, but only by the immediate context of the one-time utterance, and in written narrative such an immediate context is contained within the narrative itself.

18. Kooij has reservations about the proposed immediate constituent analysis, see pp. 64–65.

CHAPTER 3

1. See, for example, "Madame de Mauves" (1874) and "The Path of Duty" (1884).

2. Since Perry is concerned with the inverted poem, I substitute "story" for "poem" wherever necessary.

3. Some of James's stories contain literal or metaphoric descriptions of gaps. In "Sir Dominick Ferrand" (1891), for example, the hero, who has discovered unknown papers says, "There are lots of questions I can't answer, of course; lots of identities I can't establish; lots of gaps I can't fill" (*The Complete Tales of Henry James*, ed. Leon Edel, 8: 370). And the narrator of "Glasses" (1896) prefaces his story with, "The little story is all there, I can touch it from point to point: for the thread, as I call it, is a row of coloured beads on a string. None of the beads are missing—at least I think they're not: that's exactly what I shall amuse myself with finding out" (Ibid., 9: 317).

4. "And don't you think he has done them [masterpieces]?" she asks Paul in an earlier scene (p. 251).

5. The ambiguity of Marian was first brought to my attention by Dorothea Krook in a seminar on Henry James at the Hebrew University of Jerusalem.

Chapter 4

1. I owe this point to Professor Dorothea Krook, who commented on my one-sided view of the deaths in the above-mentioned article.

2. A parallel phenomenon at the verbal level is that of ambiguity resulting from ellipsis. Also similar is James's use of exophoric pronouns which have a double situational referent.

3. Perhaps there is also the possibility that the narrator will find the partial knowledge cumbersome because his intellectual resources are insufficient to discover the rest, and that Vereker's ironic pleasure derives from seeing how wide off the mark the narrator's article is.

4. Leo B. Levy interprets the end in still another way, but I find it difficult to support his interpretation by evidence from the text. According to Levy, Deane knows the secret, as it is the secret of love, and his love for Gwendolen made him know it without having to be told. His pretended ignorance is explained as an act of compassion. "We may believe (if my view is reasonable) that Deane is moved by pity, perhaps by love, to give the narrator support in his forlorn and empty quest" (1962 a, pp. 463–64).

Chapter 5

1. One could perhaps claim that the miraculous process described by the metaphor of the sacred fount is another instance of the fantastic, but this would be an extension of the term beyond Todorov's intention.

2. For a highly ingenious (but wrongheaded) interpretation of this sentence see Rubin 1963–64, p. 316.

3. Note the similar theme of "communicating a consciousness" in *The Sacred Fount*.

4. The governess then gives a "twist" to this denial, suggesting that it is doubly directed. In this connection, it is interesting to note that the present perfect tense ("I never *have*") may support a suspicion that Flora knows what is meant, since she refers to an activity that started in the past. In the immediate context (before the "twist" is taken into account), the present perfect seems a natural reaction to the possibility of habitual meetings implicit in the governess's question.

5. In the governess's mouth these epithets acquire an effect of quasi oxymoron, but they may also be taken as straightforward descriptions of real innocence. The whole question of the children's real or seeming innocence in scenes like the above belongs to the discussion of doubly directed clues.

6. Cranfill and Clark (1965, p. 98) suggest that Miles's words could yield a different meaning if the stress is put on "me" rather than, or as well as, on "bad." "I did it so that, for a change, you should think *me,* rather than Flora, bad." There is no doubt that this is a possible and plausible meaning

if we change the position of the stress, but there is grave doubt as to whether we are entitled to change the stress when James, an author so careful with his italics, put it on "bad."

7. Note that support for this view can be restrospectively gleaned from the uncle's statement that the headmaster is "an awful bore" (p. 28). Perhaps Miles's "crime" was no more than some childish prank which the stiff headmaster could not tolerate. But note also that the uncle's statements are hardly a criterion for truth, since he is such an irresponsible character and would probably call anyone who gave him trouble a bore.

8. Note that because "such doings" is not fully determined, it may add a touch of double-directedness to the affirmation. Mrs. Grose may be said to believe in "such doings" as removing the girl in order to bring about her recovery. But this is a less likely possibility, for "in spite of yesterday" clearly relates the "doings" to the lake scene which provoked Flora's hysteria.

9. Mrs. Grose's shuddering response in the same scene (pp. 58–59) may be caused either by her horrified acceptance of the governess's theory or by her shocked reactions to the perversity of the governess's imagination.

10. In reply to the governess's further insistence, Miles explains that he has to see Luke—an explanation which the governess considers "a vulgar lie" (p. 132), but which may also be true, though in no less vulgar a way. Perhaps the boy does not use Luke as an evasive pretext, but really wants to see him in order to ask him to lie about the letter.

11. Mrs. Grose's expression of "deeper dismay," which makes the governess feel that she has "found a touch of picture," may perhaps be caused by the triviality of the detail with which the governess chooses to begin the description, not by the image hovering in Mrs. Grose's mind.

12. Note that Mrs. Grose's "identification" of Miss Jessel is clearly not an identification, for it is the governess who says "My predecessor—the one who died," and Mrs. Grose only supplies the name, and even that presumably in a tone of incredulity, for the governess immediately repeats, "Miss Jessel. You don't believe me?" (p. 57). Soon afterward Mrs. Grose explicitly expresses doubt: "How can you be sure?" (p. 57).

13. If the second possibility seems less likely, the reader should notice that in the sequel Miles talks about the governess's loneliness.

14. Note that the recurrence of physical pressure is again doubly directed: on the one hand it supports the view that the sentence in question describes her as pressing Miles again, but on the other hand, only a few lines before this sentence she "spring[s] straight upon him," so perhaps now it is not Miles? Or is it Miles again, with an ever-increasing frequency of her grasps?

15. Note that this identification is further developed when the governess sees Miss Jessel in the schoolroom looking like a maid who applies herself to "the considerable effort of a letter to her sweetheart" (p. 97). Occurring a short time after the question of the governess's letter to her employer was debated, the description establishes an analogy between the two.

CHAPTER 6

1. A further twist is given by Obert's later rejection of this commonsense explanation and its replacement by something similar to, though not identical with, the narrator's initial interpretation (p. 162).

2. That people are liable to misinterpret him is suggested by Lady John's view of his relations with Mrs. Briss (p. 126).

3. The narrator is the only testing factor, as he is the only one who has the benefit of having heard her theory.

4. It can also suggest rationalization on his part, expressing fear to enter into the full commitment of a love relationship. In this sense it is a doubly directed clue of the type I shall discuss in the next section.

5. See also pp. 58, 77, 79, 102–3, 172. In an appendix devoted to James's late style, Krook has already pointed out the "persistent use of what may be called logical terms, expressions and images" (1967, p. 395), and has discussed their significance in the framework of James's "philosophy." This exempts me from further elaboration of the point. See also Blackall 1965, and Andreach 1962, pp. 197–216.

6. Newspapermen are notorious for falsifying the truth. Is the image meant to suggest falsification?

7. Similar in function is the use of "as if." May Server agrees with the narrator, "but as if speaking rather for harmony" (p. 52).

8. This, I believe, is an extension of the strict meaning of *oxymoron*. The oxymoron here is not between two consecutive words, but between a situation and the words chosen to describe it.

9. The words "absurdly" attached to himself and "benightedly" to the others also have a boomerang effect.

10. Robert Gale says, "James in 1877 met Tennyson and wrote that he had "a face of genius" (*The Letters of Henry James*, 1:53), but there is nothing in James's fiction or other writings to indicate any high regard for the laureate's poetry," and "With the imagery, it is simply a matter of James's recalling lines or situations with greater or lesser consciousness, from the better poems" (1964, p. 112). He cites examples from "Rose-Agathe" (1878), *The Golden Bowl* (1904), and "Crapy Cornelia" (1909), but says nothing about *The Sacred Fount*. I hope to have shown that the significance of the allusion to Tennyson in this novel goes beyond what Gale leads us to believe.

11. Blackall suggests a possible associative connection in James's mind between the allusion to Ludwig II and the quotation from "The Raven." In November 1866, she says, *Lippincott's Monthly Magazine* published "Ludwig of Bavaria: A Personal Reminiscence" by Lew Vanderpoole. And she goes on, "It is especially interesting to speculate that James may have seen the Vanderpoole article because its principal theme is Ludwig's admiration for Edgar Allan Poe and his attempts to explain his own temperament with reference to that of Poe. And James quotes "The Raven" in the exchange of repartee between Ford Obert and the narrator at the end of Chapter X of *The Sacred Fount*" (1965, p. 101).

12. The existence of ambiguous pronouns in Henry James's style has not escaped the notice of critics (see, for example, Izzo 1965, p. 141; Short 1946, p. 81; Dupee 1951, p. 151; Chatman 1972, pp. 62–63), but they do not relate this phenomenon to the overall ambiguity of the narrative.

13. The theme of vampires first appeared in James's work in an early story entitled "De Grey: A Romance" (1868), where the wife is "draining the blood from her husband's being" (see Edel, ed., 1962, 1:425).

14. The light tone is more prevalent in the first chapters. As the novel proceeds, the tragic overtones become more and more pervasive.

15. The French *sacré*, like its Latin predecessor *sacer*, is much more frequently used in both senses, and James's leaning toward French expressions is well known.

16. It seems completely unjustified to say that the narrator's theory is not supported by the other characters when a mere counting of evidence proves that it *is* in exactly half the cases.

17. The italics in pp. 212–17 are mine, unless otherwise indicated. From p. 218 onward italics, unless otherwise indicated, are again James's.

18. We have already observed that "her part in a relation" in the scene from which the quotation is taken is put in doubt, and thus the value of repetition (of events as well as of words) as proof is also questioned.

19. It is not stated anywhere in the novel that the narrator is an author. The critics who take him to be one probably do so because it is he who tells-writes the story. Such an implicit inference gives rise to a difficult problem, for it may turn all first-person narrators into authors.

CONCLUSION

1. It is interesting to note in this connection that Sigmund Freud discerns a similar mechanism in dreams:

The attitude of dreams towards the category of antithesis and contradiction is most striking. This category is simply ignored; the word "No" does not seem to exist for a dream. Dreams show a special tendency to reduce two opposites to a unity or to represent them as one thing. [1925, 4:184]

Bibliography

The bibliography includes only books and articles quoted or referred to in the text.

PRIMARY SOURCES

Works by Henry James

1961–64. *The Complete Tales of Henry James*. Edited by Leon Edel. 12 vols. London: Rupert Hart-Davis. Vol. 7, "The Lesson of the Master" (1963); Vol. 9, "The Figure in the Carpet (1964); Vol. 10, *The Turn of the Screw* (1964).

1959. *The Sacred Fount*. London: Rupert Hart-Davis.

1962 [1934]. *The Art of the Novel: Critical Prefaces by Henry James*. Edited by R.P. Blackmur. New York: Charles Scribner's Sons.

1968. *Henry James: Selected Literary Criticism*. Edited by Morris Shapira. Harmondsworth, Middlesex: Penguin Books. The articles reprinted in this book were first published between 1865 and 1914.

1970 [1920]. *The Letters of Henry James*. Selected and edited by Percy Lubbock. 2 vols. New York: Octagon Books.

1961 [1947]. *The Notebooks of Henry James*. Edited by F.O. Matthiessen and Kenneth B. Murdock. New York: Oxford University Press.

Works by other authors

Mosley, Nicholas. 1968. *Impossible Object*. London: Hodder and Stoughton.

Nabokov, Vladimir. 1960 [1941]. *The Real Life of Sebastian Knight*. London: Weidenfeld and Nicolson.

Pynchon, Thomas. 1966. *The Crying of Lot Forty-Nine*. Philadelphia: Lippincot.

Robbe-Grillet, Alain. 1961. *L'année dernière à Marienbad.* Paris: Minuit.

————. 1958. *La jalousie.* Paris: Minuit.

————. 1955. *Le voyeur.* Paris: Minuit.

Sarraute, Nathalie. 1956. *Portrait d'un inconnu.* Paris: Gallimard.

SECONDARY SOURCES

Anderson, Quentin. 1957. *The American Henry James.* New Brunswick, N.J.: Rutgers University Press.

Andreach, Robert J. 1962. "Henry James's *The Sacred Fount: The Existential Predicament.*" *Nineteenth-Century Fiction* 17:197–216.

Andreas, Osborne. 1948. *Henry James and the Expanding Horizon: A Study of the Meaning and Basic Themes of James's Fiction.* Seattle: University of Washington Press.

Barthes, Roland. 1964. *Essais Critiques.* Paris: Seuil.

————. 1966. "Introduction à l'analyse structurale des récits." *Communications* 8:1–27.

————. 1970. *S/Z.* Paris: Seuil.

Beardsley, Monroe C. 1954. *Thinking Straight.* New York: Prentice-Hall. A shorter version of *Practical Logic.*

————. 1958. *Aesthetics: Problems in the Philosophy of Criticism.* New York: Harcourt, Brace, and World.

Bewley, Marius. 1952. *The Complex Fate: Hawthorne, Henry James, and Some Other American Writers.* London: Chatto and Windus.

Blackall, Jean Frantz. 1965. *Jamesian Ambiguity and* The Sacred Fount. Ithaca, N.Y.: Cornell University Press.

Blackmur, R.P. 1945 [1943]. "In the Country of the Blue." In *The Question of Henry James: A Collection of Critical Essays.* Edited by Frederick W. Dupee. Pp. 191–211. New York: Holt.

Blanché, Robert. 1966. *Structures intellectuelles: Essai sur l'organisation systématique des concepts.* Paris: Librairie Philosophique J. Vrin.

Bremond, Claude. 1964. "Le message narratif." *Communications* 4:4–32.

————. 1966. "La logique des possibles narratifs." *Communications* 8:60–76.

Brooks, Cleanth. 1949. *The Well-Wrought Urn: Studies in the Structure of Poetry.* London: Dennis Dobson.

Chatman, Seymour. 1969. "New Ways of Analyzing Narrative Structure, with an Example from Joyce's *Dubliners.*" *Language and Style* 2:3–36.

————. 1972. *The Later Style of Henry James.* Oxford: Basil Blackwell.

Chomsky, Noam. 1957. *Syntactic Structures.* The Hague: Mouton.

————. 1965. *Aspects of the Theory of Syntax.* Cambridge, Mass.: M.I.T. Press.

Cixous, Hélène. 1970. "Henry James: L'écriture comme placement ou De l'ambiguïté de l'intérêt." *Poétique* 1:35–50.

Copi, Irving M. 1961 [1953]. *Introduction to Logic.* 2d ed. New York: Macmillan.

Costello, Donald P. 1960. "The Structure of *The Turn of the Screw.*" *Modern Language Notes* 75:312–21.

Cranfill, Thomas M., and Robert L. Clark, Jr. 1965. *An Anatomy of "The Turn of the Screw."* Austin: University of Texas Press.

Dawson, Sheila. 1965. "Infinite Types of Ambiguity." *British Journal of Aesthetics* 5:289–95.

Dorfman, Eugene. 1969. *The Narreme in the Medieval Romance Epic: An Introduction to Narrative Structures.* Toronto: University of Toronto Press.

Dupee, Frederick W. 1951. *Henry James.* London: Methuen.

Eco, Umberto. 1960. "L'oeuvre ouverte et la poétique de l'indétermination", translated by André Boucourechliev. *La nouvelle revue française* 8:117–24, 313–20.

————. 1968. *La definizione dell'arte.* Milan: U. Mursia.

Edel, Leon. 1959. Introduction to *The Sacred Fount,* by Henry James. London: Rupert Hart-Davis.

Empson, William. 1935. *Some Versions of Pastoral.* London: Chatto and Windus.

————. 1961 [1930]. *Seven Types of Ambiguity.* Harmondsworth, Middlesex: Penguin Books.

Erlich, Victor. 1969 [1955]. *Russian Formalism: History-Doctrine.* 3d ed. The Hague: Mouton.

Escher, M.C. 1972 [1961]. *The Graphic Work of M.C. Escher.* Translated from the Dutch by John E. Brigham. London: Macdonald and Co.

Finch, G.A. 1968. "A Retreading of James's Carpet." *Twentieth-Century Literature* 14:98–101.

Folsom, James K. 1961. "Archimago's Well: An Interpretation of *The Sacred Fount.*" *Modern Fiction Studies* 7:136–45.

Forster, E.M. 1963 [1927]. *Aspects of the Novel.* Harmondsworth, Middlesex: Pelican Books.

Frenkel-Brunswick, Else. 1954. "Intolerance of Ambiguity as an Emotional and Perceptual Personality Variable." In *The Study of Personality,* edited by Howard Brand. New York: John Wiley.

Gale, Robert L. 1962. "*The Marble Faun* and *The Sacred Fount*: A Resemblance." *Studi Americani* 8:21–33.

———. 1964. *The Caught Image: Figurative Language in the Fiction of Henry James.* Chapel Hill: University of North Carolina Press.

Gard, A. Roger. 1963. "Critics of *The Golden Bowl.*" *Melbourne Critical Review* 6:102–9.

Geismar, Maxwell. 1963. *Henry James and the Jacobites.* Boston: Houghton and Mifflin.

Goddard, Harold C. 1970 [1957; written in 1920 or earlier]. "A Pre-Freudian Reading of *The Turn of the Screw.*" In *Twentieth-Century Interpretations of "The Turn of the Screw" and Other Tales,* edited by Jane P. Tompkins, pp. 1–36. Englewood Cliffs, N.J.: Prentice-Hall.

Gombrich, E.M. 1963. *Meditations on a Hobby-Horse and Other Essays on the Theory of Art.* London: Phaidon Press.

———. 1968 [1960]. *Art and Illusion: A Study in the Psychology of Pictorial Representation.* 3d ed. London: Phaidon Press.

———. 1969a. "The Evidence of Images." In *Interpretation: Theory and Practice,* edited by Charles S. Singleton, pp. 35–104. Baltimore: Johns Hopkins Press.

———. 1969b [1965]. "Visual Discovery Through Art." In

Psychology and the Visual Arts, edited by James Hogg. Harmondsworth, Middlesex: Penguin Books.

Halliday, M.A.K.; McIntosh, Angus; and Strevens, Peter. 1964. *The Linguistic Sciences and Language Teaching.* London: Longmans.

Hirsch, E.D. 1967. *Validity in Interpretation.* New Haven: Yale University Press.

Isle, Walter. 1968 [1965]. "The Romantic and the Real: Henry James's *The Sacred Fount.*" In *Henry James: Modern Judgments,* edited by Tony Tanner. London: Macmillan.

Izzo, Carlo. 1956. "Henry James: Scrittore Sintattico." *Studi Americani* 2:127–42.

Jakobson, Roman. 1967 [1962]. "Linguistics and Poetics." In *Essays on the Language of Literature,* edited by Seymour Chatman and Samuel R. Levin, pp. 296–322. Boston: Houghton and Mifflin.

Jensen, James Peter. 1965. "The Genesis of Ambiguity." *Dissertation Abstracts* 25, 7271A (University of Washington).

Kaplan, Abraham and Ernst Kris. 1948. "Esthetic Ambiguity," *Philosophy and Phenomenological Research* 8:415–35.

Kermode, Frank. 1969. "The Structures of Fiction." *Modern Language Notes* 84:891–915.

———. 1972. "Novel and narrative." W.P. Ker Memorial Lecture. Delivered in the University of Glasgow, 9 March 1972.

King, A.H. 1941–42. "Some Notes on Ambiguity in Henry IV, part 1." *Studia Neophilologica* 14:161–83.

Kooij, J.G. 1971. *Ambiguity in Natural Language.* Amsterdam: North-Holland.

Krook, Dorothea. 1967 [1962]. *The Ordeal of Consciousness in Henry James.* Cambridge: At the University Press.

Lainoff, Seymour. 1961. "Henry James's 'The Figure in the Carpet': What is Critical Responsiveness?" *Boston University Studies in English* 5:122–28.

Leech, Geoffrey N. 1969. *A Linguistic Guide to English Poetry.* London: Longman.

Lees, R.B. 1960. "A Multiply Ambiguous Adjectival Construction in English." *Language* 36:207–21.

Lemon, Lee T., and Reis, Marion J., eds. 1965. *Russian Formalist Criticism: Four Essays.* Lincoln, Neb.: University of Nebraska Press.

Levy, Leo B. 1962a. "A Reading of 'The Figure in the Carpet.'" *American Literature* 32:457–65.

———. 1962b. "What Does *The Sacred Fount* Mean?" *College English* 23:381–84.

McMaster, Juliet. 1969. " 'The Full Image of a Repetition' in *The Turn of the Screw.*" *Studies in Short Fiction* 6:377–82.

Melchiori, Giorgio. 1965. "Cups of Gold for The Sacred Fount: Aspects of James's Symbolism." *Critical Quarterly* 7:301–16.

Mukařovský, Jan. 1964. "The Esthetics of Language." In *A Prague School Reader on Esthetics, Literary Structure, and Style,* edited and translated by Paul L. Garvin, pp. 31–69. Washington, D.C.: Georgetown University Press.

Nowottny, Winifred. 1962. *The Language Poets Use.* London: The Athlone Press.

Perosa, Sergio, trans. 1963. Introduction to *La Fonte Sacra,* by Henry James, pp. ix–xxxvii. Venice: Neri Pozza.

Perry, Menakhem, and Sternberg, Meir. 1968. "The King Through Ironic Eyes: The Narrator's Devices in the Biblical Story of David and Bathsheba and Two Excursuses on the Theory of the Narrative Text." *Ha-Sifrut* 1:263–92. (In Hebrew; English abstract: 452–449.) Discussed in Hebrew by various people in *Ha-Sifrut* 2:580–663. (English abstract: 686–679.)

Perry, Menakhem. 1968–69. "The Inverted Poem: On a Principle of Semantic Composition in Bialik's Poems." *Ha-Sifrut* 1:607–31. (In Hebrew; English abstract: 769–768).

———. 1969. "Thematic Structures in Bialik's Poetry: The Inverted Poem and Related Kinds." *Ha-Sifrut* 2:40–82. (In Hebrew; English abstract: 261–259).

Powers, Lyall H. 1961. "A Reperusal of James's 'The Figure in the Carpet.'" *American Literature* 33:224–28.

Propp, Vladimir. 1958 [1928 in Russian]. *Morphology of the Folktale.* Bloomington, Ind.: Indiana University Research Center in Anthropology, Folklore and Linguistics.

Reaney, James. 1962. "The Condition of Light: Henry James's

The Sacred Fount." *University of Toronto Quarterly* 31: 136–51.

Reed, Glenn A. 1960. "Another Turn on James's 'The Turn of the Screw.' " In *A Casebook on Henry James's 'The Turn of the Screw,'* edited by Gerald Willen. New York: Crowell.

Reichenbach, Hans. 1951. *Elements of Symbolic Logic.* New York: Macmillan.

Ricoeur, Paul. 1969. "The Problem of the Double-Sense as Hermeneutic Problem and as Semantic Problem." In *Myth and Symbols: Studies in Honor of Mircea Eliade,* edited by Joseph M. Kitagawa and Charles H. Long, pp. 63–79. Chicago: University of Chicago Press.

Rimmon, Shlomith. 1973. "Barthes' 'Hermeneutic Code' and Henry James's Literary Detective: Plot-Composition in 'The Figure in the Carpet' " *HSL* 1:183–207.

Rommetveit, Ragnar. 1968. *Words, Meanings and Messages: Theory and Experiments in Psycholinguistics.* Oslo: Universitetsforlaget.

Rubin, Louis D., Jr. 1963–64. "One More Turn of the Screw." *Modern Fiction Studies* 9:314–28.

Samuels, Charles Thomas. 1971. *The Ambiguity of Henry James.* Urbana, Ill.: University of Illinois Press.

Saussure, Ferdinand de. 1969 [1915]. *Cours de linguistique générale.* Publié par Charles Bally et Albert Sechehaye avec la collaboration de Albert Riedlinger. Paris: Payot.

Schaar, Claes. 1965. "Old Texts and Ambiguity." *English Studies* 46:157–65.

Segal, Ora. 1969. *The Lucid Reflector: A Study of the Role of the Observer in Henry James's Fiction.* New Haven: Yale University Press.

Shipley, Joseph T. 1966. *Dictionary of World Literature.* Totowa, N.J.: Littlefield, Adams and Co.

Short, R.W. 1964. "The Sentence Structure of Henry James." *American Literature* 18:71–88.

Sollers, Philippe. 1968. *Logiques.* Paris: Seuil..

Stanford, William Bedell. 1939. *Ambiguity in Greek Literature: Studies in Theory and Practice.* Oxford: Basil Blackwell.

Stephenson, Ralph, and Debrix, J.R. 1965. *The Cinema as Art*. Harmondsworth, Middlesex: Penguin Books.

Swan, Michael. 1952. *Henry James*. London: Lowe and Brydone.

Tarski, Alfred. 1940 [1936 in Polish]. *Introduction to Logic and to the Methodology of Deductive Sciences*. Translated by Olaf Helmer. New York: Oxford University Press.

Todorov, Tzvetan. 1966. "Les catégories du récit littéraire." *Communications* 8:125–51.

———. 1969. *Grammaire du Décaméron*. The Hague: Mouton.

———. 1970. *Introduction à la littérature fantastique*. Paris: Seuil.

———. 1971. *Poétique de la prose*. Paris: Seuil.

Todorov, Tzvetan, ed. and trans. 1965. *Théorie de la littérature: Textes des formalistes russes*. Paris: Seuil.

Todorov, Tzvetan, ed. 1968. *Théorie d'ensemble*. Paris: Seuil.

Ullmann, Stephen. 1957 [1951]. *The Principles of Semantics*. Oxford: Basil Blackwell; Glasgow: Jackson.

———. 1962. *Semantics: An Introduction to the Science of Meaning*. Oxford: Basil Blackwell.

Vaid, Krishna Baldev. 1964. *Technique in the Tales of Henry James*. Cambridge, Mass.: Harvard University Press.

Vernant, Jean-Pierre. 1969. "Tensions and Ambiguities in Greek Tragedy." In *Interpretation: Theory and Practice*, edited by Charles S. Singleton. Baltimore: Johns Hopkins Press, pp. 105–21.

Waldock, A.J.A. 1960. "Mr. Edmund Wilson and *The Turn of the Screw*." In *A Casebook on Henry James's "The Turn of the Screw*," edited by Gerald Willen. New York: Crowell.

West, Muriel. 1964. "The Death of Miles in *The Turn of the Screw*," *PMLA* 79:283–88.

Westbrook, Perry D. 1953. "The Supersubtle Fry." *Nineteenth-Century Fiction* 8:134–40.

Wheelwright, Philip. 1967. "On the Semantics of Poetry." In *Essays on the Language of Literature*, edited by Seymour Chatman and Samuel R. Levin, pp. 250–64. Boston: Houghton and Mifflin.

Wiesenfarth, Joseph. 1963. *Henry James and the Dramatic Analogy*. New York: Fordham University Press.

Index

Actional structure, 28–29, 36, 38, 43
Aeschylus, *The Suppliants*, 66
Agam, Yaacov, 13
Allegory, 13–14, 16
Ambivalence, 18
Ambiguity: definition of, xi, 8–9, 27, 52;
 and generative-transformational
 grammar, 40; and the fantastic, 119
Ambiguity, in Henry James: in "The
 Figure in the Carpet," 95–115; in "The
 Lesson of the Master," 79–94; in *The
 Sacred Fount*, 167–226; in *The Turn of
 the Screw*, 116–66
Ambiguity, narrative: closedness of, 16,
 57–58; concrete realization of, 41,
 50–51, 75; distinguished from cognate
 phenomena, 12–16; formative principle
 of, 9–16; propositional, 39; prospective,
 55–56, 95, 121, 123–25, 170;
 retrospective, 87–94, 120, 123–25;
 sequential, 39–40, 40–42, 75, 145–46;
 and verbal ambiguity, 72
Ambiguity, verbal: concrete realization of,
 58–75; distinguished from cognate
 phenomena, 17–25; formative principle
 of, 16–26; grammatical, 67–69, 71,
 76 (*see also* Constructional homonymity); inherent vs. contextual, 61,
 72–73, 76; lexical, 59, 64–67, 70, 76;
 phonological, 62–64, 70, 76; potential
 vs. realized, 61, 72–73; types of, 25–26,
 238 nn. 15, 19
Ambiguity, visual, ix–xi, 229, 233–34
Analogy: general, 31, 35; in "The Figure
 in the Carpet," 121; in *The Sacred
 Fount*, 168–81, 208–11, 212–20,
 221–23, 226; in *The Turn of the Screw*,
 163–64
Anaphora, 214–15
Anderson, Quentin, 115
Andreach, Robert J., 188, 213–14
Andreas, Osborne, 85
Année dernière à Marienbad, L' (Robbe-
 Grillet), 33, 45, 56, 232–33
Anti-novel, 234–35
Armature, 28, 30, 36–37, 43
As You Like It (Shakespeare), 194

Balzac, Honoré de, *Le Père Goriot*, 35

Barthes, Roland, 13, 30, 43–44, 97, 120,
 228, 234
Beardsley, Monroe C., 20, 46–48, 146
Bentley, Edmund C., *Trent's Last Case*,
 57
Benveniste, Emile, 31
Berio, Luciano, 12–13
Bewley, Marius, 163, 227
Bible (Old and New Testaments), 70, 207
Blackall, Jean Frantz, 179, 181, 183, 195,
 208, 210–11
Blackmur, R. P., 85, 115, 205, 229
Blanché, Robert, 7–8
Bremond, Claude, 32, 37–39, 43
Brissenden, Grace (in James's *The Sacred
 Fount*), 52, 167, 169, 170–75, 177–82,
 184–85, 187–88, 190–94, 196–204,
 206, 209–10, 212, 215, 217–23
Brissenden, Guy (in James's *The Sacred
 Fount*; often called "poor Briss"), 167,
 171–78, 181–82, 185–86, 189–91,
 199–206, 209–11, 215–16, 221–22,
 225–26
Brooks, Cleanth, 24
Bunyan, John, *Pilgrim's Progress*, 13–14
Burroughs, William, *Naked Lunch*, 12

Calder, Alexander, 13
"Canonization, The" (Donne), 24
Catalyse, 39, 43
Catullus, 19
Chance (Conrad), 45
Chatman, Seymour, 108, 229
Chiasmus, 216–17
Chomsky, Noam, 29, 40–41, 69
Cicero, 24
Cixous, Hélène, 115
Clayton, Jack, *The Pumpkin Eater* (film)
 33
Clues. *See* Gap-filling clues; Hermeneutic
 clues
"Coat, A" (Yeats), 68
Common sense, 208–9
Competence, 29
Complexity, 21–22
Conjunction: in ambiguity, 8, 26, 75; in
 complexity, 22–23; definition of, 3, 5;
 in double and multiple meaning, 14, 22.
 See also Logical operations

253